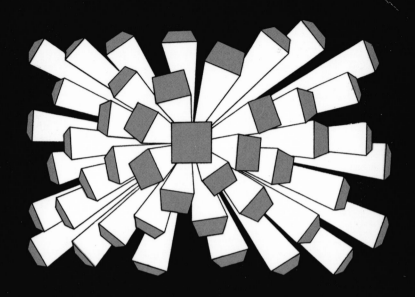

Philosophical Alternatives in Education

Gerald Lee Gutek

A publication in the Merrill Coordinated Teacher Preparation Series,
under the editorship of Donald E. Orlosky

PHILOSOPHICAL
ALTERNATIVES
IN EDUCATION

A publication in the
Merrill Coordinated Teacher Preparation Series
under the editorship of
DONALD E. ORLOSKY

PHILOSOPHICAL ALTERNATIVES IN EDUCATION

Gerald Lee Gutek

Loyola University of Chicago

Charles E. Merrill Publishing Company
A Bell & Howell Company
Columbus, Ohio

published by
Charles E. Merrill Publishing Company
A Bell & Howell Company
Columbus, Ohio 43216

International Standard Book Number: 0–675–08926–3

Library of Congress Catalog Card Number: 73–76802

Printed in the United States of America

1 2 3 4 5 6 7 8—79 78 77 76 75 74

Preface

Philosophical Alternatives in Education, which resulted from my
teaching philosophy of education at Loyola University of Chicago, is
designed to meet the needs of: (1) prospective teachers enrolled in
undergraduate teacher education programs; (2) undergraduate
students in the liberal arts and sciences; (3) graduate students in
professional education programs.

The book follows a pattern of including descriptive analyses that
examine the major features of each philosophy considered.
Selections from the writings of the major proponents of the
particular philosophy are then presented so that the student can
directly confront the sources of the philosophy. The selections are
preceded by brief biographical sketches that indicate the background
and position of the philosopher who wrote the material.

For the prospective teacher, the course in educational philosophy
may mark the first encounter with the humanistic foundations of
education. Philosophy of education courses frequently are structured
as examinations of one systematic philosophy of education, as
inquiry into specific educational problems, or as the study of a
number of philosophies of education. *Philosophical Alternatives in
Education* follows the third approach. On the student's initial
encounter with the discipline, it seems premature to restrict
philosophy of education to a single point of view. While it may be
desirable, commitment to a particular philosophy should come when
students have had an adequate opportunity to consider the major
schools of thought. While educational issues should be examined for
their most general consequences, I believe locating these problems in
their philosophical context places them in perspective. After teaching

educational philosophy as both an introduction to a particular system and as inquiry into problems, I returned to the method that examines a variety of philosophical alternatives in education. Although this is somewhat conventional, it enables students to become familiar with the major contributions to philosophical thought in education. It presents alternatives that can serve as a prelude to commitment to a particular philosophy of education. It also provides perspective into the problems of education in their most general form.

Students in the liberal arts and sciences who may not be identified with teacher preparation programs often select philosophy of education as an elective course. These students have commented that philosophy of education has given them insights into their own educations and has helped them to integrate the various components of their education into a whole. I believe that philosophy of education, like the history of education, can be a liberal as well as a professional study. Of course, it is useful in that it provides perspective into the humanistic foundations of education that have personal and social implications.

Graduate students in professional education are enrolled in programs such as administration, supervision, curriculum, guidance and counseling, and higher education, as well as in the various foundations of education. These students are generally experienced classroom teachers or school administrators who recognize the need for the reflective examination of education. The study of philosophies of education enables them to reflect upon their own practices as teachers and administrators and to speculate on the general consequences of their actions.

I wish to express my deep appreciation to the Committee on Faculty Appointments of Loyola University for generously providing a leave from my teaching responsibilities that enabled me to complete my work on the manuscript. I also wish to thank John M. Wozniak, Dean of the School of Education, and Rosemary V. Donatelli, Chairman of the Foundations of Education Department at Loyola University, who have always encouraged my projects.

I am grateful to the students who enrolled in my classes in philosophy of education at Loyola University. Their interest, questions, and criticisms helped me to shape this book.

I wish to thank Elizabeth Cronenwett, who typed the manuscript with patience and care.

It was a pleasant experience to work with Denny Rea, Tony Samuolis, and Frances Heisel of the Charles E. Merrill Publishing

Company who encouraged, edited, and prepared the manuscript for publication.

I appreciate the understanding of my wife, Patricia, who was so helpful in the writing of this book.

Gerald Lee Gutek

Loyola University
Chicago, Illinois

for my mother and my father
Irene and Albert Gutek

Contents

one

PHILOSOPHY AND EDUCATION

During a person's first experience as a teacher, he has little time to examine the general or theoretical implications that result from his presence in a school. All too frequently, teaching is a hurried and often frustrating series of episodes in which the teacher reacts to the immediate demands of students, parents, administrators, colleagues, and community and school organizations. In the first years of a teaching career, the teacher must meet the day-to-day demands of planning lessons, meeting classes, and attending conferences both in and out of school. Little time is available for reflection on the enterprise of education with which he is involved. For the teacher who wishes to become a genuine professional, an exclusive attention to daily routine and detail is insufficient. Every teacher knows that education is a powerful instrument for the shaping of individual lives and of society. When the teacher begins to reflect upon his role, he is beginning to pass from preoccupation with the immediately practical to an examination of the theory that underlies and sustains practice. As the moral enterprise which it is, teaching requires the careful blending of theory and practice. Theory without practice is insufficient; practice which is not guided by theory is aimless.

As a blending of theory and practice, teaching is a reflective activity which has effects beyond the immediate teaching-learning episodes that occur in the classroom. The way in which the teacher relates to his students depends upon the conception that the teacher has of human nature and its purpose. Instruction is about something; it is about a skill or about knowledge. The teaching of a skill depends upon its social utility and involves the teacher in an examination of societal needs. Knowledge depends upon one's view of reality. When the teacher begins to reflect upon his conception of man, of society, and of reality, he is involved in philosophy of education.

AREAS OF SYSTEMATIC PHILOSOPHY

In its broadest and most general terms, philosophy is man's attempt to think most speculatively, reflectively, and systematically about the universe in which he lives and his relationships to that universe. Philosophers have divided their speculations into four basic areas. These are metaphysics, epistemology, axiology, and logic.

Metaphysics, the study of the nature of ultimate reality, deals with man's speculation into the nature of existence. It asks the question: After all of the nonessentials of existence have been stripped away, what is it that is genuinely real? In their speculations into the nature of reality, metaphysicians have drawn varying conclusions. While an Idealist defines reality in nonmaterial, spiritual terms, a Realist sees reality as an order of objects that exists independently of man. A Pragmatist, in contrast, holds that man's conception of reality is determined by his experience.

Metaphysics relates to educational theorizing and practice in many ways. The subjects, experiences, and skills that are included in the curriculum reflect the conception of reality that is held by the society which supports the school enterprise. Much of formal schooling represents the attempt of curriculum makers, teachers, and textbook authors to describe certain aspects of reality to students. For example, subjects such as history, geography, and chemistry describe certain phases of reality to students.

The area of epistemology, the theory of knowing and of knowledge, is of crucial importance for educators. Dealing with man's most general and basic conceptions of knowing, epistemology is closely related to methods of teaching and learning. For example, an Idealist may hold that man's knowing, or cognitive process, is really the recall of ideas that are latently present in the mind. The appropriate educational method would be that of the Socratic dialogue, in which the teacher attempts to stimulate or to bring latent ideas to the student's consciousness by asking leading questions. Realists hold that knowledge originates in the sensations which men have of the objects which are part of the environment. From his sensations, they hold, each man arrives at concepts. Through abstraction upon sensory data, he builds concepts that correspond to these objects in reality. A teacher who wishes to structure a method of instruction based upon the Realist sensation-abstraction formula might develop a set of classroom demonstrations that will explain natural phenomenon to students. The Pragmatist, in turn, holds that man creates knowledge by acting and interacting with his environment in a series of problem-solving episodes. Thus, problem solving is the appropriate method of learning for those who accept the Pragmatist's view of knowledge.

Axiology is concerned with value theory and attempts to prescribe what is good and right conduct. The subdivisions of axiology are ethics and aesthetics. Ethics is the philosophic study of moral values and conduct. Aesthetics is concerned with the study of values in the realms of beauty and art. While metaphysics is concerned with attempts to describe the nature of ultimate reality, axiology refers to prescriptions of moral behavior and beauty. Educators have always been concerned with the formation of values in the young and with the encouragement of certain kinds of preferred behavior.

In a common-sense way, each man is subjected to those who seek to shape his behavior along certain lines. Children are continually told that they should or should not do certain things. Statements such as "you should wash your hands before eating," "you should not break the school's windows," or "you should love your country" are all obvious value statements. In the process of growing to maturity, an individual encounters countless attempts to mold his behavior along preferred modes of action. In a very direct way, parents, teachers, and society reward or punish behavior as it conforms to or deviates from their conceptions of correctness, goodness, or beauty.

Modern man finds himself in a world of clashing values. Internationally, the nationalistic value patterns of the various nation-states have led to conflict and to war. Within nations, there are clashes of values on class or group lines. Sociologists of education have written volumes on the dilemma that faces public schools in the wake of the clash between the values of the middle and lower socioeconomic classes. Traditionally value systems have been codified and ritualized in the ethical principles of the various world religions. In the United States, where one finds racial, religious, social, and economic pluralism, the school is a place of value tensions.

The classical conflict in values can be identified as that of objective versus subjective value theory. Those who subscribe to an objective value theory assert that what is good is rooted in the universe itself and is applicable everywhere for all time. In contrast, subjectivists assert that values are group or personal preferences—likes or dislikes—that depend on particular circumstances, times, and places. For them, values are not universally valid but are relative in that they depend on particular situations.

The aesthetic dimension of life has frequently been overlooked in American education. In its broadest sense, aesthetic theory refers to the cultivation of taste and a feeling for that which is beautiful. Although aesthetic theory is concerned with man's attempt to objectify his insights and feelings in various art forms, it is equally concerned with the cultivation of persons whose lives are harmonious, balanced, and beautiful. While aesthetic values have an obvious place in art, drama, music, and dancing classes, they are relevant to the cultivation of the public taste and style of life that represents the perspectives of a people.

Logic is concerned with the rules or patterns of correct and valid thinking. It examines the rules of valid inference which enable us to frame our propositions and our arguments correctly. Deductive logic is that reasoning which moves from general statements or principles to particular instances and applications. Inductive logic is reasoning which moves from particular instances to generalizations.

EDUCATION

Education refers very broadly to the total social processes that bring a person into life in a culture. The human species reproduces biologically as do all other living organisms. Biological reproduction, however, is not cultural reproduction. By living and participating in a culture, the immature human being gradually becomes a recipient of and a participant in a culture. Many people and social agencies are involved in the process of enculturation of the young. The family, the peer group, the community, the media, the church, and the state all have formative effects on the individual person. Through living with other people, the immature child learns how to deal with them. He takes on their language, their manners, and their behavior. Educational theorists and philosophers have long recognized the educative role of interactions of man and society. They have tried to indicate the outlines of the kind of social order that is based upon and fulfills man's potentiality.

Education, in a more formal and deliberate sense, takes place in the school, a specialized social agency established to cultivate preferred skills, knowledge, and values in the learner. The school is staffed by teachers who are regarded to be experts in the learning processes. Informal, or milieu education, is related to schooling, or formal education. If the school is to succeed in its program of instruction, its curriculum and methods of instruction must be related to and viable in terms of society.

Curriculum   As the focus and vital center of the school's educational efforts, the curriculum is the locus of the sharpest controversies. Decision making in curricular matters involves considering, examining, and formulating the ends of education. Those concerned with curriculum planning and organization ask such questions as: What knowledge is of most worth? What knowledge should be introduced to the learner? What are the criteria for selecting knowledge? What is it that is valuable for the learner as a person and as a member of society? The answers to these questions will determine what is included in and what is excluded from the instructional program of the school. These answers rest ultimately on assumptions about the nature of the universe, of man, of society, and of the good life.[1] In the philosophies that will be examined in this book, there are a variety of basic and general assumptions that provide alternatives that are applicable to the making of the curriculum.

Curriculum has been defined in various ways. Throughout most of the history of education, the curriculum consisted of the tool skills of reading, writing, and mathematical computation at the primary or elementary level and the arts and sciences at the secondary and higher levels. For many educators, the curriculum remains essentially a program of studies, skills, and subjects which is offered in a formal sequence. Since the appearance of the activity or experience approach in the twentieth century, many educators have moved to a more generalized and extensive conception of curriculum. For them, the curriculum includes all of the experiences of the learner for which the school assumes responsibility.

In the broadest sense, the curriculum can be defined as the organized experiences that a student has under the guidance and control of the school. In a more precise but restricted sense, the curriculum is the systematic sequence of courses or subjects that forms the school's formal instructional program. These two major definitions of curriculum, as well as the variations that lie between them, are based upon particular conceptions of knowledge and value. The philosophies of education that will be examined later in this book involve conceptions of the curriculum that range in scope from the broad view, which includes all of the learner's experiences, to the more restricted one, which construes it to be bodies of intellectual subject matters.

There can be no question that curriculum designers, regardless of their philosophical convictions, attempt to seek that which is of the greatest worth to the learner. The problem is one of identifying and agreeing as to what is of the greatest truth, beauty, and goodness. This problem has metaphysical, epistemological, and axiological dimensions. Philosophers and educational theorists, however, have responded to this question with different answers, and these disagreements have produced the varieties of curricula.

---

1. For an excellent discussion of the curriculum in relation to philosophy of education, see Tom C. Venable, *Philosophical Foundations of the Curriculum*. Chicago: Rand McNally & Co., 1967.

For the Idealist, Realist, Thomist, Perennialist, and Essentialist philosophers, the curriculum consists of skills and subject matters. The basic skills are regarded as necessary tools for the later study of the more sophisticated subject matters that are derived from learned disciplines, such as history, mathematics, geography, and physical science, which have been developed by scientists and scholars. For these more traditional philosophies, the preferred curricular design is one of subject matter. Their major goal is the transmission and preservation of the cultural heritage. The curriculum is the means of transmitting the heritage, in learnable units, to the immature, so that they can participate in the culture. The survival of civilization is believed to hinge on the ability to teach tested truth and value to the young. The subject matter curriculum is a form of the conscious and deliberate transmission of the adult view of reality to children. Although children may be initially imposed upon, the acquisition of knowledge will lead to their eventual freedom by multiplying their alternatives of action. The subject matter curriculum is arranged in a hierarchy with priority given to subjects that are regarded as more general, and hence more significant, than other subjects. The arrangement of the subject matter hierarchy depends upon the particular conception of reality and values that is a background for the construction of the curriculum.

In contrast to a subject-matter design, other forms of curriculum have been proposed. Experimentalists, Progressives, and Reconstructionists have been more concerned with the process of learning than with the acquiring of the bodies of information that comprise the learned disciplines. The process-oriented curricular design has been referred to as the *activity,* the *experience,* or the *problem-solving curriculum.* According to John Dewey's experimental mode of learning, there is a method of scientific inquiry which can be applied to all human problems. The curriculum which follows this idea is a series of problem-solving episodes which are determined by the learner's interests and needs. The process-oriented curriculum is then concerned with developing methodological skills that are useful in a variety of situations. The content of the disciplines is used when it is needed to solve problems.

Methodology of Instruction   The method of instruction is closely related to the goals or ends which are specified in the curriculum. Methodology is the processes of teaching and learning by which the learner is brought into relationship with the skills or knowledge that are specified and contained within the curriculum. In the school, methods are the means or procedures that a teacher uses to aid students in having an experience, mastering a skill or process, or acquiring an area of knowledge. If efficient and effective, the methods of instruction will achieve the desired end.

John Colman has defined method as "an ordered system by which a teacher puts educative agents to work on humans to produce certain changes or results." He further has identified five necessary elements in instructional methodology: (1) an aim, or the specific objective or purpose of instruction; (2) an introduction that relates the particular lesson to previous learning or experiences; (3) content, or that which is the substance or the subject of a lesson; (4) a summary to reinforce the particular learning; and (5) an evaluation that determines if the particular aim has been achieved by the learner.[2]

Since teaching implies the use of a technique or method of instruction to secure a desired objective, educators at all levels are involved in methodological questions. Programs of teacher education include courses in techniques and methods of teaching. For example, there may be courses in teaching reading, language arts, science, social studies, mathematics, music, and art. Supervised student or practice teaching is designed to provide the prospective teacher with experience in integrating content and methodology in a classroom situation. Experienced teachers are involved in programs of inservice training designed to familiarize them with new methods. School administrators devote much of their time and resources in introducing and experimenting with methodological innovations. Even a cursory examination of the literature of professional education gives evidence of keen interest in methodology. There are articles on the Socratic method, the project method, the discovery method, the inquiry method, and many other approaches to instruction.

Methods of teaching and learning are most closely related to epistemology, or knowing, and to logic, the correct patterns of thinking. Once again, the study of systematic schools of educational philosophy provides clues to learning strategies that relate to the conception of knowing that is part of the philosophical system. If knowledge, or ideas, are innately present in the mind, then the most effective learning strategy would be a means of bringing them to consciousness. The Socratic method is an example of stimulating the learner to recall ideas. If learning is a transaction between man and his environment, as Dewey states, then the most effective method of instruction would be a means of making experience an efficient instrument in dealing with environmental problems. Although methods of instruction vary according to their

2. John E. Colman. *The Master Teachers and the Art of Teaching.* New York: Pitman Publishing Corp., 1967. pp. 5–11.

preferred contents and sequence, they all involve a set of procedures that are carried out with some aim.

Teacher and Learner Formal education involves a teacher and a learner. The conception of the nature and function of the teacher and of the learner depends upon the view of man that one holds. If man is regarded as an "incarnate spirit-in-the world," as the Thomists suggest, then the conception of his purpose and destiny is likely to be very different from the Pragmatic conception that man is a biological–sociological–vocal phenomenon. If man creates his own essence, as the Existentialists say, then the view of teacher and learner will be different from the philosophies that see man as a category in a metaphysical system.

The teacher–learner relationship is also based upon roles in the learning process. In the context of the subject-matter school, the teacher is a mature person who is expert in the content and the teaching of a body of knowledge. The learner is an immature person, in regard to that knowledge, and is present in the school to acquire and to master it. Thus, the method of instruction and the teaching–learning relationship depend substantially on the logic of the subject matter's organization.

In contrast to the subject-matter approach, the Progressive educator looks to the child's interests to provide the basis for the teacher–learner relationship. The child and not the subject matter is the center of the relationship. The teacher is a guide to the learning process and does not dominate it.

The assumptions that are made about the learner influence the teacher's behavior toward him and determine the curriculum that is planned for him. Assumptions about the nature of man influence the type of curriculum, the particular method of instruction, and the general climate of the school. The chapters that follow will examine the various philosophical assumptions about the nature of man and the education that is appropriate for him.

PHILOSOPHIES OF EDUCATION

Idealism, Realism, and Thomism are three of the major philosophies of education that have had a long history in Western civilization. They are still vital philosophies that guide educational processes and give substance to various forms of curricular design. Closely related to these rather traditional philosophies are the educational theories of Perennialism, which emphasizes man's rational character, and Essentialism, which stresses basic education.

In contrast to the more traditional philosophies, John Dewey's Pragmatic Experimentalism emphasizes the process of education as a transaction between man and his environment. Among the theories of education which bear a relationship to Experimentalism are Progressivism and Reconstructionism. Progressivism, which started as a reaction against traditionalism in education, stresses the liberation of the child's interests and needs. Reconstructionists urge that the school play a significant role in cultural criticism and change.

Contemporary education has witnessed the rise of two new approaches to educational theory: Existentialism and Philosophical Analysis. The Existentialist is worried about the rise of a mass society and school which dehumanizes man by reducing him to an object or a function. Philosophical Analysis seeks to find meaning in the language that is used in both common and scientific discourse.

It is valuable for students of education to be aware of the various philosophies of education, in order to identify educational programs, curricula, and methods in their relationship to particular philosophic positions. This may help them to examine and criticize educational proposals and policies. Although the philosophies may not be found in their pure forms in school practices, knowledge of the basic content of the various philosophical positions may be helpful in examining the consequences that are likely to result from the implementation of particular curricular or methodological designs.

The study of schools of educational philosophy should stimulate teachers to think about education in terms general enough that they may resist the temptation of subscribing to the promises of panaceas or to propagandistic slogans. Perhaps an examination of the schools of philosophy of education will help teachers to recognize that mechanical and organizational innovations can be used for many purposes and can have many consequences. The study of philosophy of education should encourage teachers to examine and formulate the broad personal and social aims that should guide educational practice.

Philosophical inquiry may aid the educator in examining his immediate decisions and problems. In turn, philosophy of education may draw heavily from the experiences, practices, and observations of the educator. For example, educational goals, practices, methods, and ends can be extrapolated from such systems of philosophy as Idealism, Realism, and Thomism. The converse is also true. It is possible to create educational philosophies by examining educational practices and generalizing about their most general consequences for personal and social growth, as the Essentialists, Progressives, and Perennialists have done.

Throughout history, and particularly in recent years, education has been the subject of debate and conflict. In many ways, the presence of divergent views and of debate is a sign of health and vitality. As a social institution, the school is the focal point of conflicts. This degree of interest and involvement shows that schools are relevant institutions. If one reads the literature of educational controversies, numerous recommendations are made for school reform. Some have even suggested that the school be abandoned as society's primary educational institution. Some argue that schools should deliberately instill religious and spiritual values in the young; others plead for an emphasis on law and order; still others proclaim that they must return to the intellectual virtues, to the liberal arts and sciences, or to basic education. Some people see schools as agencies of social criticism or social and political reform. For each platform and program that is advanced, there is a reaction and a counter-proposal. Behind each of these plans, programs, and platforms for the use of the school, there are underlying assumptions about the nature of the universe, man, life, and society. By examining these assumptions in their philosophical matrices, these various alternatives in education may be examined and illuminated.

FURTHER READING

Brown, L. M. *General Philosophy in Education.* New York: McGraw-Hill Book Company, Inc., 1966.

Brubacker, John S. *Modern Philosophies of Education.* New York: McGraw-Hill Book Company, Inc., 1969.

Colman, John E. *The Master Teachers and the Art of Teaching.* New York: Pitman Publishing Corp., 1967.

Frankena, William K. *Philosophy of Education.* New York: The Macmillan Company, 1965.

Kneller, George F. *Introduction to the Philosophy of Education.* New York: John Wiley & Sons, Inc., 1971.

Lucas, Christopher J. *What is a Philosophy of Education?* Toronto: The Macmillan Company, 1969.

MacDonald, John. *A Philosophy of Education.* Glenview, Ill.: Scott, Foresman and Company, 1965.

Morris, Van Cleve. *Modern Movements in Educational Philosophy.* Boston: Houghton Mifflin Company, 1969.

Nash, Paul. *Authority and Freedom in Education.* New York: John Wiley & Sons, Inc., 1965.

O'Neill, William F. *Selected Educational Heresies: Some Unorthodox Views Concerning the Nature and Purposes of Contemporary Education.* Glenview, Ill.: Scott, Foresman and Company, 1969.

Park, Joe (ed.). *Selected Readings in the Philosophy of Education.* New York: The Macmillan Company, 1968.

Phenix, Philip. *Philosophies of Education.* New York: John Wiley & Sons, Inc., 1961.

Reid, Louis A. *Philosophy and Education: An Introduction.* New York: Random House, Inc., 1965.

Rich, John Martin. *Readings in the Philosophy of Education.* Belmont, Calif.: Wadsworth Publishing Co. Inc., 1966.

Runes, Dagobert D. *Living Schools of Philosophy.* New York: Philosophical Library, Inc., 1948.

Shermis, S. Samuel. *Philosophic Foundations of Education.* New York: American Book Company, 1967.

Starkey, Margaret M. *The Education of Modern Man: Some Differences of Opinion.* New York: Pitman Publishing Corp., 1966.

Venable, Tom C. *Philosophical Foundations of the Curriculum.* Chicago: Rand McNally & Co., 1967.

Walker, Wanda. *A Philosophy of Education.* New York: Philosophical Library, Inc., 1963.

two

IDEALISM

Idealism's origins are usually traced to the ancient Greek philosopher Plato. Although only a few comtemporary philosophers of education can be classified as Idealists, the study of Idealism provides valuable historical perspective. Despite its current decline, Idealism has enjoyed several periods of great popularity in the past. In eighteenth and nineteenth century Germany, such Idealists as Fichte, Schiller, and Hegel dominated philosophy. Hegel's monumental works influenced the development of philosophical thought both in Germany and elsewhere. Both Karl Marx and John Dewey were students of Idealism in their early careers as philosophers. Friedrich Froebel, the founder of the kindergarten, attempted to create an educational method based on Idealist tenets.

In the United States Idealism has enjoyed moments of popularity. The New England Transcendentalists, the most famous of whom were Ralph Waldo Emerson and Henry David Thoreau, used Idealist metaphysical propositions in framing their own ontology, which was based upon the Oversoul, or Macrocosm. The nineteenth century educational administrator William Torrey Harris expounded a philosophy which recast basic Hegelian concepts in terms of the American experience.

Certain current educational practices have their origins and rationales in the Idealist framework. The notion that education is a process of unfolding that which is present but latent in the child is grounded in Idealist epistemology. The concept of the teacher as a moral and cultural model, or exemplar, has its origin in philosophical Idealism, as does the use of the Socratic method.

IDEALIST METAPHYSICS

In its basic terms, Idealism refers to any theory that asserts the crucial importance of the Mind, the spiritual, and the ideal in reality. It affirms that reality is essentially spiritual (the embodiment of the mental) and denies the possibility of knowing anything except the mental. As a means of explaining the Universe, Idealism posits ultimate reality in and solely within the mind and concludes that the universe is an expression of a highly generalized intelligence and will.[1]

In explaining human nature, the Idealist holds that man's spiritual essence is durable and permanent. The mind is the life force that gives man his vitality and dynamism. Mind is evidenced by doubting; doubting is thinking; thinking gives evidence of the presence of intellect or of mind.

Man's real Self is nonmaterial, spiritual, or mental. Selfhood, an integrating core of personal values, provides identity for the person, since it separates that which is from that which is not the self.

Although the universe may contain nonmental entities, it is the spiritual realities that are irreducible and hence really existent. The universe definitely contains distinctive mental realities. Reality is spiritual in substance rather than material. Spirit is more inclusive than matter and encompasses it. Matter is dependent upon spirit, since spirit enervates and vitalizes matter.

Although it is the spiritual which is ultimately real, it is possible to speak of the "real" world and the world "appearance" in the Idealist setting. The real world of mind and ideas is eternal, permanent, regular, and orderly. Representing a perfect order of reality, the eternal ideas are inalterable, since change is inconsistent and unnecessary. It is possible, then, to assert the existence of absolute truth and value.

There is also that which appears to the senses, the apparent world of everyday sensory experience. The apparent is characterized by change, imperfection, irregularity, and disorder. In terms of the real and the apparent, the educational task is that of redirecting the student from sensation to that of the reality of Ideas. Education becomes a kind of conversion to the reality of ideas.

Idealist metaphysics involves a transition from the notion of an individual, spiritual self to the assumption that the entire universe is of the same nonmaterial substance and is also a larger and more comprehensive spiritual self. Through the principle of relationship, the individual self is related to other selves. In other words, the individual self realizes

---

1. For treatments of Idealism, see J. Donald Butler, *Idealism in Education.* New York: Harper & Row, Publishers, 1966; and Sarvepalli Radhakrishnan, *An Idealist View of Life.* London: Unwin Books, 1932.

that what is transpiring in the universe is also transpiring within the self. This leads to a recognition that only mind can know mind. As a self, the subjective individual mind can know other selves, other minds, and can interpret them. In order to know and interpret other selves, there must be an order of intelligibility which is capable of being comprehended. This leads to the assumption that there is a Universal Self, an all-encompassing Entity, in which all reality is posited and organized. Thus, the individual human mind is related to and is of the same substance as the universal self.

The principle of intelligibility or relationships of spiritual selves to each other leads to the concepts of the Macrocosm and the Microcosm. Idealists have given various names to the concept of the macrocosmic mind and have referred to this universal ground of being as the Absolute Self, the World Mind, the First Cause, or the Universal. Regardless of the name used by the particular Idealist, the macrocosmic mind is the whole or totality of existence and the ground of all being. The universe is one, all-inclusive, and complete self of which the lesser selves are genuine or identical parts. The universal, macrocosmic mind is an absolute person, which is continually thinking, feeling, perceiving, and willing. The macrocosmic mind or self is both a substance and a process. Although the language may be vague or poetical, the macrocosm can be said to be thought thinking, contemplation contemplating, and will willing.

Although of the same substance as the whole, the microcosm is a limited part of the whole, an individual, lesser self. A qualitative relationship exists between the absolute macrocosmic mind and the individual microcosmic self. Although mind is universal, there are degrees of mind based upon its completeness. The individual self, or mind, is a complete entity insofar as it is a self. However, in relationship to the universe, it is a part of the whole. In the sense that the part is less than the whole, the individual self is qualitatively less than the whole.

The Nature of the Whole and the Part   A basic metaphysical problem for Idealists has been the question of the relationship of the part to the whole, the microcosm to the macrocosm, or the one to the many. Since Idealists share the basic working premise that the ultimate reality is nonmaterial or spiritual, the basic question has had to do with the relationship of the various parts to the unifying principle, or to the whole. This problem has contributed to the rise of a variety of Idealist philosophies. For the Spiritual Monist, reality is a single spiritual unity which possesses a dynamism that enervates and motivates all the individuated selves. All existence is permeated by a single unifying principle and force. According to the Spiritual Monists, the individual human self is a dependent part of the whole. To the Spiritual Pluralist, reality is a community in which the many selves reach out, embrace, and transcend each other. Such transcendence culminates in a mental or spiritual community in which all the individual selves are related to each other. The Absolute Idealists, such as Hegel and Harris, see the absolute objectifying itself in time and space through a dialectical process of unfolding. Hegelians used the now-classic formula of thesis, antithesis, and synthesis to explain the unfolding of the absolute reality.

Although there are subtle metaphysical differences running through the various Idealist schools, a number of major agreements can be found in them as the underlying basis of Idealist philosophy. Among them are: (1) the universe is spiritual and contains distinctively mental, or nonmaterial, realities; (2) these mental realities are personal; (3) the universe is one, all-inclusive, and complete part in which the lesser selves are genuine and identical parts or constituent members.

IDEALIST EPISTEMOLOGY

The absolute mind is a consciousness which is eternally thinking thoughts and ideas. The finite mind, or the microcosmic individual mind, is of the same substance as the absolute mind. Although limited in its completeness, the individual mind is capable of communicating with and of sharing the ideas of the absolute self or the macrocosmic mind, whose reach is ultimate and whose knowledge is complete. The microcosmic self is an emergent mind which is limited by being a part. As an emerging personality, the microcosmic, individual human mind seeks to be united in the absolute.

In Idealism, the process of knowing is that of recognition or reminiscence of latent ideas which are preformed and already present in the mind. The microcosmic individual human self may discover the ideas of the macrocosmic absolute mind in his own thoughts and feelings. Through intuition or introspection or short flashes of insight, the individual self looks within his own mind and therein finds a copy of the absolute. Thus, knowing is essentially a process of recognition, a recall and rethinking of Ideas that are latently present in the mind. What is to be known is already present in the mind. The learning task is that of bringing this latent knowledge to consciousness.

For the Idealist, the basic logic which underlies the metaphysical and epistemologic processes is that of relationships between the whole and the part. Mind is essentially a process by which relationships are ordered on the basis of whole–part logic. Truth exists within the macrocosm, or the absolute; it is an order or pattern that is logical, systematic, and related. Each proposition is related to a larger and higher proposition. While the whole includes the parts, the parts must be consistent with the whole. As an ordering process, mind organizes ideas, concepts, and propositions according to a pattern of systematic consistency.

According to the Idealist coherence principle of truth, truth is a set of closely related, orderly, and systematic relationships. To "be," or to exist, means to be involved systematically in the whole–part or macrocosmic–microcosmic relationship. As an assimilator and arranger, mind locates consistency and exposes inconsistency. The task of mind is to establish a perspective which is based upon the relatedness of the parts to the whole. The world mind, or the macrocosmic mind, views the universe according to a total perspective which orders time and space. The properly functioning individual mind strives to imitate the universal mind, in that it seeks to establish a coherent perspective into the universe. The consistent mind is one that is able to relate the parts —time, space, circumstance, event—into a coherent pattern or whole. Inconsistency in the finite mind occurs when time, place, circumstance, and condition are unrelated and cannot be ordered into a perspective.

Idealist Epistemology and the Educative Process   According to the principles of Idealist epistemology, the major educational task is that of assisting the learner to achieve a more vital and fuller identification with the absolute mind. Learning is the process whereby the learner comes into a gradually larger expression or apprehension of mental awareness. Learning is both a qualitative and quantitative expansion of the self which is accomplished by self development. The learner seeks a broad and general understanding, or perspective, into his universe.

As a highly intellectual process, learning is the recalling of and the working with ideas. If reality is mental, then education should be concerned with concepts or ideas. It has already been mentioned that reality is nonmaterial and is of ideas. Mind, again, is the process by which ideas are brought to consciousness and are arranged according to a system in which the part is related to the whole. Mind is thus a systematizer.

The Idealist educator is quite at home with the subject-matter curriculum in which various ideas or concepts are related to each other. The academic disciplines contain necessary concepts which are related to each other and which are referred to through symbols. For example, a word is a symbol of something. Symbols refer to or point to concepts. Learning is a self-active process which occurs when the learner recalls the concept to which the symbol refers. Any of man's symbolic systems are orderly designs or structures which rest on concepts which are present in the mind.

Through the course of human history, man has arrived at sets of conceptual systems such as the clusters of linguistic, mathematical, and aesthetic systems. Each conceptual system has a set of symbols which refer to its various concepts. While there seem to be many conceptual systems and their corresponding disciplines, all of these various subject matters are related into a synthesis. The subject matters represent the varying dimensions of the absolute. However, their cause, origin, and culmination are in the one underlying Unity. For example, the liberal arts are arranged into many conceptual systems, such as history, language, philosophy, mathematics, and chemistry. The highest degree of knowledge is that which sees the relationships of these various subject matters and is able to relate them into an integrated unity.

IDEALIST AXIOLOGY

In Idealist axiology, values are more than mere human preferences; they are real existents which are inherent intrinsically in the structure of the universe. Value experience is essentially an imitation of the Good which is inherent in the absolute. As real existents, values are absolute, eternal, unchanging, and universal. Goodness, truth, and beauty are found within the universal structure. Most Idealists deny that evil is a real existent. Rather, evil can best be described as the absence of organization, system, and completion.

As man searches to discover values, he finds an ethical core in the wisdom of the human race which has endured over time. Ethical conduct grows out of the permanent aspects of a social and cultural tradition which, in reality, is the wisdom of the past functioning in the present. The rich sources of value education are found in such cultural subjects as history, literature, religion, and philosophy. These are the subjects which reflect the unfolding of the absolute throughout man's historical experience.

For the Idealist, the aesthetic experience rests on the idealization of the world about us. The work of art is a concretizing or objectification of our ideas about reality. Art succeeds insofar as it captures the idealized representations of that which looks commonplace in our life. Art succeeds when it builds perspective and harmony. Like the work of art, an aesthetic personality is one which is harmonized and balanced. In aesthetic education, the student should be exposed to the great works of art and literature.

THE EDUCATIONAL IMPLICATIONS OF IDEALISM

The major aim of Idealist education is to assist the individual self, or learner, to achieve the good, unification with the absolute. To achieve the good means that one must first recognize and be directed toward it. Idealist education aims at nothing less than a conversion to the good, true, and beautiful.

The individual student has potentialities that are inherent in his ideational structure. Education is an instrument which aids in the unfolding and self-development of these potentialities. Based upon the assumption that the absolute has been revealed through the gradual unfolding of history and through human culture, idealism says that the learner is exposed to the cultural possibilities that are inherent in the cultural heritage. The man who wishes to cooperate in the process of his own growth recognizes that the relationship between the private man and the public man is reciprocal. As a social institution, the school cultivates the growth of the individual human personality and also the social self.

The Idealist Curriculum   The Idealist sees the curriculum as a body of intellectual subject matters which are ideational and conceptual. These various conceptual systems explain and are based on particular manifestations of the absolute. However, all conceptual systems culminate and participate in one unifying and integrating concept, one idea, or one cause.

The conceptual systems which are derived from the universal absolute have been revealed to man through the unfolding of history and constitute his cultural inheritance. The Idealist curriculum can be viewed as a hierarchy in which the summit is occupied by the most general of the disciplines, philosophy and theology, which explain man's most basic and general relationships to God and to the Cosmos. According to the principle of the hierarchy, the more particular subjects are justified by the more general subjects. The more general subject matters are abstract and transcend the limitations of particular time, place, and circumstances. Since they are general and abstract, they have the power of transferring to a wide variety of situations. Mathematics, in its pure form, is a very useful discipline since it provides methods for dealing with abstractions. History and literature are also ranked high in the hierarchy of the curriculum. In addition to being cognitive stimuli, the historical and literary disciplines are value-laden. History, biography, and autobiography can be examined as sources for moral and cultural models and heroes. The historical dimension can be seen to be the record of the absolute unfolding over time and in the lives of men, especially those men and women who are of heroic dimension. Somewhat lower in the curriculum hierarchy can be found the various sciences, which are concerned with particular cause-and-effect relationships. Since it is the key to communication, language is a necessary tool skill which is cultivated at the elementary level.

The Attitudinal Dimension of Education Since the ethical core is contained within and is transmitted with the cultural heritage, those cognitive subject matters such as philosophy, theology, history, literature, and artistic criticism are also rich sources of value. These subjects, in which the cognitive and the axiological are fused, represent the generalized ethical and cultural conscience. They are the bearers of man's moral traditions. The humanistic subjects can be closely studied and used as sources of cognitive stimulation. At the same time, these historical and literary sources can be absorbed emotionally and used as the basis for the construction of models of value. Value education, according to the Idealist conception, requires that the student be exposed to worthy models and exemplars so that their style might be imitated and extended. Therefore, the student should be exposed to and should examine critically the classics of art and of literature.

Idealist Methodology The Idealist's conception of the educative process is directly related to his conception of epistemology. The process of thought is essentially that of recognition, an introspective self-examination in which the learner examines the contents of his own mind and therein finds the truth which is shared by all others, because it is a copy of the truth which is present in the world mind. Idealist educators such as Friedrich Froebel have emphasized the principle of the learner's own self-activity. All learning takes place within the mind of the learner, who must actively seek truth. Although learning is a product of the learner's own activity, the learning process is made more efficient by the stimulation which comes from a teacher and school environment. Schooling is regarded as an efficient means of stimulating the learner's latent interest. Therefore, all education is essentially self-education. Immersion in the cultural heritage via the curriculum is a part of the formal school in the Idealist context. The cultural heritage is a means of stimulation rather than of transmission.

The learner's own activity is related to the student's interests and to his expenditure of effort. Students have intuitive self-interest which attracts them to certain acts, events, and objects. With such intrinsic interest, no external prodding is needed. When interest is intrinsic, or internal to the learner, then the positive attraction of the task is such that no conscious exertion is needed.

Although the learner has his own interests, not all learning is easy. The student may be deluded by the world of appearance and may seek ends which are not genuinely related to his own self-development. It is at such a time that the teacher, a mature model of cultural values, acts to encourage the student's redirection to truth. At times effort may be required, when the task does not elicit sufficient interest on the student's part. After an expenditure of interest and the application of self-discipline, the student may become interested in the learning task. Again, the cultural heritage comes into play to affect the student's interests. The broader the exposure to the cultural heritage, the more likely it is that the student will have a variety of interests. The more interests that are present, the greater the possibilities for further self-development.

The Idealist educational method is designed to stimulate the learner's own intuitive and introspective self-exploration. The process of growth or development is from the interior to the external. There is no one method that is used exclusively in stimulating the learner. Indeed, the idealist teacher should be conversant with a variety of methods and should use the particular method that is most effective in securing the desired results.

Although no one particular method can be specified, the Socratic dialogue is certainly appropriate to the Idealist learning situation. The Socratic dialogue is a process in which the mature person acts to stimulate the learner's awareness of ideas. The teacher must be prepared to ask leading and stimulating questions about crucial human concerns. When the Socratic dialogue is used in a classroom situation, the teacher must be able to use the group process so that a community of thought develops in which all students are willing to participate. The Socratic method requires skillful questioning on the part of the teacher. It is not a simple recall of facts that have been memorized in previous assignments. However, memorization may be a necessary first step so that the dialogue does not degenerate into a pooling of ignorant and uninformed opinion.

The use of Idealism might be illustrated by the following example of a high school English teacher discussing Mark Twain's *Huckleberry Finn* with students who had just finished reading about the moral dilemma that Huck encounters when he must either follow the enacted law of the state or the higher law of his conscience. Specifically, Huck must decide if he should surrender the escaped slave Jim to the authorities for return to his slave master, or if he should assist Jim on his way to a free state. Huck's dilemma reveals the conflict that can occur between general and abstract values and those that are more immediate and particular.

The teacher uses *Huckleberry Finn* to represent a classic work of the American experience—whose basic theme has persisted in attracting generations of readers. The book is one that has withstood the test of time and represents values that are perennial to man's life and destiny on the planet. It is important that the teacher place the book in its historical and literary context so that the students are aware of its relationship to the American experience. The relationships of the book to the history of the Dred Scott decision and the fugitive slave law should also be made clear to the students.

It is important that the students have read the book before discussing it. While the Idealist teacher welcomes a free flowing discussion, he does not encourage misinformation or permit unfounded opinion to obscure the necessary essentials of the learning episode. Once the students are aware of the author's life story, the context of the book, the characters and plot, then the serious and exploratory learning can take place through the asking and framing of stimulating questions. Avoiding those questions that can be answered with a simple yes or no, the teacher asks questions which have answers which lead to still other questions.

The conflict between the enacted and higher law is the crucial issue that has persisted throughout human history. What should man do when the law of the state and the dictates of his conscience conflict? Should there be a distinction between the good man and the good citizen? Should man follow his conscience and take the risks attendant to such a decision? Should he seek to change the enacted law? Is the inner law of conscience part of a universal and higher law that binds all men?

Once the students have explored the theme of man's conflict presented by Huck's dilemma, then other instances of the same conflict can be illustrated by pointing to examples of civil disobedience as practiced by Henry David Thoreau, Mohandas Gandhi, and Martin Luther King. The moral questions raised by the Nuremberg trials of the Nazi leaders and the My Lai massacre in Viet Nam can be examined and explored to illustrate the current and yet persistent aspects of this broad moral question.

Imitation of the exemplar is also a part of the Idealist methodology. The student is exposed to valuable lessons which are based on worthy models from history, literature, religion, biography, autobiography, and philosophy. He is encouraged to study and to examine the model so that the particular person being studied serves as a source of value. The teacher is also a constant model in that he is a mature embodiment of the highest values which are present in the culture. Although the teacher should be selected for competency in both subject matter and pedagogy, he should be an aesthetic person who is worthy of imitation by the immature. The student imitates the model by incorporating the exemplar's value schema into his own life. Emulation does not mean mimicry, but is an extension of the good into one's own life.

Teacher–Learner Relationship   In the teacher–learner relationship, great emphasis is placed on the central and crucial role of the teacher. As a mature person, the Idealist teacher should be one who has established a cultural perspective. He should be an integrated person who has blended his various life roles into an harmonious orchestration of values. It is clearly recognized that the learner is immature and is seeking the perspective that the culture can provide. This does not mean that the student's personality is something to be manipulated by the teacher. It is a simple recognition that the student is striving toward maturity, toward a perspective into his own personality. As in the case of all men, the learner's nature is spiritual and his personality is of great worth. The teacher should respect the learner and should see his role as that of assisting the learner to realize the fullness of his own personality. As indicated, the personalities of the teacher and student are of immense value. Since he is a model and mature representative of the culture, the selection of the teacher is of great importance. The teacher should embody values, love students, and be an exciting and enthusiastic person.

J. Donald Butler, in *Idealism in Education,* has emphasized the crucial role of the teacher by citing some of the desired qualities of the good teacher. According to Butler, the teacher should: (1) personify culture and reality for the student; (2) be a specialist in human personality who knows his students; (3) as an expert in the learning process, be capable of uniting expertise with enthusiasm; (4) merit his students' friendship; (5) awaken the desire to learn in his students; (6) realize the moral significance of his work since he is a coworker with God in perfecting men; (7) aid in the cultural rebirth of each generation.[2] Although this list mentions only some of the qualifications cited by Butler, it is evident that much is expected of the Idealist teacher. He should be both a skilled professional educator and a warm and enthusiastic person. According to such a conception of the role of the teacher, teaching is a demanding blending of expertise, competence, culture, and personality. It is an art as well as a science.

CONCLUSION

Idealism is a philosophy that proclaims the spiritual nature of man and the universe. It holds that the good, true, and beautiful are permanently part of the structure of a related, coherent, orderly, and unchanging universe. The Idealist educators prefer a subject-matter curriculum that emphasizes truths gained from man's enduring theological, philosophical, historical, literary, and artistic works. The following concepts, rooted in Idealist philosophy, have a special relevance for current educational practice: (1) education is a process of unfolding that which is

---

2. Butler, *Idealism in Education,* p. 120.

latently present in the person; (2) learning is a discovery process in which the learner is stimulated to recall the truths that are present within his mind; (3) the teacher should be a moral and cultural exemplar of values that represent the highest and best expression of personal and humane development.

SELECTION

J. Donald Butler

J. Donald Butler, one of the major contemporary advocates of Idealist philosophy of education, was born in Nebraska in 1908. He received his bachelor's degree at the University of Omaha in 1929. In 1933, he received a Master of Religious Education from the Biblical Seminary in New York and received his Doctorate of Philosophy at New York University in 1937. He has been active in the fields of religion and education. He taught history and philosophy of education at Princeton Seminary from 1944 through 1958 and was professor of Christian education at the Austin Presbyterian Theological Seminary from 1958 to 1961. In 1961, he became James Wallace Professor of Religion and Chairman of the Department of Religion at Macalester College. The following selection, from Butler's *Four Philosophies and Their Practice in Education and Religion,* examines the educative process from an Idealist perspective.

*   *   *

Bogoslovsky proposes a novel arrangement of the curriculum in his *Ideal School.* Not liking the sharply segregated subjects of study in the conventional school, he proposes four general areas of study and development, all interrelated. Even the structure housing the school is to be designed to give a distinctive place to each of these four phases. Viewed from the air the building will be a perfectly symmetrical cross, each arm of which will house one of these four main departments. The first, the *universe* division, is to be an enlarged science department in which students study the "inanimate forces of nature, the origin of our solar system, the developing of life, all background of the human drama." The second section is the *civilization* division, offering an inclusive study of the social sciences. "By civilization," Bogoslovsky explained, "we mean all the activities,

From pp. 215–216 and 217–219 in FOUR PHILOSOPHIES AND THEIR PRACTICE IN EDUCATION AND RELIGION by J. Donald Butler, 3rd Ed. Copyright, 1951, 1957, by Harper & Row, Publishers, Inc. Copyright © 1968 by J. Donald Butler. By permission of Harper & Row, Publishers, Inc.

achievements, and institutions of humanity, which control our environment so as to provide the necessities of life, security, and comfort—all that we do to get rid of dangers, fears, and privations. Food, clothing, shelter, technology, communication, and government are all within this field." In the *culture* division, which is the third, "philosophy, art, literature, religion, interpretation and evaluation of environment" are to be included. The fourth section, named the *personality* division, offers study of "the physical, physiological, emotional, and intellectual factors that together make up human beings . . . different types of personalities and . . . the most interesting individuals who have actually existed or have been created by art." These four divisions are to be closely tied together by the *personality building* section housed where the four arms of the cross converge. In this central division is "the final summing up, coordination, or integration of everything that is done in the other sections in terms of helping students systematically and persistently, to build continuously better and better personalities."

Without drawing such a blueprint, Demiashkevitch claimed that the public secondary school should give an enriching and stimulating general cultural education. In making his brief for the informational side of school learning, he outlines three objectives to be fulfilled by it: (1) The student should acquire enough general information to know how and when to search for reliable information on problems he will have to face. (2) He should come to possess "sufficient knowledge of the fundamental truths, moral, social, and scientific, ignorance of which would make him dangerous to himself and others." And (3) the mind of the pupil should be imbued with "standards of lucid, profound, fruitful, and careful reasoning," inculcating in him "the habit of hard and accurate thinking." . . .

The final aspect of idealist education now to be considered is a practical one, namely, teaching methods. What method or methods will the idealist teacher use? Could you spot an idealist by catching him doing things in certain characteristic ways in the classroom?

First of all, idealists are likely to insist that they are creators and determiners of method, not devotees of some one method. Contrasting themselves to the experimental tendency in recent times and the wide adoption of the project method, they may say something like this:

"Yes, we believe in experimentation, activity, and the project. But we insist that doing is just one among many methods, not *the* method. There are various methods from which we can select those that best serve our purposes at the time."

Still speaking in general terms, we can say that the idealist prefers that an informal dialectic be in process in the classroom most of the time. Instead of students being confronted constantly by specific directions in which a definite path of action or thought is laid out for them, he prefers that there always be alternatives of thought, at least, if not alternatives of action. Since it is the self-activity of the pupil in which genuine education and development take place, he wants the student to be confronted by decision and selection as much of the time as is practicable. Certainly he doesn't want the pupil's will crippled by having all his decisions and selections made for him.

1. Because of this, questioning and discussion are probably the prime methods for many idealists, at least when the subject under study involves thinking and readily lends itself to this treatment. In leading discussion the teacher can do many things by careful use of thought-provoking questions. He can lend significance and meaning to the content being studied. He can confront the student with alternatives evoking his judgments. The teacher can open to him alternatives of thought that might not otherwise occur to him. And he can represent to the student something of the breadth of ideas and opinions he will face when he goes out into the world on his own. Parenthetically, it should be remarked that the idealist teacher uses questions not so much to find out what the student knows as to cultivate the student's judgment.

In addition to the teacher's ability to create dialectical situations by means of question and discussion, the students themselves, by virtue of their various backgrounds and unique individualities, will create their own dialectic, usually without knowing or intending it. The skillful teacher is the one who will make the most of these resources of the students, letting the conflicts of their own thinking have free course, using these resources fully and never substituting his own questions or ideas for them. These latter are reserves of initiation to be used when, for one reason or another, the thoughts of the students do not strike fire.

Care should be taken, however, that discussion does not degenerate to the level where it is little more than an ill-prepared pooling of ignorance or a clearing house for empty words. Horne readily acknowledges that discussion can be wasteful unless in the hands of a skillful leader. "Successful use of it," he says, "not only requires a good leader, but presupposes experience, study, observation, and knowledge on the part of those participating."

2. Lecture is another method idealists may use, but here again there are precautions in its use. There is a legitimate place for

good expository presentations by the teacher in which accurate representations of objective information are made or in which precepts, beliefs, or interpretations are wisely offered as counsel. The dangers to be avoided are that the lecture may become a phonographic recitation of facts or ideas, on the one hand, or an autocratic institution, on the other, allowing no place for student questioning, response, or judgment.

Another legitimate use of the lecture, according to idealists, which of course comes as an accompaniment, is as a creative work of art inspiring students and evoking their response much as a painting, poem, or symphony might do it. Bishop Grundtvig's influence in the Danish Folk High Schools, which brought glorification of the lecture into those schools, is an instance of this kind of practice. Often students were requested not to take notes, so that there would be no artificial device separating student and lecturer, the spoken word being given free course as medium of communication and response.

3. A third important method of idealism is, of course, the project, in which students, singly or in groups, pursue a constructive task themselves. Observation and experimentation there will be, at least in the physical and biological sciences, starting with problems and religiously following the steps of scientific method. Excursions and projects beyond the walls of the school will occasionally supplement book learning by face-to-face relation with real community and social situations. There will be essays to be written, notebooks to be assembled, all kinds of reference leads to follow in libraries, creative writing, sketching and painting, sculpturing, and numberless other engaging occupations to be used whenever they grow out of the unit of study at hand.

FURTHER READING

Butler, J. Donald. *Four Philosophies and Their Practice in Education and Religion.* New York: Harper & Row, Publishers, 1968.

_____. *Idealism in Education.* New York: Harper & Row, Publishers, 1966.

Gentile, Giovanni. *The Reform of Education.* New York: Harcourt, Brace and Co., 1922.

Greene, Theodore M. "A Liberal Christian Idealist Philosophy of Education," in *Modern Philosophies of Education,* 54th Yearbook, Part I, National Society for the Study of Education. Chicago: University of Chicago Press, 1955.

_____. *Liberal Education Reconsidered.* Cambridge, Mass.: Harvard University Press, 1953.

Horne, Herman H. *The Democratic Philosophy of Education.* New York: The Macmillan Company, 1932.

————. "An Idealist Philosophy of Education," in *Philosophies of Education,* 41st Yearbook, Part I, National Society for the Study of Education. Chicago: University of Chicago Press, 1942.

————. *The Philosophy of Education.* New York: The Macmillan Company, 1905.

Radhakrishnan, Sarvepalli. *An Idealist View of Life.* London: Unwin Books, 1932.

Thomson, Merritt M. *The Educational Philosophy of Giovanni Gentile.* Los Angeles: University of Southern California Press, 1934.

three

REALISM

Although there are various schools of Realistic philosophy, such as Scientific Realism, Classical Realism, Natural Realism, and Theistic Realism, certain basic common threads run through all these various positions. John Wild best illustrated the basic Realist position when he wrote:

Our common sense tells us, first that we inhabit a world consisting of many things which are what they are, independent of any human opinions and desires; second, that by the use of reason we can know something about these things as they actually are; and third, that such knowledge is the safest guide to human action. . . .

These basic beliefs of mankind are also the three basic doctrines of realistic philosophy: (1) there is a world of real existence which men have not made or constructed; (2) this real existence can be known by the human mind; and (3) such knowledge is the only reliable guide to human conduct, individual and social.[1]

While educational philosophers have devoted much energy to interpreting John Dewey's Pragmatic Experimentalism, much of their discussion has remained purely theoretical and academically abstract in that it has not affected school practice. In contrast, the subject-matter curricula of secondary and higher education show a Realist orientation. In many secondary schools and colleges, the curriculum consists of bodies of such discretely organized, separate subject matters as history, language, mathematics, and science. These various subject matters are con-

---

1. John Wild. *Introduction to Realist Philosophy.* New York: Harper and Brothers, 1948. p. 6. By permission of Harper & Row, Publishers, Inc.

strued to represent man's carefully organized and systematic exploration of his world. High school and college students read textbooks written by experts in the disciplines and attend classes taught by specialists in the various subject matters. This chapter examines the basic principles of Realist philosophy and analyzes its educational implications. Realism may be defined as any philosophical position that asserts: (1) the objective existence of the world and beings in it and relations between these beings, independent of human knowledge and desires; (2) the knowability of these objects as they are in themselves; (3) the need of conformity to the objective reality in man's conduct.

ARISTOTELIAN ORIGINS

The origins of Realist philosophy can be traced to the ancient Greek philosopher Aristotle, who elaborated a form of natural Realism. While Plato was concerned with a private world of perfect forms or ideas, Aristotle used methods of common-sense observation to investigate a public world. As a result of his empirical study, Aristotle developed a metaphysical system which construed Being to be a uniting of Actuality and Potentiality. While Actuality is that which is complete and perfected, Potentiality is the capability of being perfected. In his explanation of Reality, Aristotle referred to four formal Causes. He defined a cause as that which in any way influences the production of something, of an object. The Material Cause, or matter, is that out of which a being is made. As the substratum of Existence, matter is indeterminate but capable of determination. It is potency. Form, or the Formal Cause, is that into which a thing is made. Form, the principle of actuality, is the design which shapes and gives structure to an object. In terms of knowing, form is the object of intellectual knowledge, or the essence of a being—that which remains unchanged despite alterations or accidental qualities. For Aristotle, it is the union of form and matter that constitutes individual concrete substance. From form come the objects' essential or unalterable qualities; from matter come the objects' imperfections, limitations, and individuating qualities. The Efficient Cause is the agency of production which brings about the action, or motion, from potentiality to actuality. All natural processes are developmental actions that bring out the latent possibilities by bringing into actuality those perfections which are already contained as potency in matter. The *Final Cause* refers to that on account of which the effect is produced, or the direction toward which the object is tending.

Throughout the Aristotelian metaphysical system there is a pronounced predilection to dualism—the tendency to view reality as composed of two constituent elements. For example, Aristotle viewed existence as the uniting of the two elements of actuality and potentiality, of form and of matter. As will be pointed out later, this dualistic conception of reality profoundly affected Western thought. Man could be viewed as a composite creature composed of spirit and flesh or mind and matter. Based upon such a dichotomous view of human nature, distinctions could be made which had pronounced educational consequences. Knowledge could be separated into the theoretical and the practical arts; aesthetic experience could be viewed in terms of the fine and applied arts; education could be distinguished as being either liberal or vocational. In the context of these basic dualisms, that which was abstract, theoretical, fine, and liberal was given priority over that which was practical, applied, and vocational. In part, John Dewey's attack on dualism (which appeared in *The Quest for Certainty*) was a critique of this tendency to view reality, man, and human experience in terms of two planes of existence.

The Aristotelian conception of a dualistic universe can also be seen in terms of the categories of Substance and Accident. *Substance* refers to that which exists of and by itself, without a supporting structure. It is the stable element in existence. In contrast, *accident* refers to the variable changes which do not alter the essence of a being but which serve to individuate it.

To Pragmatists, reality is in a constant state of flux or change. The Realist would observe that to have or to measure change, there must first be something which is changing. For the Realist, that which undergoes change is substantial. The changes themselves are accidental.

When Aristotelians and other Realists refer to the Nature of a thing or, in the case of man, to human nature, they refer to those universal elements of man that are unchanging, regardless of time, place, and circumstances. It is these universals that constitute the crucial and basic elements in the education of man. For example, when Aristotelians refer to human nature, they define man as a rational being who is endowed with the "given" of an intellect that enables him to abstract from his experience and to frame and to act on various alternatives. Regardless of their race, nationality, occupation, or sex, all human beings have the power to reason. Nevertheless, particular men live at different times and in different places. Varying climates and conditions give rise to a variety of human experiences which result in cultural particularities. Although particular men may be American, Chinese, Russian, or African because of the accident of being born in a particular place, all men share a common human nature. As a result of the very important accident of being born in a certain location, different men will speak different languages; but regardless of their particular language, all men will use language as a means of expression and communication.

Robert Hutchins in *The Higher Learning in America* clearly described the educational implications of the Aristotelian distinction between substance and accident:

One purpose of education is to draw out the elements of our common human nature. These elements are the same in any time or place. The notion of educating a man to live in any particular time or place, to adjust him to any particular environment, is therefore foreign to a true conception of education.

Education implies teaching. Teaching implies knowledge. Knowledge is truth. The truth is everywhere the same. Hence education should be everywhere the same. I do not overlook the possibilities of differences in organization, in administration, in local habits and customs. These are details. I suggest that the heart of any course of study designed for the whole people will be, if education is rightly understood, the same at any time, in any place, under any political, social, or economic conditions. Even the administrative details are likely to be similar because all societies have generic similarity.

If education is rightly understood, it will be understood as the cultivation of the intellect. The cultivation of the intellect is the same good for all men in all societies. It is, moreover, the good for which all other goods are only means. Material prosperity, peace and civil order, justice and the moral virtues are means to the cultivation of the intellect. So Aristotle says in the *Politics:* "Now, in men reason and mind are the ends towards which nature strives, so that the generation and moral discipline of the citizens ought to be ordered with a view to them." An education which served the means rather than their end would be misguided.[2]

Hutchins' reference to Aristotle is a telling one. It reveals the Realist's conception that man as a rational being should live according to reason's dictates. According to such a conception of human nature, the task of education is to cultivate and to exercise man's rational potentiality so that it might be actualized. In *de Anima* and the *Nichomachean Ethics,* Aristotle asserted that certain general principles of human nature and behavior were discernible. With other animals, man shared the functions of nutrition, locomotion, reproduction, and respiration. But as a more complex and sophisticated being, man also has functions of sense, imagination, habit, pain, and pleasure. Following his dualistic world view, Aristotle described the two planes of human existence. As a

---

2. Robert M. Hutchins. *The Higher Learning in America.* 1936; New Haven: Yale University Press, 1962. pp. 66–67.

rational being, man is an abstractive, symbolic, and choice-making creature. However, there is also a nonrational component in human nature
in that the same man who is rational is also emotional and volitional.
In nature's scheme, there is a place for man and a reason for his existence. Man's reason-for-being is to recognize, to cultivate, to develop,
and to use his rationality. His greatest source for happiness comes in the
active cultivation of his rationality, which contributes to his own self-
actualizing, or self-cultivation and self-perfection. The man who truly
acts as a human being is one who is governed by his highest and defining
power—his reason. Although man's emotions are the means of experiencing pleasure and his will is the instrument of obtaining his ends, both
the emotions and the will are governed properly by reason. When
governed by his appetites, emotions, and will, man acts unintelligently
and debases his own essential humanity. When governed by reason,
man can develop that excellence of moral character which is a mean
between the extremes of repression and uninhibited expression or indulgence of passions and appetites.

In the *Politics,* Aristotle postulated his doctrine of general education,
which recognizes a reciprocal relationship between the properly educated man and the properly educated citizen.[3] Education is to be an
instrument of cultivating man's basic rationality. The rational man
should also be the worthy citizen of the *polis,* or society. For civil welfare
it is necessary to secure the proper education of youth. Education is to
cultivate both the self-governing man and the harmoniously governed
civil society.

Education was conceived by Aristotle to be a means of aiding man in
his quest for happiness *(Eudaimonia).* Man's greatest happiness is in
possessing excellence or perfection of any kind. The most important
kind of excellence is that of being a truly humane person, a genuinely
reasoning being. Education aids man in achieving his quest for perfecting his reason. As his reason is perfected, so is man a total human being.
According to the Aristotelian position, education is always towards an
end, toward the perfection of human nature. Education has the function
of developing the best part of human nature as well as man's lower
faculties. When education is directed to the perfection of rational inquiry, it takes on the added dimension of aiding men in shaping their
own futures through deliberation and action.

Aristotle believed that the curriculum should follow the patterns of
growth and child development. Infants are to have the opportunities for

---

3. For a well-written essay on Aristotelian education, see Robert S. Brumbaugh and
Nathaniel M. Lawrence. "Aristotle: Education as Self-Realization," in *Philosophers on
Education: Six Essays on the Foundations of Western Thought.* Boston: Houghton Mifflin
Company, 1963. pp. 49–75.

play and physical activity and should be exposed to proper studies. Before adolescence, the major educative emphasis is directed to the cultivation of proper values and predispositions. Attention is also given to physical activities which lead to bodily exercise. Little is attempted in the cognitive area, with one exception: the child learns the fundamental operations needed by literate men—reading and writing.

For adolescents and youths, Aristotle's curriculum design stresses intellectual studies such as arithmetic, geometry, astronomy, music, grammar, literature, poetry, rhetoric, ethics, and politics. After age twenty-one, the most sophisticated intellectual disciplines, such as physics, cosmology, biology, psychology, logic, and metaphysics, are introduced.

REALIST METAPHYSICS

Based upon its origins in Aristotelian principles, Realist philosophy stresses a belief in the reality of a material world that is real and exists independent of and external to the minds of the observers. Understanding of that which is genuinely real is based in a world of physical objects and in man's perceptions and experiences of those objects. All objects are composed of some material, or matter, which is at the base of all existence. Since it includes the "principle of potentiality" within it, matter has the potential of being shaped and organized into any kind of being. In order to become an object, matter must be encased in a design or form and has to assume the design of a particular object before it can actualize its potentiality. Although the concepts of matter and form are logically separate, they are not experientially separate.

REALIST EPISTEMOLOGY

Realist metaphysics is based on the assumption that there exists an objective order of reality which consists of objects that are independent of man's knowing of them. These objects are independent to and antecedent of man's knowing or experiencing of them. However, man is capable of knowing these objects through his senses and his reason. As he comes to know the order of reality, man comes to know the nature of things such as the structure of the universe, of man, and of society.

For the Realist, *knowing* is to have knowledge about an object. Cognition or knowing involves an interaction of the mind and the world outside of the mind. Such an interaction is between man's sensory-mental apparatus and the energy which emanates from the object.

Sensation is the beginning of knowledge but not the end of knowing. The origin of man's knowledge of an object begins with sensations of energy in the form of light, sound, pressure, heat, cold, vapor, or taste, which emanate from an object. Each of man's external senses has a proper object of sensation. Touch apprehends pressure or physical resistance; sense of temperature reveals whether the object is hot or cold; taste, localized in the tongue, is a specialized development of the sense of touch which apprehends flavors; smell is a sense localized in the nasal passages which apprehends odors; the object of hearing is sound; sight, the highest and most objective sense, has color as its proper object. Sensation, then, first involves the physical action of something impinging on man's sensory apparatus.

The mind first apprehends the immediate qualities emanating from the object (color, odor, taste, hardness, softness, pitch, etc.). The qualities are immediate and need no other senses to mediate for them. They are conveyed to man from the outside by the different energy patterns that activate the sensory organs. The mediate sensory qualities of size, distance, position, shape, motion, and weight are borne to the mind by the immediate sensory qualities. Sensation is about the material component of an object—about matter. Since the material is changing, sensation varies from time to time and from place to place. It is contingent and circumstantial.

As a result of sensation, man has sense experience of the object. The products of sensation, sensory data, are sorted by the mind like a computer. Man's common sense, or power of abstraction, sorts out the perceptions into those qualities which are always present in an object, or necessary conditions of that object, and those which are sometimes found in the object, its contingent conditions. Those qualities which are always present in the object are essential to it and are the basis of a concept of the object. A concept is a meaning that applies to all things of the same class. It has qualities which it shares with other objects in the same class but with no other objects.

For the Realist, man knows by a two-fold process which involves sensation and abstraction. This corresponds to the Realist conception of a dualistic universe. Man's senses encounter objects and come to play on the material aspects of these objects. Through the senses of touch, taste, smell, sight, and sound, data about the material component of an object are conveyed to the mind. Once in the mind, these sensory data are sorted out, classified, and catalogued. Through the process of abstraction, the mind arranges the data into two sorts of conditions: those that are necessary, or always found in an object, and those that are contingent, or sometimes found in an object. Those that are always present in an object are essential to that object; they constitute the form of that object. Form is the proper object of abstraction. Those qualities or conditions that are sometimes present in the object are those that reside in the material component. Conceptualization results when the mind has abstracted the form of an object and has recognized the object as belonging to a class. Objects are classified when they are recognized as having qualities which they share with other members of the class but not with other objects belonging to a different class.

Perhaps an example will illustrate the Realist epistemological strategy. In his experience, man encounters other men. These men are of varying skin pigmentation—some are white, others are black, still others are red or yellow. Men are of different heights and weights; they speak different languages and are of different ethnic origins. They are of different nationalities. However, underlying the variations which result from color, size, weight, height, ethnic origin, and nationality, there is something, some "whatness" or "quidity" which is common to men of all kinds and types. There is a common human nature which identifies them as belonging to the class "homo sapiens" and not to other classes of objects. A man is different from a horse, a tree, a house, or a rock.

The Realist epistemological strategy has sometimes been called a "Spectator Theory." Simply put, man is viewed as a careful observer of reality who seeks to know through an organized, systematic, and structured way of viewing reality. The Realist is concerned with the plan or design of the universe. What is the structure or design of reality? Man's epistemological problem is that of extracting or abstracting the structures which explain the operations of the universe, of man, and of society. For example, linguistics is the study of the structure of language, which can be extracted from studies of various languages. The natural and physical sciences deal with the structure and patterns of natural and physical reality. The various social sciences have as their objects knowledge about the structure of human interaction. According to the Spectator Theory, man's knowing quest is to find the structure in reality. The finding of structure consists in carefully extracting it from the matter which conveys it. Man knows by being a spectator who observes the world in the hope of finding the patterns which it contains. Organized spectating, for the Scientific Realists, deals with the discovery of principles and laws. Natural laws can be discovered, and they can be used to guide men's conduct.

As a spectator, the Realist is a discoverer of reality that is pre-existent, independent, and antecedent to his experiencing of it. Through careful observation, man can discover the structures of objects and can discover how these objects interact with each other. He can frame generalizations which are based on the patterns and regularities that occur in these interactions between objects. For example, he can observe and record daily temperatures. As a result of his careful observation, it is possible to detect variations in temperature and to plot temperature ranges. When the plotting of temperatures has been done for an extended period of time, it is possible to generalize about temperature variations and to speak about "seasons." Such generalizations form the theory which is basic to meteorology. The theory is derived from experience and can be used to guide such practical activities as the planting of crops, the wearing of clothes, and the constructing of dwellings.

The Realist theory of knowledge is also referred to as the "Correspondence Theory." Our ideas are true when our concepts conform to or correspond to the object in reality. Our statements about reality conform to or correspond with the way things really are. In other words, the idea in our minds corresponds perfectly with the object being known.

According to the Realist correspondence theory, knowledge conforms to reality and that which is taught should also conform to reality. For example, Newton's law of universal gravitation conforms to the way the universe actually is in its operations. It is true and worthy of being transmitted to the young. For the Realist, the extent of agreement of our knowledge with the actual object as it exists in the real world determines the truth or falsity of our knowledge claims.

The Realist Curriculum   The Realist conception of reality is that of an objective order of reality. The objects that comprise reality can be classified on the basis of their structural similarities. The disciplines of history, geography, language, mathematics, biology, botany, and chemistry, for example, consist of clusters of related concepts and of generalizations which interpret and explain interactions between the objects which these concepts represent. Each discipline is a conceptual system which has a structure. A structure is a framework of related conceptual meanings and their generalizations which explain physical, natural, social, and human realities. For example, the discipline of biology consists of a number of necessary concepts which are appropriate to the study of plants and animals. Any discipline consists of a number of related concepts that constitute the necessary structure of the discipline.

The role of the expert scientist and scholar is crucial in defining the areas of the curriculum. The scholar or the scientist is an expert because he studies and carefully observes certain restricted and well-defined aspects of reality. For example, the historian studies man's past and scrutinizes the documents which relate to it. By using the historical method, he judges evidence and draws certain generalizations or interpretations about past events. The expert is such because he has mastered a particular area of reality. He knows the limits of his expertise to the degree that he is aware of that which is appropriate to his field of study and that which is unnecessary to it. He also is skilled in the method of inquiry which is the most efficient mode of discovery in his particular area of research. Through monographs, lectures, and books, the scholar makes his findings available to other experts in his field. These findings are subjected to criticism from within the field. Although scholars and scientists may disagree on interpretations, they are expected to share the methodology of inquiry and agree on the necessary concepts of their respective disciplines.

Scientists and scholars are often, but not always, found in colleges, universities, or research centers. In particular, universities are expected to support research and teaching. The scholar and the scientist are expected to make their findings known publicly and to publish the results of their research. They are expected to contribute to the literature which explains and elaborates disciplines. Underlying scholarly activity is the assumption that generalizations about reality can best be made by experts who carefully examine certain selected aspects of reality. In universities, these experts are usually organized into academic departments of history, language, chemistry, physics, English, political science, and so on. Students attend the institutions of higher learning to study with and to obtain the knowledge which the expert can provide. Prospective teachers, especially secondary teachers, study academic subject matters. They, in turn, will take the information, the concepts, the generalizations provided by the expert and organize this subject matter into teachable units for their students.

Basic to the Realist curriculum is the idea that the most efficient and effective way to find out about reality is to study it through organized, separate, and systematically organized subject matters. The liberal arts and science curriculum of the undergraduate college and the departmentalized secondary school curriculum provide evidence of the subject-matter approach to curriculum. The conventional subject-matter curriculum consists of two basic components: (1) the body of knowledge which is the structure of a discipline; (2) the appropriate pedagogical ordering of the subject matter so that it fits the readiness and maturation of the learner. In such a plan, the teacher is expected to be skilled in both the subject matter that he teaches and the method of teaching it to students.

Also present in the Realist conception of curriculum is what can be referred to as the "Percolation Theory," in which knowledge is discovered by experts who transmit it to others. Formal schooling involves the transmission of knowledge from experts to those who are inexpert and who wish to know something about reality.

REALIST AXIOLOGY

The Realist theory of value is an objective one that asserts that man is capable of estimating the value nature of objects through knowledge. The value of an act lies in the object or in the relationship among objects in such a way that it can be known, judged, or estimated. In contrast to emotive theories that rely merely on subjective feelings, the Realists assert that every act or object is intrinsically good or evil, right or wrong, beautiful or ugly.

As has been indicated, the Realist tends to view the operations of the universe as regular, purposeful, and patterned. There are operations which follow a design and are for an end. By using his rationality, man can discover the design of the universe and can come to know its operations and laws. The purpose of knowledge is to assist man to recognize the patterns operative in reality and to encourage his conformity to these patterns.

Prizing rationality as man's distinguishing characteristic and defining power, the Realists seek to encourage man to shape his values in terms of the structures of reality. By knowing the structures of physical, natural, social, and human reality, man can frame realistic and viable alternatives. Through knowledge, he can rationally frame choices about his life. The presence of such choices constitutes the liberal (or liberating) aspect of an education.

THE SCHOOL AND TEACHER IN A REALIST CONTEXT

The Realist position asserts that the school is a specialized environment which is designed to advance the cultivation of rationality. It is a formal institution which is staffed by competent teachers who possess knowledge of a subject or skill and who know how to teach it to people who are immature in terms of the knowledge that is to be acquired. The school has the definite and specific function of transmitting bodies of knowledge and inquiry skills to students. The school's task is primarily an intellectual one. Although the school may from time to time perform recreational, community, and social functions, these are ancillary to the primary task and should not be allowed to interfere with the efficient performance of that task. In such a setting, the educational administrator's role is that of seeing that the faculty of a school is not detracted from performing its intellectual task of cultivating and stimulating the knowledge of the learner. The administrator is especially charged with maintaining the freedom of his faculty to teach and his students to learn.

The Realist curriculum at the elementary level involves the acquiring of the tool skills of reading, writing, mathematics, and study habits that are necessary for the more advanced and systematic inquiry into the learned and systematic disciplines. The secondary and collegiate curricula consist of the bodies of funded knowledge that are regarded as containing the wisdom of the human race, as determined by the most authoritative scholarship.

The teacher is to be a person who possesses a body of tested knowledge and who is capable of transmitting it to students. The teaching–learning relationship always involves the teaching of some knowledge or skill to someone. It is the teaching of reading, or of history, or of chemistry, to a student. Teaching, in the Realist context, is not permitted to degenerate into polemics or indoctrination. Nor should teaching become merely a set of personal interactions which do not involve the learning of a skill or area of knowledge. Although personal interaction is certainly recognized as necessary to the learning of a skill or subject, the presence of knowledge and the acquiring of such knowledge is what defines the art of teaching.

CONCLUSION

Once again, the Realist posture in education is clearly summarized by John Wild, who wrote:

Education is the art of communicating truth. It has not been fully achieved until this truth not only lies within but actually possesses the mind and heart of the student.

By way of summary, we may say that the aim of education, as the realist sees it, is four-fold: to discern the truth about things as they really are and to extend and integrate such truth as is known; to gain such practical knowledge of life in general and of professional functions in particular as can be theoretically grounded and justified; and, finally, to transmit this in a coherent and convincing way both to young and to old throughout the human community.[4]

---

4. John Wild. "Education and Society: A Realistic View," in *Modern Philosophies and Education,* 54th Yearbook, National Society for the Study of Education, Part I (Chicago: University of Chicago Press, 1955), p. 31.

SELECTIONS

Harry S. Broudy

Harry S. Broudy, a respected defender of classical Realism in education, was born in Poland in 1905. His higher education was in American institutions. He received the Bachelor of Arts from Boston University in 1929, and was awarded the Master of Arts in 1933 and the Doctor of Philosophy in 1935 by Harvard University. He taught philosophy and education at Massachusetts State Teachers College at North Adams and then at Framingham before coming to the University of Illinois in 1957 as a professor of education. Among his books are *Paradox and Promise* (1961), *Building a Philosophy of Education* (1961), *Enlightened Cherishing: An Essay on Aesthetic Education* (1972), and *The Real World of the Public Schools* (1972). With John Palmer, he wrote *Exemplars of Teaching Method* (1964).

The selection that follows is from *Building a Philosophy of Education.* Here, Professor Broudy discusses reality and knowledge from the perspective of Realist philosophy. Among the topics treated are: (1) the objective order of reality; (2) the form-matter hypothesis; (3) sensation and perception; and (4) conceptualization.

* * *

Being and Knowledge Knowledge is *about* something—about an object. That object may be a cow, a set of insurance statistics, the state of the stock market, or a problem in algebra. And the aim of knowledge is to bring into awareness the object as it *really* is. Sometimes, of course, it is more comforting not to know the truth, but ignorance is bliss only when ignorance is complete. The moment we suspect that the doctor may have deceived us about our health or the instructor about our grades, the bliss is gone. Our concern to know objects as they really are shows that there is a possibility that we can be deceived and that some of our judgments may be false. A false judgment will not make us aware of the object as it really is, but as it *appears* to be. Consequently, if we can indicate the conditions under which our judgments are true (epistemology), we are at the same time setting up the standards by which we can distinguish appearance from reality (metaphysics).

We have no choice but to begin with our experience and the standards of correct thinking. We have no choice but to judge A and B as different if we can find nothing important common to both of

Harry S. Broudy, BUILDING A PHILOSOPHY OF EDUCATION, Second Edition © 1961. Reprinted by permission of Prentice-Hall, Inc., Englewood Cliffs, New Jersey. pp. 106–111.

them, and to say they are somewhat alike if we do. We have no choice but to accept one of two contradictory statements and to reject the other. In short, if we rely on our human powers, experience plus the laws of evidence are all we have to go on in the search for what is really real and what is really true.

Using these two resources, we find that the world divides itself into a multitude of different objects interacting in countless ways. If we now ask for the most fundamental distinction we can make among all the objects of experience, it would seem to be the difference between the concrete objects that occupy space, come into being, and pass away, on one hand, and the images and ideas by which we are aware of them, on the other.

Awareness is a peculiar transaction. When A is aware of X, X is present to A, but it is a strange presence, for X is not physically inside A. I am aware of the keys of my typewriter flicking up to the paper, yet neither the paper nor the typewriter is inside of me. Nor does my being aware of the typewriter do anything to the machine. In the world of things such transactions are not to be found. If your automobile and mine collide, we both shall probably have repair bills. When two elements unite to form a compound, the result is different from each of them, and neither comes out of the ordeal unscathed. To be sure, my nervous system discharges some energy whenever I am aware of anything, but it is very doubtful that it discharges twice as much energy when it is aware of two men than when it is cognizing one. The image of the Grand Canyon bulges my skull no more than the image of a flea.

Just as remarkable is another feature of awareness. If we take the color out of a piece of cloth, another color appears beneath it. We cannot take the size out of a suit of clothes without destroying the suit itself. We cannot take the hardness out of iron without performing drastic operations upon its shape and other properties. Yet the mind performs all of these feats of extraction without disturbing the object in the least. For awareness is always a process of abstraction, of concentrating on some aspects of things and ignoring others.

We have already discussed still another characteristic of the mind. It is its ability to combine its images, perceptions, and concepts into patterns with extraordinary freedom. None of us thinks it a very remarkable feat to invoke into our presence the picture of a grandmother who is no longer alive and the notion of tomorrow's breakfast which is not yet cooked. All physical things are chained to the present; yesterday and today have no meaning for an automobile or a bag of beans.

Putting these features together, we have to conclude that in awareness the human mind operates in a way and with elements that to some extent, at least, are non-material. The kind of being ideas have is not the same as the kind of being trees, stones, and birds have. Meanings, ideas, concepts have their being simply in pointing to or disclosing the natures of things, but they are not things themselves. Plato believed that meanings or concepts exist in a world of their own—the world of forms. Aristotle and others held that they are abstracted by the mind from our sense experience, that is, from the interaction of our sense organs with the external world. We shall call this type of being (of ideas) noetic or cognitive being.

Although all noetic being is abstract, not all of its elements are equally so. My image of the fire hydrant outside the window is abstract, yet it is the resemblance of a particular object. When we remember and imagine, it is still with images of particular things. On the other hand, when we decide to *define* a fire hydrant, the resulting *concept* leaves out its redness, its somewhat dignified stance, and its particular location outside my window. The notion of fire-fighting instruments leaves out still more of my hydrant, but makes up for it by referring to the multitude of hydrants wherever they may be.

For some of our mental constituents we depend on physical objects and physical processes that furnish us with images retained by memory and aroused in imagination. And some of its objects the mind invents, e.g., the square root of minus one, quadratic equations, diverse hopes and aspirations, the perfect circle, and the perfect marriage. Nevertheless, the ultimate origin of all our knowledge lies in our awareness of the external world, and it is the nature of this kind of knowledge that sets up the most persistent problems in epistemology.

Science and Metaphysics   This external world is a world of space. Things in it have a location and happen at a certain time. When and where are always pertinent questions to ask about anything that is said "to exist." All real individual things exist and in this sense forms or concepts do not exist even though it is by their means that we become aware of "what" does exist.

All real individuals in the world of our experience are changing. Things are in continuous transformation, changing their size, location, and qualities. Our world is the domain of existence, that is, of changing Being. To understand changing Being is the function of both science and metaphysics. The difference lies in the nature of the questions each asks.

Science wants to know what variables are involved in a specific kind of change, for example, what variables are involved in the growth of plants and animals; what variables are involved in juvenile delinquency or in keeping a satellite in orbit? Science also wants to answer the question as to how variables vary with respect to each other. For example, is an increase in national income accompanied by a decrease in crime? Does the earning power of American males vary with the amount of schooling they have received? Does the speed of aircraft vary with the temperature of the atmosphere?

As science develops it wants to know whether there is any law or general formula that describes how one variable changes with respect to others. Pressure of a gas, to be sure, changes with volume and temperature, but in what ratio? How much of a change in one will be accompanied by how much of a change in the others? Is there a law, one might ask, that tells how crime or the birth rate or trips to Europe vary with changes in *per capita* income of Americans?

Science, therefore, is interested in finding formulas or the most general forms wherewith to describe specific changes in the world. Each science is concerned with its own domain of changes: chemistry, physics, biology, economics, psychology have their own domain of events which they try to describe and understand.

The test of truth for science is called *empirical verification.* This means that when a scientist can by his formula predict how a change in one variable will be accompanied by a change in other variables, he is on the way to being satisfied that his formula is reliable. But this satisfaction is increased as he or other workers test the predictions and find them to be as predicted. The spectacular predictions of astronomers about eclipses; the success of chemists in making new compounds so that they will have the properties we want them to have, for example, were dramatic verifications of the *formulae* these scientists were testing.

It will be noticed that the inner nature of a thing or an event need not be understood or even talked about so long as the formula "works." If wearing blue neckties were to reduce delinquency in cities, we might proceed to furnish all adolescent boys with blue neckties without knowing why they were so effective in reducing crime. It would not be long, however, before scientific curiosity would impel investigators to search for factors within the blue ties and the crime in order to account for the efficacy of the neckwear. They would be taking a step toward discovering the "nature" of blue ties and crime. How far into the "real nature" of things will science go? This much we can predict: science will go as far as it must to verify the formulas it has constructed and as far as it can to discover new formulas that predict better than the old ones.

Metaphysics, on the other hand, asks a somewhat different set of questions about changing Being. To understand change metaphysically is to find a formula that describes features which are essential to any change whatsoever, that is, which make the very idea of change understandable.

Thus in one of the most famous metaphysical analyses of change Aristotle argued that to "think" change we have to think of something that changes, that is, something that persists through the change as the house persists when we change its color, or the horse persists as it grows from colt to yearling. Aristotle called what makes this persistence possible "matter."

Matter is not made up of little hard particles, but is to be thought of as a principle or kind of being that can be spread out in space and that can take on new forms. It never exists apart from some form, but it is not irrevocably wedded to any particular form. Therefore, matter is a relative term. The bar of steel can be matter for a pair of scissors or a girder for a building, and the girder may be matter for the builder. If, however, we reduce the steel to molecules, and these to atoms, and these to electrons and protons, we are gradually getting to the notion of what the ancients called a "prime" matter, or matter with a minimum of form.

By the forms that give each individual thing its character or "whatness" we can mean:

1. Such qualities as shape, position, size, weight, motion—commonly called the primary qualities.

2. Such qualities as color, odor, taste, hardness, softness, hotness, pitch—commonly called the secondary qualities.

3. Such qualities as beautiful and ugly, propitious or threatening, attractive or repulsive—sometimes called the tertiary qualities.

4. Certain structures that give the object power to affect other objects in particular ways, e.g., that of an acid or of a man.

5. A definition that isolates what is indispensable to its being the sort of thing it is, and certain accompanying characteristics that it always has (necessary accidents) or sometimes has (contingent accidents).

There are many kinds of change, ranging from the drifting of a grain of sand on the beach to nuclear fission. Some changes merely substitute one surface quality for another, e.g., as when a lady changes the color of her lips, cheeks, or hair. Other changes, such as we call growth, follow a fairly regular pattern. Birth and death are more radical changes; wholly new forms come into being and pass away. But without the notion of a matter that is hospitable to many forms, we could have only creation and annihilation—not change. To understand change is to be able to indicate:

(1) the state or form of matter out of which the present thing came,
(2) the agency that brought about the transition,
(3) the form or structure that it now has, and
(4) the direction toward which the thing is trending.

Metaphysics does not seek to control things but rather to discover and describe the most general features of Being. It does not ask: "How does X vary with Y?" Nor, "How does X affect Y?" These are scientific questions. It does ask: "What does it mean to say that anything exists?" "How does one describe change as such?" Cause, agency, substance, attribute, matter, form, actuality, potentiality and purpose—these are some of the categories or notions Aristotle felt were needed to describe what it means for anything to exist.

Some of these terms are not needed in the special sciences but when we include "human being" or the kind of existence human beings lead along with the way stones and stars exist, it is difficult to talk about Being meaningfully without the ideas of actuality and potentiality; matter-form; cognitive being and changeable Being. In Aristotle's system all things were given some of the characteristics of "human being." For example, Aristotle thought of each thing as a composite of matter and form, that is, of the potential becoming actual according to some built-in design. For Aristotle the universe and everything in it was trying to achieve a goal or end natural to it. Such a teleological mode of Being modern science denies to physical objects, although "purpose" is hard to dispense with in discussing human behavior.

*   *   *

William Oliver Martin
William Oliver Martin was born in Ohio in 1903. He received the Bachelor of Arts degree from Wittenberg College in 1925, his Master of Arts from Ohio State University in 1929, and the Doctorate of Philosophy from Harvard University in 1934. From 1936 until 1949, he was a professor of philosophy and mathematics at Ohio University. Since 1949 he has served as professor and chairman of the Philosophy Department at the University of Rhode Island. He is a Realist in educational thought and has written the following books: *The Order and Integration of Knowledge* (1957), *Metaphysics and Ideology* (1959), and *Realism in Education* (1969). The following excerpts from *Realism in Education* illustrate the teaching-learning relationship from a Realist perspective.

*   *   *

The activities of learning and teaching are so closely related that in considering the rights and duties of the student we have already had to mention the duties of the teacher. What does it mean for a teacher to have academic freedom? In what sense is it a right? And what duties go with it?

The student's duty to learn implies the teacher's freedom to teach the kind of knowledge the student is supposed to learn. The obviousness of this in principle is likely to blunt awareness of the fact that this is not always observed in practice, especially in the teaching of "controversial subjects." The right to teach also implies the right to have others respect his authority in his own field of knowledge in so far as he knows it. In any given case, of course, this may be difficult to determine. It means at least this, however, that the teacher should be free of social pressures which would require him to distort or withhold relevant knowledge in a course. For example, in a class in "agriculture" in college, the truth about margarine and butter should not be withheld because a member of the board of trustees owns a dairy business and has indirectly been concerned about "what has been going on in a certain class." Even in more controversial subjects, usually those called "value subjects," the teacher must have freedom to teach within the restrictions set by the kind of knowledge he is supposed to teach. To rescue this from an innocuous truism, it is necessary to point out that this freedom makes quite a demand upon the teacher, for to know the limitations of his own special subject is to have a kind of knowledge other than that subject. The judgment of how well this principle is acted upon, whether made by the teacher or by his superior, will turn out to be prudential, and often a matter of debate.

Does a teacher have the right to teach any truth even in his own subject matter? A simple illustration will point up the prudential aspect. Let us suppose a teacher of the second grade, in the course of dealing with the history of the Colonies and with George Washington, stresses the fact that Washington wrote love letters to another man's wife, and made some money in shady land deals. When the protests come in from parents, he pleads academic freedom. Is it justified? The issue is not the truth of the statements, but rather whether he should tell *those* truths. Are no truths to be withheld from a student at any age? If one maintained this, then he

From pp. 75–80 in REALISM IN EDUCATION by Wm. Oliver Martin. Copyright © 1969 by Wm. Oliver Martin. By permission of Harper & Row, Publishers, Inc.

would have to hold that the age-level of the student is irrelevant to what may be taught—which, of course, is admittedly a false proposition. It would seem, then, that prudence demands the withholding of truths at certain ages, the reason being the danger that their presentation at a given age may lead more to misunderstanding than to understanding. Is there any school, at any place in the world, and at any time, that has not done this?

This problem is a little more subtle than it appears. For one may ask whether it is justifiable to teach falsehoods, if they lead to more knowledge than not teaching them. The whole truth about Washington is not being presented, hence to that degree a relatively false image of Washington is being created in the minds of the students. Let us ask another question: can it be otherwise? What solution does the teacher really propose? Taken literally, it is a pure contradiction, hence nonsense, to say that a teacher's function is to teach falsehoods instead of truths. But is the selection of truths, that of not giving the whole truth, that kind of falsehood? In high school chemistry, the whole truth about valence cannot be told. The student really only understands it when he comes much later, if at all, to physical chemistry. Again, to make the problem more complicated, can something that is relatively false be used to communicate a truth? Obviously not. Yet, in the first or second grade, look at the drawing of the earth going around the sun. It is a long ellipse with the foci far apart. Now the earth does not really move that way. If the drawing were accurate, the ellipse would be so close to a circle that in appearance the student would confuse it with a circle, hence not understand the elliptical orbit.

When it comes to matters of prudence, there are no rules for the automatic and simple solution of problems. Prudence is the virtue concerned with the art of applying principles. When singular cases of alleged infringement of academic freedom arise and call for judgment, then, however clear the right to teaching-freedom may be in principle, for better or worse that judgment must be prudential. Whatever uncertainty is involved usually stems from the complexity of the existential circumstances. And it cannot be mentioned too often, that in the absence of a great deal of moral integrity on the part of the teacher there can be no solutions to such problems.

Infringements upon the freedom of teaching are roughly proportional to the scale in the education ladder, being more frequent on the upper levels. There is a reason for this. As the student grows older and matures, he merits the right to learn that which, for prudential reasons, was withheld from him in the earlier years. As these truths gradually emerge in the teaching activity, there may arise pressures, social and otherwise, to have them suppressed. If so, then there is genuine interference with the freedom of teaching, which is not morally justifiable. But, even this cannot properly be understood unless the duties as well as the rights of the teacher are considered.

Pedagogical books are sometimes filled with detailed lists of what a teacher ought to do, including keeping a classroom well ventilated. Such a list of rules and duties has its function, and is not to be deprecated. But the problem here is concerned with the duties of a teacher in a more basic sense, having to do with ethical principles.

The first duty of a teacher is to "know his stuff." The school exists primarily for the student and not the teacher. The purpose of teaching is primarily to help the student to "get to know," to learn some specific kind of knowledge. The teacher was once a student, too, and had the freedom to learn. If he merits the right to teach, then he has of necessity acquired the knowledge which he hopes to convey to the student. The right to teach implies the duty to know one's special subject that is to be taught. If this seems like belaboring the obvious, it is sometimes forgotten that one may believe, sincerely but mistakenly, that he knows more than he really does. An example may illustrate. A very wealthy man, retired at an early age, was not only disappointed but somewhat offended because a business school would not give him the right to teach "marketing." Had he not made his fortune marketing the farm machinery of a certain manufacturer? Did he not know "marketing"? Of course, yes and no. What he failed to understand was that the subject included a lot more knowledge than he had.

The teacher has the duty, and not merely the right, to insist that what he teaches is knowledge, *in some sense or other*. And he should understand and be sensitive to the qualification. For there are "degrees of knowledge," and there are degrees of certainty based upon the extent of the evidence. He has the duty to separate good guesses and personal prejudice from opinions based on a modicum of evidence, and these in turn from propositions having a high probability of truth or having practical if not theoretical certainty. A proper understanding of this obligation would require him to have not merely a knowledge of his own special field, but also of that part of philosophy which is concerned with logic, epistemology, and the order of knowledge. At least, he should not be naive about these matters.

The teacher also has an obligation not only to know those pedagogical methods that can help make him an effective teacher, but also to be alert to new techniques. This may not be necessary for a person in his role as a research worker, but it is his duty in so far as he is a teacher.

Also, a teacher has the obligation to recognize the authority of others in their own fields. This is a moral demand, and it requires some humility and self-discipline on his part. An example may relieve the abstractness of this principle. In higher education, a professor of biology should not argue that to have peace there must be, of necessity, a world government; for nations are like cells in an organism, and if cells were separated from the organic whole there would be only disintegration and death, etc. etc. The reader may say that such "things" and their equivalents go on in classrooms all the time. Unfortunately, this is correct; which simply says that a great deal of immorality and intellectual nonsense goes on under the guise of teaching a kind of knowledge.

The exact issue here should be understood. The issue is not whether world government is desirable and is necessary to achieve peace in the world; nor is there any question about the right of the professor to know what he is talking about, and to know the limitations of his own special field. But there is a lack of justice in the classroom in such a leap from biology to international politics.

In the first place, he does not know where his subject begins and where it ends; for in advocating and trying to "prove" the necessity of world government he has stepped outside the field of biology, in which he is an authority, without warning the students of the fact. Thus, there is an illegitimate shift of authority. Second, he has used bad logic by using what is called a "false analogy," thus demonstrating his lack of knowledge of another field which he ought to know. Third, he has misled students into thinking that biology can prove more than it can, namely, that biological evidence can prove something in political science or international affairs— which, of course, is not merely false but plain nonsense. What the teacher is doing, then, is imposing his own ignorance on students under the guise of wisdom, and by virtue of his status he renders them rather helpless.

Helpless? Cannot the students protest, or at least correct him? However innocent or naive the question is, the answer is yes. Since this is not a hypothetical example, one very brilliant student did attempt to correct him, and he "learned" the following—that there are two approaches, the biological and that of political science, that there is a difference of opinion on such matters, but that this is good, for it is the mark of a *live* university and surely the student would not want it otherwise.

Now, of course, that was the final sophistry. If that is multiplied by a few million, day in and day out, one may get a rather accurate image of contemporary education. These ethical principles we have stated, which are intrinsic to the very nature of teaching, may seem in the abstract to be truisms. Therefore, why belabor the obvious? They are truisms. However, when once the full implications are examined, it turns out that to many, if not to most, they are not at all immediately obvious; and perhaps they need some belaboring.

To be most effective as a teacher, one should have goodwill, be a seeker of truth, have intellectual humility. He should love his students as fellow human beings, and not use them as instruments of his egotism. And so on. If teaching is one kind of moral activity among others, then the teacher must be just, must be moral. It is not sufficient merely to have piled up credits in courses on "teaching."

FURTHER READING

Breed, Frederick S. *Education and the New Realism.* New York: The Macmillan Company, 1939.

Broudy, Harry S. *Building a Philosophy of Education.* Englewood Cliffs, N.J.: Prentice-Hall, Inc., 1961.

Brumbaugh, Robert S. and Nathaniel M. Lawrence. "Aristotle: Education as Self-Realization," in *Philosophers on Education: Six Essays on the Foundations of Western Thought.* Boston: Houghton Mifflin Company, 1963.

Martin, William O. *Realism in Education.* New York: Harper & Row, Publishers, 1969.

Whitehead, Alfred N. *The Aims of Education and Other Essays.* New York: The Macmillan Company, 1929.

Wild, John. "Education and Society: A Realistic View," in *Modern Philosophies and Education,* 54th Yearbook, Part I, National Society for the Study of Education. Chicago: University of Chicago Press, 1955.

_____. *Introduction to Realist Philosophy.* New York: Harper and Brothers, 1948.

four

THOMISTIC PHILOSOPHY

The Theistic Realism of Saint Thomas Aquinas has important educational implications. Since the late middle ages, Thomism has been the dominant philosophy associated with Roman Catholicism. Although Aquinas did not concentrate his efforts on constructing an educational theory, his philosophy, Thomism, has usually been identified with Roman Catholic educational institutions.[1] In addition, it has attracted support from individuals such as Robert Hutchins and Mortimer Adler, who are not associated with Roman Catholicism.

In terms of philosophical classifications, Thomism is one variety of religious, or theistic, realism. While accepting the basic metaphysical and epistemological tenets of Aristotelian natural realism, Thomists also embrace Christian principles. The Thomist accepts the following parts of Aristotelian natural realism: (1) the objective existence of the world and beings in it and relations between these beings, independently of human knowledge and desires; (2) the knowability of these objects as they are in themselves; (3) the necessity of human conformity to objective reality in man's thought and conduct. Thomistic epistemology also accepts the basic Realist strategy of cognition, that there are objects or persons which man can come to know through a two-fold knowing process of sensation and abstraction.

In contrast to purely natural realism, Thomism embraces supernaturalism. It includes Revelation as a source of divinely inspired truth. Thomists assert that man is destined for the beatific vision, or communion with God, which constitutes man's final and most complete happi-

---

1. For a very readable account of the life and educational theory of Thomas Aquinas, see John W. Donohue, S.J. *St. Thomas Aquinas and Education.* New York: Random House, Inc., 1968.

ness. However, through his own free will, man sinned and was alienated from God, his Creator. This "estrangement" or "alienation" was overcome through the redemptive act of Jesus Christ, the Son of God, who instituted grace and founded a new "People of God." As a free agent, man can choose either to cooperate or to oppose the work of his own salvation.

Thomism draws from both Aristotelian natural Realism and from Catholic Christian theology; and as a system, it represents the interpenetration of the two. In Thomism, reality has both a spiritual and a material dimension. Man, possessing both a body and a soul, is also seen to exist on both a supernatural and a natural plane. God, the First Cause and Creator, regarded as the Source of all existence, is a personal and caring Creator and not an impersonal "ground of being."

The interpenetration of realistic philosophy and Christian theology can be made clear by referring to several current works in educational philosophy which draw support from Thomistic principles. In *Catholic Viewpoint on Education,* Father Neil McCluskey discusses both the theological, or revealed bases of Catholic education, and the philosophical, or perennial bases of Catholic education.[2] According to McCluskey's account, the theological bases of Catholic education are the following: (1) God gave man a supernature by which he would be enabled to experience divine life; (2) through sin, man fell from grace; (3) Jesus Christ, the Son of God, redeemed man and restored him to God's grace and to the promised supernatural life; (4) Christ represented the perfect human being and serves as a moral exemplar for the Christian who seeks to live the Christ-like life; (5) the supernatural order is complementary to the natural order and in no way diminishes the value of reason and nature. It does not diminish the natural rights of the individual, the home, and society.

McCluskey also comments on the philosophical bases of Catholic education when he asserts: (1) there is a personal God whose existence can be demonstrated by reason; (2) man has a purpose for existing which is in keeping with his nature; (3) as a person, each man is a free and rational being; (4) man's perfection lies in knowing and possessing truth, beauty, and goodness; (5) man's material body gives him a continuity with nature, and his spiritual soul promises a destiny that transcends the purely material and temporal natural order.

Father William Cunningham in *Pivotal Problems of Education* has referred to this synthesis of Realism and Theism as Supernaturalism.[3]

---

2. Neil G. McCluskey, S.J. *Catholic Viewpoint on Education.* New York: Image Books, 1962. pp. 57–79.
3. William F. Cunningham. *Pivotal Problems in Education.* New York: The Macmillan Company, 1940.

Cunningham asserts that man, consisting of a soul and body, is properly guided by faith and reason. For Cunningham, education has a perennial and unchanging character. An educational philosophy which is founded upon Supernaturalism can specify certain educational aims in terms of the origin, nature, and destiny of man. Man's origin was from God through the act of creation; man's nature is fashioned in the image and likeness of God; man's destiny is to return to the God from which he came. In asserting the value of a Supernatural philosophy of education, Father Cunningham claims that it can specify ultimate and proximate aims, goals, and ends. This is in contrast to the purely naturalistic forms of Experimentalism, Pragmatism, and Progressivism which ignore or deny the existence of man's spiritual nature and his spiritual destiny.

The interpenetration of Realism and Theism in Thomistic philosophy has some pronounced educational implications. Education will have a two-fold but complementary set of aims which derive from man's dualistic nature. Education should: (1) provide the knowledge, exercise, and activities which contribute to the cultivation of man's spirituality; and (2) provide the knowledge, exercise, and activities which cultivate man's rationality. Thus, educational aims, practices, and goals can be organized upon this dualistic conception of man and reality.

EDUCATIONAL IMPLICATIONS OF THE THOMISTIC CONCEPTION OF MAN

Aquinas defined man as a "spirit-in-the-world," an incarnate spirit who possesses the essential unity of animated body. Man is unique because he is composed of a corporeal and spiritual substance and is set between two worlds, with his soul situated on the boundary between heaven and earth. Man possesses an immortal, deathless, and immaterial soul which vitalizes the principle of self-awareness and freedom. Man's soul requires embodiment and has an historical and social existence, a temporal and spatial context, in which man knows, loves, and chooses.

In continuity with Nature, each man is shaped by his particular time and place and participates in writing his own biography. Man is a social being who is born, grows, matures, and dies within families and social communities. As a social and communicating animal, man has developed formal speech, writing, and reading. These patterns of community and communication are acquired and must be learned. Schools as social agencies contribute to man's development as a reasoning and communicating participant in community life.

Thomists recognize that each man lives in a particular place at a particular time. Because there are historical variations and social adaptations to changing conditions, there are various cultures and nations.

Despite his recognition of these variations, the Thomist avoids cultural relativism. He asserts that there is a commonality to human nature and culture which is more important than these variations. All men possess a common human nature which is what it is because of the underlying spiritual and material realities in which all men participate. The Thomistic conception of human nature or spirit-in-the-world provides a basis for curriculum construction. In curriculum development, the principle of the hierarchy of generality is operative. Those aspects of existence that are most general, abstract, and durable are located at the summit of the hierarchy. Those aspects of life that are particular, specific, and transitory are located in a lower position. Should there be conflict in the lower rungs of the curricular hierarchy, it is adjudicated in terms of agreement or disagreement with the more general and higher areas of the curriculum. Since man's soul is immortal and destined for the perfect happiness of the beatific vision of God, those studies and exercises that contribute to spiritual growth and formation are given curricular priority. Theological, scriptural, and religious studies should be emphasized. Since man is a rational being who is a free agent, knowledge and exercises that contribute to the cultivation and exercise of rationality are emphasized so that each man will prepare to exercise his freedom of choice. Man lives in a natural and a social environment and possesses a material body. That knowledge and skill which enables man to sustain his bodily and physical existence should also be included in the curriculum. As a product of history, man creates his own biography. Living in society, he needs ethical, legal, political, and economic systems which contribute to his personal and social well being. Since he is a social and communal being, the language and literary skills that contribute to communication and community form a major foundation of formal education. The skills of reading, speaking, and writing are an important part of man's basic education.

Although there have been more recent statements on Catholic education which emphasize ecumenism and social justice, the statement of Pope Pius XI, "On the Christian Education of Youth," is worth examining since it contains a clear view of Thomistic educational principles. In speaking of the nature of Christian education, Pius said:

Since education consists essentially in preparing man for what he must be and for what he must do here below, in order to attain the sublime end for which he was created, it is clear that there can be no true education which is not wholly directed to man's last end. . . . Christian education takes in the whole aggregate of human life, physical and spiritual, intellectual and moral, individual, domestic, and social.[4]

4. Pius XI. *Christian Education of Youth*. Washington, D.C.: National Catholic Welfare Conference, 1936. p. 36.

THOMISM AND KNOWLEDGE

As has been previously indicated, the Thomistic conception of epistemology basically follows Aristotelian patterns. Man is immediately conjoined to material reality through his senses. Through sense experience, a necessary condition of knowing, man can sense objects and other persons. The senses are bodily powers which unite men directly with individual objects of sensation. Man's mind gives him the power to conceptualize from this sensory experience by abstracting and sorting the characteristics or qualities present in objects. Concepts are formed by the mind when their universal, or essential qualities, are liberated from the restrictions of concrete materiality. Concepts are immaterial constructs or abstracts which can be manipulated by man's reasoning mind. By organizing concepts, man can generalize from his experience and can construct possible alternatives of action. When he exercises his freedom of choice, man weighs and chooses from various possible alternatives.

Like Aristotle, Aquinas asserted that man's highest human activity was that of rationality, of exercising his intellectual and speculative powers. Through his defining rational powers, man can come to distinguish himself from other objects and can come to know himself. Man's intelligence enables him to transcend the limitations of the material by abstracting the universal, essential, and necessary qualities of an object. Through thought, or conceptualization, man can overcome the restrictions of a primitive and natural determinism and can transform his own natural environment. In transforming the environment, man must formulate plans and structure ends. These ends are the intelligent projection of hypotheses into the environment for the purpose of altering that environment. Through the means of experimentation, art, science, and technology, man can use his intelligence to transform his material environment.

Aquinas agreed with Aristotle that man acted most humanely when engaged in speculation. However, Aquinas qualified his agreement on the point. Although reason is man's highest and most satisfying earthly power, it is not a complete and perfect happiness. Man cannot achieve perfect happiness until after death when, through the gift of divine elevation, he experiences an immediate cognitive and affective union with God.

Thomistic educators emphasize the intellectual function of the school. In this aspect, they are like other Realist educators who emphasize the role of the school in cultivating and exercising human reason. In *Pivotal Problems of Education,* Father Cunningham asserts that the function of the school is primarily but not exclusively intellectual. He asserts that the Catholic school's specific function is the intellectual development of youth. As an intellectual agency, the Catholic school is most concerned with the transmission and the use of the liberal arts and sciences to exercise and cultivate man's rationality. Although primacy is given to intellectual development, physical, social, and religious development is not neglected.

As is the case with most Realist educational conceptions, the process of formal schooling is occupied with the transmission of bodies of subject-matter disciplines. The Thomistic conception of subject matter is that of "scientia," or bodies of funded, accumulated, demonstrated, and organized knowledge. A subject-matter discipline, so conceived, consists of a body of knowledge which contains first premises that are either self-evident, based on experimentation, or derived from a higher science. Those bodies of knowledge, or subject matters, are transmitted by teachers, who are expert in the disciplines which they teach, to students, who are expected to use their intellectual powers in understanding, mastering, and applying the principles that are contained in the subject matter. It is anticipated that the arts and sciences will contribute to the intellectual formation of those to whom they are communicated.

THOMISTIC DISTINCTIONS: TEACHING AND LEARNING

Thomistic educational philosophy can supply some useful distinctions and qualifications of the meaning of education, even to those educators who do not share its theological premises. American educators have often failed to provide precise distinctions between informal education, which relates to the complete formation of a person, and formal education, which is done by means of deliberate instruction within the school context. Thomistic educational theory clearly defines the distinctions between education and schooling.

Education, or *educatio,* is defined as one's general formation. In the case of the child, education refers to the child's total upbringing or rearing. Education, the total process of human development, encompasses more than formal instruction, which takes place in the school's more limited environment. Since a person's total formation rests upon forces that are informal as well as formal, the work of the school must be considered in relationship to total development.

In the school, one is exposed to deliberate instruction or to training, *disciplina,* as when a teacher teaches something to a learner. The success or failure of such deliberate instruction depends upon its relationship to that general formation that is taking place outside of the school.

In the Thomistic context, the teacher is a person who possesses a body of knowledge or some skill and through instruction seeks to impart this to a learner. Instruction is a highly verbal process by which the teacher carefully selects the appropriate words and phrases to illustrate the principles or demonstrate the skill that the learner is to acquire. It is the student who must be active in the teaching–learning relationship since he possesses the potentiality for intellectually grasping and appropriating knowledge. The teacher's language is a stimulus which serves to motivate and to explain so that the student can exercise his intellect. The Thomistic teacher must be a skilled communicator, a polished rhetorician. In order to communicate effectively, the teacher has to select the correct words, use the proper speaking style, and select appropriate examples and analogies. As a skilled communicator, the teacher must also exercise caution that instruction does not degenerate into idle verbalism or preaching in which the words used are meaningless to the learner's experience. Instruction should always begin with that which the student already possesses and should lead to that which is new. Teaching involves a careful structuring and organizing of the materials to be taught.

Thomas Aquinas saw teaching as a vocation, a calling to serve mankind. Because of his desire to serve, the good teacher is motivated by a love of truth, a love of man, and a love of God. Unlike the emotionalism of such romantic naturalist educators as Rousseau and Pestalozzi, who also preached a doctrine of love, the Thomistic teacher prizes the cultivation of rationality. As true Aristotelians, the Thomists emphasize that genuine love comes from knowing and is based upon reason. Therefore, teaching is not allowed to degenerate into merely an emotional personal relationship. It is always about some knowledge, about some truth, that is worthy of being transmitted and worthy of being known by a learner.

In the Thomistic conception of the teacher, the art of teaching is a rare blending of the contemplative and the active life. As a contemplative, the teacher must spend time in research and in discovery. He is to know his subject matter thoroughly, be it theology, mathematics, or science. Much of this research takes place in the quiet of a cell or a library. The teacher is also an active person who is involved with his students and who communicates his knowledge to them.

MORAL EDUCATION

Thomistic education, especially in the Roman Catholic school, is intended to be an education which is committed to supernatural values. It is intended to educate Christ-like individuals. Theology and religious education are certainly a part of such an education. Value formation takes place not only in religious education in the formal sense but also in the school milieu and activities which involve an exposure to religious practices, habits, and rituals.

Aquinas was careful to point out, however, that knowledge does not necessarily lead to morality. Although a person may know the principles of religion and may know about religious observance, knowledge cannot be equated with goodness. While rationality is not goodness, only intelligent men and women can distinguish between moral right and wrong. As a free agent, man has alternatives. The exercise of freedom means that man possesses the ability to frame, to recognize, and to evaluate alternative courses of action.

In the Thomistic context, moral education is properly a process of habituating the learner to a climate of virtue. Such an environment should contain models of value which are worthy of imitation. The Christian school milieu should provide the exercises and conditions that are conducive to the forming of dispositions that are inclined to virtue.

CONCLUSION

Thomistic education is based upon premises that are found in Aristotelian philosophy and Christian scriptures. Based upon its theistic antecedents, Thomism asserts that education should aid man to merit supernatural life. Following Realism, it asserts that man's distinguishing characteristic is reason and that education should contribute to a life that is intellectually excellent. A complete education should also facilitate every man's active participation in his own culture and history. Although it recommends an education that is primarily intellectual, Thomism recognizes that man is a manipulator of the natural environment and a creator of culture. As a worker, man is also a practical being who needs some preparation for professional and occupational life.

SELECTION

Neil McCluskey

Father Neil McCluskey, member of the Society of Jesus, was born in Seattle on December 15, 1920. His Bachelor of Arts (1944) and Master of Arts (1945) degrees were earned at Gonzaga University. Father McCluskey received his doctorate from Columbia University in 1957. He has taught at Seattle University, Gonzaga University, and the University of Notre Dame. From 1955 to 1961, he was editor of *America*. Among Father McCluskey's publications are *Catholic Education in America* (1964), and *Catholic Education Faces Its Future* (1969). In the selection from *Catholic Viewpoint on Education* which follows, Father McCluskey examines: (1) the philosophical and theological bases of Catholic education; (2) the mutual rights and relationships of the church and state in education; (3) the value of a Christian education.

* * *

One of the clearest statements of the purpose and scope of Catholic education was written thirty years ago by Pius XI in his encyclical letter, "The Christian Education of Youth" (*Divini Illius Magistri*). The entire letter repays careful study for its well-balanced explanation of the nature of education, the division of rights in education, the subject and environment of education, and the end and object of Christian education. We have selected here a few central passages of this authoritative statement that will serve as a starting point for a discussion of the theological and philosophical bases of traditional Christian education.

Its Nature. Since education consists essentially in preparing man for what he must be and for what he must do here below, in order to attain the sublime end for which he was created, it is clear that there can be no true education which is not wholly directed to man's last end. . . .

Impact of Revelation. In the present order of providence, since God has revealed Himself to us in the Person of His Only Begotten Son, who alone is "the way, the truth and the life," there can be no ideally perfect education which is not Christian education.

The Common Goal. The proper and immediate end of Christian education is to co-operate with divine grace in forming the true and perfect Christian, that is, to form Christ Himself in those regenerated by baptism. . . .

The Result. The true Christian, product of Christian education, is the supernatural man who thinks, judges and acts constantly and consistently in accordance with right reason illumined by the supernatural light of the example and teaching of Christ.

Broad Scope. Christian education takes in the whole aggregate of human life, physical and spiritual, intellectual and moral, individual, domestic and social. . . .

Supernatural Perfects the Natural. [Christian education takes in the whole aggregate of human life] not with a view of reducing it in any way, but in order to elevate, regulate and perfect it, in accordance with the example and teaching of Christ.

Some of the fundamental truths stated or implied here by the Pontiff are propositions of the natural order, whose truth man can reason to unaided by revelation, and others are of the supernatural order that have been revealed in the sacred scriptures. Together they form a perennial unchanging charter which, from the beginning of the Christian era, has guided Catholic education and can be called the solid core of its philosophy. These might be briefly set down as follows:

Philosophical Bases
1. There is a personal God whose existence can be proved by reason.
2. Man was put upon earth by God for a purpose in keeping with man's nature.
3. Man is a "person," that is, a rational free being whose perfection consists in knowing and possessing truth, beauty and goodness.
4. Though man's material body gives him a continuity with nature, his spiritual soul indicates a destiny that transcends the purely material and temporal order.

Theological or Revealed Bases
1. God gave man the added gift of a "supernature" by means of which he would be able to share, after a trial, in the divine life.
2. Adam, the first man, fell from God's favor and, as head of the human race, lost for his descendants the conditionally promised supernatural life.
3. The eternal Son of God became incarnate to redeem man and to restore him to God's grace and the supernatural life. This restoration takes place by man's incorporation into Christ.
4. Accordingly, the educated Christian is formed in the example and teaching of Christ, the perfect man.
5. The supernatural order does not extinguish nor diminish the values of right reason and the natural order, nor the natural rights of the individual, the home or society itself in what regards education.

The starting point in the Catholic philosophy of education, then, is the reality of the supernatural as revealed through and in Jesus Christ. The Catholic belief that man is a creature of God destined to share in the divine life answers the two questions upon which every philosophy of education is built: What is man? What is his purpose? This sharing in the divine life is actually begun at the moment of baptism, when sanctifying grace and the virtues of faith, hope, and charity—man's supernatural faculties—are infused into the soul. That life, begun on earth through faith, is consummated in a beatific union with God in glory hereafter. For a Catholic this truth is not only the ultimate purpose and final objective of education; it is the theological integrating principle, the philosophical guide, and the basic sanction of the moral order.

Little wonder is it that this uncompromising supernatural bias in Catholic education has always been a scandal and an affront to humanists and secularists. As the late William J. McGucken, S.J., has penetratingly written:

Nothing is more irritating to the modern than this dogma of the supernatural, a dogma that cannot be proved by anthropology, history, psychology or any other human science. Yet nothing is more certain than this, that all traditional historic Christianity is inextricably bound up with it. It cannot be demonstrated by human reason; it requires God's revelation to bring to our knowledge this fact that man is super-naturalized.

The Catholic concept of education situates man against the backdrop of the total society in which he lives and develops. The involved process by which man arrives at adult perfection in society is *education*. Since education is as extensive as human life itself, different agencies in society share rights and responsibilities in this broad field. For man is born into three societies of the large society: the family, civil society (including the state), and the Church. Each has distinct rights, yet all are properly ordered to ensure balance and harmony within the total educational process. . . .

Control over the education of their children belongs primarily to parents, since those who bring children into this world must assume the primary responsibility for their proper rearing and schooling. The duty of parents certainly includes seeing that their children receive proper instruction for both their temporal and spiritual destinies. No matter how radically philosophies of education differ, every one of them agrees that education includes formation or the inculcation of values. Education of the young is for Catholics, particularly a spiritual and religious concern.

Catholics believe that education, as a basically ethical undertaking, is necessarily connected with man's supernatural goal. Since the Church was established by Christ to guide men to that goal, education becomes a proper function of the Church. By making His Church the gateway to eternal life, God has endowed His religious society with essential rights over the education of the baptized. God set up His Church precisely to provide, largely through religious instruction and training, the means to learn the supernatural truths He has revealed and the practices of the Christian religion He has made obligatory.

The Catholic Church, therefore, possesses the pre-eminent right in education—pre-eminent precisely because of the primacy of the supernatural order. The Church holds that her right to teach is a power vested in her directly by her Divine Founder Himself. She is not, therefore, like other voluntary associations in society dependent upon the civil power for the privilege of teaching.

She cannot admit, therefore, that any earthly power can deprive her of her right to teach. That right inheres in her very nature as an autonomous society, one whose constitution is altogether independent of the state. If the Church were not allowed to teach she would be bereft of one of her basic functions: she would be condemned, as under Communist totalitarianism today, to a twilight existence and, by every human augury, to gradual extinction.

Parents who recognize the divine authority of the Church are therefore obliged to follow its teachings and regulations regarding the education of their children.

In ideal, all these rights—those of parent, Church, and state—work in harmony for the benefit of the individual. The supernatural order, to which the Church owes her rights, does not annihilate the natural order, to which pertain the rights of parent and state, but completes and elevates it. The reason for this harmony, as Pope Pius said, "is because both come from God, who cannot contradict Himself: 'The works of God are perfect and all His ways are judgements.' "

What are the principal benefits that a Catholic parent and pastor find in a Catholic education? They can be grouped around these four points.

1. The child learns systematically and thoroughly about his religion. He obtains a formal knowledge of the truths of Christian revelation, including the existence and nature of God, Christ's Incarnation and Redemption, Christ's Church and the workings of the Holy Spirit within it, the history of the chosen people and of the Church.

2. He enjoys regular opportunities, direct and indirect, for the deepening of his sense of religious dedication. He has ready access to the Mass and the sacraments; he learns to live a fuller life of prayer; he acquires a practical knowledge and love of the Church's liturgical life.

3. The child learns an ordering of knowledge in an atmosphere in which the spiritual and the supernatural hold the primacy in the

hierarchy of temporal and eternal values. He learns that his faith is not something apart but is related to the whole texture of life.

4. He acquires a "Catholic" attitude or outlook on life based upon the firm knowledge of his duties and privileges as a follower of Christ; he gains pride and love in—and loyalty to—his Catholic heritage.

These four categories cannot, however, be treated as if they were independent of one another. They are closely related, for each is an aspect of Christian growth, each fuses with and reinforces the others. The result is Christian education in all its dimensions—than which no loftier or more perfect educational ideal has ever been conceived.

Knowledge is not faith, but since faith is an intellectual virtue, the two go hand in hand. Acquaintance with the object of belief and an awareness of one's motives for belief are the ordinary prerequisites for firm assent. So systematized instruction has importance here. A person learns religion in somewhat the same way he learns a language. If he is fortunate enough to be raised in the country where the tongue is spoken, he will almost always have a far better grasp of the language than he would through intense self-instruction or private tutoring or enrollment in a special class. It is axiomatic that residence in a country facilitates the acquisition of a second language. Here is the learner's great advantage, when instruction in the Catholic faith takes place within a Catholic school. He not only gets a more complete and systematic instruction in the formal truths of his religion, but he is "in the new country" and the atmosphere reinforces and hastens the process of learning.

Despite the fact that religion is taught formally for only brief periods, its influence pervades other areas of the curriculum. Religious themes receive proportionate treatment in other courses where they are integral to the subject. This will occur particularly in literature, history, and social studies. A student receives and organizes new knowledge according to his previous disposition. If he is convinced that man is only the accidental outcome of 10,000 millennia of nature's fluid evolutionary process, his receptivity will differ markedly from that of a Christian believer. Faith is never departmental: all things fall within its purview. This suggestion of the late Pius XII, made in a talk to a group of teachers in 1957, illustrates the point:

When you study nature, remember that "it was through Him that all things came into being, and without Him came nothing that has come to be" (John

1:3). When you study history, remember that it is not a simple enumeration of more or less bloody or edifying facts, because one can easily detect a pattern which becomes a subject of profound study in the light of universal Divine Providence and the unquestionable human freedom of action. Note especially how you would look upon the events of the past 2,000 years with other eyes, if you would consider them as the development of Christian civilization, starting with those events which marked the dawn of the Church, dwelling upon the great unsurpassed syntheses made in ancient times and during the Middle Ages, reflecting upon the distressful apostasies but also the great modern discoveries and looking with confidence at the signs of rebirth and recovery.

   The encyclical on "The Christian Education of Youth" speaks of the educational environment of the Church as embracing "the sacraments, divinely efficacious means of grace, the sacred ritual, so wonderfully instructive and the material fabric of her churches whose liturgy and art have an immense educational value." This brings in the parish. A thorough religious education can result only from the joint effort of all agencies concerned with the child's formation—home, school, and parish. Hence the liturgical life of the Church into which the child is initiated is lived not only in the parish church but in the school and the home as well. The parochial school is deliberately situated near the parish church, and this proximity makes for close co-operation in religious education and formation. If a school is distant from the church, it probably has its own chapel.
   Each year the liturgical cycle of the Church recounts the story of God's two great interventions in time: creation and salvation. But the liturgical cycle is more than the re-enactment of history. God's dialogue with mankind continues in the Mass and the sacraments. As one writer has put it, "By taking part in the life of the liturgy and by following the cycle of the Church year, the Christian enters into the vast stream of grace set in motion by God since the foundation of the world. Thus an historical catechesis is made complete only by a liturgical catechesis." Prayer and religious devotion are a natural growth of parochial school life. Group participation in liturgical practices and sacramental rites, when they are part of the school routine, gives them complete normalcy and acceptability. These observances fit easily into the school day and follow a natural rhythm in the school calendar.
   The Mass and the reception of the sacraments are central to the devotional life of a Catholic. Accordingly, the Catholic child is carefully instructed during the first two grades of elementary school to prepare him for his first confession and communion. The

beautiful ceremony of the First Communion traditionally occurs at a parish Mass on Mother's Day or on some other Sunday in spring. When the children are older and have been more fully instructed in the faith, they are qualified to receive the sacrament of confirmation from the bishop. This occasion, too, is an important milestone in the life of the young Christian.

Pupils are encouraged to attend the daily Mass in the parish church before the opening of the school day, especially on important feast days and during the liturgical seasons of Lent and Advent. Some schools require daily Mass attendance. Others prescribe Mass on one day of the week, but most schools leave the children free in this matter at all times. A few schools begin the regular school day with Mass as the opening period, a practice borrowed from some European countries. In many parishes the school children attend their own Sunday Mass, at which a special instruction or sermon is given. On one school day of each month the children are allowed a special period to visit the church to receive the sacrament of confession or, if they prefer, merely to enter the confessional to ask for the priest's blessing.

During his parochial school days a Catholic youngster is closer to the liturgy than at any other period in his life. From September to June he acquires a familiarity in his daily living with the saints and seasons of the Church. Along with the heroes of his country's history, the youngster gets acquainted with the great men and women of the Church world. He observes the season of Advent in preparation for the Birthday of Christ, Christmas, and the season of Lent in preparation for the Resurrection of Christ, Easter. The boys learn to assist at Mass and other liturgical functions, while the girls —often the boys too—learn to sing the sacred chants and choral music that accompany these ceremonies. These activities, however, when they are not extracurricular, are confined to the period regularly assigned for religion study or music study. Seasonal classroom decorations are other reminders of the liturgical year; for example, that November is dedicated to the Suffering Souls in Purgatory, that May is dedicated to the Blessed Virgin Mary. The classroom bulletin boards and displays tell in picture and poster about the missionary work of the Church at home and abroad, of the creation of new cardinals or the canonization of a new saint.

Probably the most distinctive, certainly the most important, benefit of education within a Catholic school is the ordering of knowledge in an atmosphere wherein the spiritual and the supernatural are properly ordered in the hierarchy of values. The

Catholic philosophy of education is based on the reality of the supernatural and its primacy in the total scheme of things. The values, goals, and ideals of the natural order—important and worthy of pursuit as these may be—are subordinate in Catholic eyes to those of the supernatural order. For in reality the order created by God was never a purely natural order, but from its inception was elevated to the supernatural. The lapse of Adam from grace did not destroy this fundamental ordering; it did result in an antagonism between the material and spiritual orders, particularly within man himself.

Nor is the Fall of man one of those sectarian items which can be dismissed as not really relevant to the large questions in education. William J. McGucken has called attention to the fact that two modern philosophers, Friedrich Foerster, a devout Lutheran, and Bertrand Russell, the modern skeptic, both have arrived independently at the same conclusion: that in the last analysis all theories of education are dependent on the views taken of the dogma of original sin. For all theories hinge on the nature of the person to be educated. Calvinism and Lutheranism held that, in consequence of the Fall, human nature was depraved; Catholicism teaches that human nature was deprived of the supernatural life; Rousseau and Dewey attempted to dismiss the whole notion.

The Catholic school shares with the home and Church the responsibility of teaching the child that "his chief significance comes from the fact that he is created by God and is destined for life with God in eternity." In order to live in a modern society where "social, moral, intellectual and spiritual values are everywhere disintegrating," the child needs the integrating force of religion—a force that will arm him with a complete and rational meaning for his existence.

The Catholic bishops of the United States in their annual statement for 1950 described in detail the effects of this religious force:

First of all, it will arouse in him a consciousness of God and of eternity. His vision will be opened out upon a supernatural world revealed by faith which differs from the world of nature his senses reveal.

Secondly, it will give him a continuing purpose in life, for it will teach him that he was made to know, love and serve God in this world as the condition for meriting eternal happiness.

Thirdly, it will induce in him a deep sense of responsibility for those rights and obligations he possesses by reason of his citizenship in heaven as well as on earth.

Finally, religion will challenge him to sanctify whatever walk of life he chooses and to seek and accept the Will of God in whatever way it may be manifested. Thus, as a principle of integration, religion will help the child to develop *a sense of God, a sense of direction, a sense of responsibility,* and *a sense of mission* in this life.

These principles are not taught day by day by means of blackboard diagrams and class recitations. In a gentle imperceptible manner, however, their meaning is absorbed and they become quietly operative in the life of the Catholic child. Certain traditional religious symbols silently telling of God, the Incarnation of His Son, man's Redemption by Christ, and the life of the blessed in heaven help to establish this atmosphere of the supernatural. The cross above the school building, the crucifix hanging in every classroom, and other religious symbols that adorn the walls serve constantly to remind the pupils of things that transcend this world. Even the clerical garb of the priest and the religious robes of the Sisters and Brothers—symbolizing dedication to the loftiest values of the spirit —contribute to this effect.

The function of the Catholic school is not merely to teach the formulas of the Catholic religion but, as Father George Bull of Fordham University once said, "to impart in a thousand ways, which defy formularization, the Catholic attitude toward life as a whole." It is Catholicism as a culture, not as a conflicting creed, which is at odds with the spirit of the modern world and in a sense makes Catholics a people apart. A Catholic's belief implicitly affects his whole life, and in many areas of life this puts him at odds with accepted conduct. A culture is not what Ortega y Gasset has called "some sort of ornamental accessory for the life of leisure." Rather, as the same modern philosopher has said:

Culture is an indispensable element of life, a dimension of our existence, as much a part of man as his hands. True, there is such a thing as man without hands; but that is no longer simply man: it is man crippled. The same is to be said of life without culture, only in a much more fundamental sense. It is life crippled, wrecked, false.

Christian or Christ-centered culture is the supreme integrating principle from which proceeds all activity within a Catholic school. Justice Robert H. Jackson of the U.S. Supreme Court inadvertently gave the reason that above all justifies the existence of a separate Catholic school, when he wrote in his dissent in the *Everson* case:

"Our public school, if not a product of Protestantism, at least is more consistent with it than with the Catholic culture and scheme of values." The Catholic community agrees.

FURTHER READING

Cunningham, William F. *Pivotal Problems in Education.* New York: The Macmillan Company, 1940.

Donohue, John W. *St. Thomas Aquinas and Education.* New York: Random House, Inc. 1968.

Gulley, A. D. *The Educational Philosophy of Saint Thomas Aquinas.* New York: Pageant Press, 1965.

Hampsch, John H. "Integrative Determinants in the Philosophy of Education of Saint Thomas Aquinas," *Educational Theory, 9* (January, 1959). pp. 31–40.

Johnston, Herbert. *A Philosophy of Education.* New York: McGraw-Hill Book Company, 1963.

McGucken, William J. *The Catholic Way in Education.* Milwaukee: Bruce Publishing Company, 1934.

————. "The Philosophy of Catholic Education," *Philosophies of Education.* Bloomington, Ill.: Public School Publishing Company, 1942.

McCluskey, Neil G. *Catholic Viewpoint on Education.* New York: Image Books, 1962.

Pius XI. *Christian Education.* New York: American Press, 1936.

Redden, John D. and Francis A. Ryan. *A Catholic Philosophy of Education.* Milwaukee: Bruce Publishing Company, 1942.

five

PERENNIALISM

The Perennialist philosophy of education draws heavily from the Realist and Thomist positions. In regard to metaphysics, the Perennialists proclaim the intellectual and spiritual character of the universe and man's place within it. Following the Aristotelian premise that man is a rational being, the Perennialists conceive of the school as a social institution which is specifically designed to contribute in the development of man's intellectual or cognitive features. The name "Perennialism" comes from the assertion that the basic principles of education are changeless and recurrent. In the Perennialist context, the educational philosopher's first problem is to examine man's nature and to devise an educational program that is based upon his universal characteristics. Man's intellect enables him to frame alternative propositions and to choose those that fulfill the requirements of his human nature. Since he can frame and choose between rational alternatives, man is a free agent. However, the basic human values derive from man's rational power, which defines him as a human being. Man frames his thought in symbolic patterns and communicates them to his fellows. Although there are cultural particularities, men everywhere have framed ethical principles that govern their individual and corporate lives. Throughout the world, men have developed religious and aesthetic modes of experience and expression.

Since human nature is constant, so are the basic patterns of education. Foremost, education should aim to cultivate man's rational powers. Basically the universal aim of education is truth. Since that which is true is universal and unchanging, a genuine education should also be universal and constant. The school's curriculum should emphasize the universal and recurrent themes of human life. It should contain cognitive materials which are designed to cultivate rationality; it should be highly logical and acquaint students with the use of the symbolic patterns of thought and communication. It should cultivate ethical principles and encourage moral, aesthetic, and religious criticism and appreciation. The Perennialist educational philosophy, when put into practice, develops the intellectual and spiritual potentialities of the child to their fullest extent through a subject-matter curriculum that is inclined to such disciplines as history, language, mathematics, logic, literature, the humanities, and science. These subjects, regarded as bearing the funded knowledge of the human race, are the tools of civilized people and have a disciplinary effect on the mind.

Perennialist educational theory emphasizes the humanities as works of man that provide insights into the good, true, and beautiful. In these works, man has caught a glimpse of the eternal truths and values. Such insights, found in science, philosophy, literature, history, and art, persist as they are transmitted from generation to generation. Works such as those of Plato, Aristotle, and Mill, for example, possess a quality that makes them perennially appealing to men living at different times and in different places. Other ideas which may be popular to a particular time fail to meet the test of time and are discarded.

These general principles associated with Perennialism can be seen in the educational ideas of Robert M. Hutchins and Jacques Maritain. While Hutchins represents a secular variety of classicial humanism, Maritain has been identified with the religious Perennialism associated with neo-Thomism. Although there are certain important variations in the philosophical positions of Hutchins and Maritain, they agree on the following basic principles: (1) there is a body of truth which is universally valid regardless of circumstances and contingencies; (2) a sound education will contribute to the pursuit of truth and to the cultivation of the permanent principles of right and justice; (3) truth can best be taught through the systematic study and analysis of man's past—as portrayed in the great works of religion, philosophy, literature, and history.

ROBERT MAYNARD HUTCHINS

Robert Maynard Hutchins has long been an articulate spokesman for the position that education is properly devoted to the cultivation of man's intellect. Hutchins was born in 1899 and received his higher education at Yale University. He was a professor of law at Yale from 1927 to 1929. At thirty-one, he became president of the University of Chicago and served in that capacity until he became chancellor of that University in 1945. In 1954, Hutchins became president of the Fund for the Republic. He is now associated with the Center for the Study of Democratic Institutions, a nonprofit educational enterprise established by the Fund for the Republic to promote the principles of individual liberty in a democratic society. He is a frequent speaker and author on behalf of the cause of liberal education. His major educational works include *The Higher Learning in America,* 1936; *Education for Freedom,* 1934; *Conflict in Education in a Democratic Society,* 1953; *University of Utopia,* 1953; and *The Learning Society,* 1968. When asked his opinion as to the ideal education, Hutchins replied:

Ideal education is the one that develops intellectual power. I arrive at this conclusion by a process of elimination. Educational institutions are the only institutions that can develop intellectual power. The ideal education is not an *ad hoc* education, not an education directed to immediate needs; it is not a specialized education, or a pre-professional education; it is not a utilitarian education. It is an education calculated to develop the mind.

There may be many ways, all equally good, of developing the mind. I have old-fashioned prejudices in favor of the three R's and the liberal arts, in favor of trying to understand the greatest works that the human race has produced. I believe that these are the permanent necessities, the intellectual tools that are needed to understand the ideas and ideals of our world. This does not exclude later specialization or later professional education; but I insist that without the intellectual techniques needed to understand ideas, and without at least an acquaintance with the major ideas that have animated mankind since the dawn of history, no man may call himself educated.[1]

This quotation reveals some of the basic principles of Hutchins' educational philosophy: (1) cultivation of the basic foundational tool skills of reading, writing, and arithmetic are indispensable for literate and civilized man; (2) a liberal education should contribute to man's understanding of the great works of civilization; (3) professional and specialized education should be deferred until one has completed the requirements of general education, that education which every man should have as a rational human being.

In 1936, Hutchins wrote *The Higher Learning in America,*[2] which was both a critique of higher education and of general education as well. Commentary on this work is useful in establishing Hutchins' educational perspective.

Hutchins bases his educational philosophy on two basic concepts: (1) man's rational nature and (2) a conception of knowledge based on

---

1. Robert M. Hutchins. *A Conversation on Education.* Santa Barbara, Calif.: The Fund for the Republic, Inc., 1963. pp. 1–2.
2. Robert M. Hutchins. *The Higher Learning in America.* New Haven: Yale University Press, 1962.

eternal, absolute, and universal truths. His educational theory assumes the presence in human nature of essential and unchanging elements. Since rationality is the highest attribute of man's nature, the development of his intellect by the cultivation of the intellectual virtues is education's highest goal. The intellectual virtues lead man to discover the great truths that are to be found in the classic books of Western civilization.

Unfortunately, American education has failed to devote its energies to the pursuit of truth and to the cultivation of intellectual excellence. American higher education, in particular, has become misdirected because of confusion in the conditions of life that are external to education. Three factors, Hutchins asserts, have contributed to this general confusion: (1) love of money; (2) an erroneous conception of democracy; (3) a false notion of progress. Emersed in materialism and catering to the shifting whims of donors, students, business, alumni, and politicians, the university has lost its integrity in the search for operating funds. Contemporary America has witnessed the rise of a university which is like a service station. In contrast, Hutchins argues for a university whose sole purpose is to pursue and discover truth.

Hutchins believes that a confused conception of democracy has resulted in the commonly-held attitude that everyone should receive the same amount and degree of education. He would reserve the opportunity for higher education to students who have the interest and ability necessary for independent intellectual activity. A false notion of progress has led to the rejection of the wisdom of the past, which has been replaced by a belief that advancement comes only from empiricism and materialism. Superficial empiricism equates knowledge with the mere collection of facts and data. This confusion produces an antiintellectualism which regards the most worthwhile education as that bringing the greatest financial return.

American higher education is not only beset by the confusion that comes to it from external sources, but it also has its own internal conditions of disintegration that take the form of professionalism, isolation, and antiintellectualism. Professionalism, resulting from the surrender of the universities to vocational pressures, is motivated by the perverted utilitarianism which equates money-making with knowledge. Hutchins' attack on premature professionalism is based on three main arguments: (1) the methods of school instruction lag behind actual practice; (2) it is foolish to try to master constantly changing techniques; (3) direct experience is the most efficient source of practical wisdom.

Overspecialization has isolated specialist from specialist. Without the integrating core of a common education, specialists lack the ideas and language that come from shared and communicable experience. Antiintellectualism stems from an emphasis on the purely utilitarian at the sacrifice of theory and speculation. Hutchins asserts that theoretical knowledge is essential to man's rational nature. American education has grown confused. Vocationalism and specialized education have entered the curriculum prematurely and have distorted the purpose of general education. An overemphasis on the empirical and the vocational has pushed the liberal arts out of the general curriculum. Some educators have tied education to specific political and social programs that lead either to superficiality or to indoctrination, rather than to the cultivation of critical intelligence.

The Curriculum: The Permanent Studies   Hutchins argues that the curriculum should be composed of permanent studies which reflect the common elements of human nature and which connect each generation to the best thoughts of mankind. He particularly recommends the study of the great books—the classics which are contemporary in any age. The great books of the Western world embrace all areas of knowledge. Four years spent in reading, discussing, and digesting the great books will cultivate the intellect and will prepare one for later professional study. A critical reading and discussing of the great books will cultivate standards of judgment and criticism and will prepare students to think carefully and to act intelligently.

In addition to recommending a curriculum based on the reading of the great books of western civilization, Hutchins recommends the study of grammar, rhetoric, logic, and mathematics. Grammar, the analysis of language, contributes to the understanding and comprehension of the written word. Rhetoric provides the student with the rules of writing and speaking so that he is capable of intelligent expression; logic, the critical study of reasoning, enables one to think and express himself in an orderly and systematic fashion. Mathematics is of general value since it represents reasoning in its clearest and most precise form.

In order to restore the rule of rationality in higher education, Hutchins recommends the revitalizing of metaphysics. As the study of first principles, metaphysics pervades the entire range of intellectual pursuits. Proceeding from the study of first principles to the most current concerns, higher education should deal with man's fundamental problems. While the social sciences embrace the practical sciences of ethics, politics, and economics, the natural sciences deal with the study of natural and physical phenomena.

Hutchins, who is critical of the specialization that has occurred in teacher education, believes that prospective teachers should have a good general education in the liberal arts and sciences. Such an education contains the basic rules of pedagogy. The liberal arts—grammar, rhetoric, logic, and mathematics—are potent instruments in preparing the prospective teacher to organize, express, and communicate knowledge.

RELIGIOUS PERENNIALISM

Like their more secular confreres, the ecclesiastical Perennialists, who are often associated with Roman Catholic education, believe that there are universal truths and values. They believe in the permanent or perennial curriculum which is useful for all men regardless of the contingencies of differing cultures. The religious Perennialists, in contrast to their secular colleagues, believe that the universe and man within were created by a Supreme Being who is a knowing and a loving God. They see divine purpose operating within the laws of the universe and within the life of man. The religious variety of Perennialism finds expression in the philosophy of Jacques Maritain, who has also been classified as a neo-Thomist or Integral Realist.

JACQUES MARITAIN

Maritain was born in 1882 in Paris and was educated at the University of Paris. He was born into a Protestant family but became a convert to Roman Catholicism in 1906. Dissatisfied with the skepticism that was popular among academic philosophers, Maritain was attracted to the philosophy of Henri Bergson. He later came to urge a reconciliation of faith and reason in philosophy, as exemplified in the works of Saint Thomas Aquinas. Maritain is an astute proponent of neo-Thomist integral realism and has written extensively on that subject. His books include *Education at the Crossroads* (1943), *Man and the State* (1951), *On the Use of Philosophy* (1961), and *Integral Humanism* (1968).

Education at the Crossroads Maritain's philosophy of education is clearly expressed in his book *Education at the Crossroads,* where he indicates that the purposes of education are two-fold: (1) to educate man in those things which will cultivate his humanity; (2) to introduce man to the requirements and particularities of his cultural heritage. Priority, however, is given to the cultivation of the rationality and spirituality which are man's defining qualities. Particular cultural, vocational, and professional education is secondary and should be subordinate to the cultivation of the intellect.

Like Hutchins, Maritain sees modern education beset by a number of misconceptions which have caused confusion and have distorted its true purposes. Influenced by Pragmatism and Experimentalism, modern education has overemphasized means and has neglected to distinguish between means and ends. The concentration on means has resulted in an aimless, and often mindless, education which has no guiding directive goals. Maritain asserts that the proper end of education is to educate man so that he can realize his human potentialities. Genuine education rests on a true conception of human nature which is derived from the religious-philosophical view of the Judeo-Christian heritage. According to Maritain:

We may now define in a more precise manner the aim of education. It is to guide man in the evolving dynamism through which he shapes himself as a human person—armed with knowledge, strength of judgment, and moral virtues—while at the same time conveying to him the spiritual heritage of the nation and the civilization in which he is involved, and preserving in this way the century-old achievements of generations. The utilitarian aspect of education—which enables the youth to get a job and make a living— must surely not be disregarded, for the children of man are not made for aristocratic leisure. But this practical aim is best provided by the general human capacities developed. And the ulterior specialized training which may be required must never imperil the essential aim of education.[3]

In emphasizing the cultivation of man's spiritual and rational potentialities, Maritain takes issue with the advocates of what he terms "voluntarism." Theorists such as Rousseau and Pestalozzi and their modern followers have emphasized man's volitional–emotional character. In seeking to educate the good-hearted man, the voluntarists neglected or minimized the cultivation of intelligent judgment. In contrast, Maritain argues that a simplistic emotionalism is inadequate. Indeed, the properly functioning man is governed by intellect rather than emotionalism. Even more dangerous than Rousseauean voluntarism is the modern emphasis that argues for the complete liberation of the emotions and would make education a matter of feeling rather than thinking.

Maritain sees the teacher as an educated, cultivated, mature person who possesses knowledge that the students do not have but wish to acquire. Good teaching begins with what the student already knows and leads him to that which he does not know. The teacher is a dynamic agent in the learning process.

The student, a rational and free being possessed of a spiritual soul and a corporeal body, is endowed with an intellect that seeks to know. The good teacher is one who establishes an orderly but open climate of

---

3. Jacques Maritain. *Education at the Crossroads*. New Haven: Yale University Press, 1960. p. 10.

learning that avoids the excesses of both anarchy and despotism. The anarchical teacher rejects any kind of discipline and, with a false permissiveness, caters to childish whims. The despotic teacher, using fear of corporal or psychological punishment, reduces the students' individuality to a standardized conformity in which spontaneity and creativity are punished.

It is then the teacher's task to foster those fundamental dispositions that will enable the student to realize his humane potential. According to Maritain the basic dispositions to be fostered by education are: (1) love of truth; (2) love of goodness and justice; (3) simplicity and openness with regard to existence; (4) sense of a job well done; (5) sense of cooperation. These five basic dispositions are to be cultivated by teachers who are capable of fostering the growth of the student's mental life.

Maritain's Curriculum Maritain follows what is basically a subject-matter curriculum based on the various sytematic disciplines. Primary education cultivates the basic tool skills which are needed for the successful study of the more systematic disciplines. Maritain argues against the view that the child is a miniature man. The child's world is one of imagination. Primary teachers should begin their instruction with the child's own world of imagination and with stories which lead the child to explore the objects and values of the rational world. Although the child's initial stimulus comes through his imagination, he gradually comes to exercise his intellect in grasping the realities of the external world.

Secondary and higher education are devoted to the cultivation of judgment and intellectuality through the study of the humanities. Secondary education, in particular, should introduce the adolescent to the world of thought and to the great achievements of the human mind. Among the subjects that Maritain recommends for study in the secondary schools are grammar, foreign languages, history and geography, and the natural sciences.

The college curriculum is divided into four years of study: (1) the year of mathematics and poetry, when the students study mathematics, literature, poetry, logic, foreign languages, and the history of civilization; (2) the year of natural science and fine arts, which is devoted to natural sciences, fine arts, mathematics, literature, poetry, and the history of science; (3) the year of philosophy, which includes the study of metaphysics, philosophy of nature, epistemology, psychology, physics and natural science, mathematics, literature, poetry, and fine arts; (4) the year of ethical and political philosophy, which includes the examination of ethics, political and social philosophy, physics, natural science, mathematics, literature, poetry, fine arts, history of civilization, and the history of science.

Relationship between Theology and Philosophy Maritain is concerned that modern society, with its stress on specialization, has destroyed the sense of integration that gives order and purpose to life. Hutchins, who shares a similar concern, recommended that metaphysics be revitalized as the discipline which would rationally integrate the natural and social sciences. In recommending an education that will contribute to human integration, Maritain emphasizes that philosophy, dealing with man's basic relationships to the universe, and theology, dealing with his relationships to God, be placed at the summit of the hierarchy of learned disciplines. As the most basic, general, and integrating of the disciplines, theology and philosophy will supply the unity that will overcome the disintegrating tendencies of overspecialization.

CONCLUSION

Perennialists of both the secular and religious varieties subscribe to a number of principles which exemplify their educational beliefs. They assert: (1) permanence is of greater reality than change; (2) the universe is orderly and patterned; (3) the basic features of human nature recur in each generation of man; (4) human nature is universal; (5) education aims to cultivate that which is humane in man; (6) the basic goals of education are universal and timeless; (7) man's defining characteristic is rationality, and it is education's task to cultivate human reason; (8) the funded wisdom of the human race can be found in certain classic works.

SELECTIONS

Robert M. Hutchins

Robert Maynard Hutchins was born in Brooklyn, New York, on January 17, 1899. He began his undergraduate studies at Oberlin College and completed them at Yale University, where he received the Bachelor of Arts degree in 1921 and the Bachelor of Law degree in 1925.

In 1921, Hutchins began his teaching career as a teacher of English and history at the Lake Placid School in New York. He became a lecturer in the Law School of Yale in 1925, served as acting dean in 1927, and was made dean in 1928. He was also professor of law at Yale from 1927 to 1929. In 1930, Hutchins became president of the University of Chicago at the early age of thirty-one. From 1945 to 1951, he served as Chancellor of that university. He was associate director of the Ford

Foundation from 1951 to 1954. Since 1954, he has been president of the
Fund for the Republic.

Hutchins has been a forceful critic of the pressures of vocationalism
and specialization which would tend to dilute the quality of general
education. He adovcates a liberal education which centers on the great
classics of western civilization. Among his books on philosphy, education, and society are: *The Higher Learning in America* (1936), *Education
for Freedom* (1943), *The State of the University* (1949), *Conflict in Education
in a Democratic Society* (1953), *University of Utopia* (1953), *Some Observations on American Education* (1956), *Dialogues in Americanism* (1964), and
The Learning Society (1968). In the selection that follows, Hutchins refers
to general education as that which every person should have as a human
being. An education based on the cultivation of the intellectual virtues
will draw out the elements of man's common nature and connect him
with his cultural heritage.

*   *   *

Our erroneous notion of progress has thrown the classics and the
liberal arts out of the curriculum, overemphasized the empirical
sciences, and made education the servant of any contemporary
movements in society, no matter how superficial. In recent years this
attitude has been accentuated by the world-wide depression and the
highly advertised political, social, and economic changes resulting
from it. We have been very much upset by all these things. We
have felt that it was our duty to educate the young so that they
would be prepared for further political, social, and economic
changes. Some of us have thought we should try to figure out what
the impending changes would be and frame a curriculum that
embodied them. Others have even thought that we should decide
what changes are desirable and then educate our students not
merely to anticipate them, but also to take part in bringing them
about.

One purpose of education is to draw out the elements of our
common human nature. These elements are the same in any time or
place. The notion of educating a man to live in any particular time
or place, to adjust him to any particular environment, is therefore
foreign to a true conception of education.

Education implies teaching. Teaching implies knowledge.
Knowledge is truth. The truth is everywhere the same. Hence
education should be everywhere the same. I do not overlook the
possibilities of differences in organization, in administration, in local

Robert M. Hutchins. *The Higher Learning in America.* New York: Yale University Press,
1936. pp. 65–68; 77–81.

habits and customs. These are details. I suggest that the heart of any course of study designed for the whole people will be, if education is rightly understood, the same at any time, in any place, under any political, social, or economic conditions. Even the administrative details are likely to be similar because all societies have generic similarity.

If education is rightly understood, it will be understood as the cultivation of the intellect. The cultivation of the intellect is the same good for all men in all societies. It is, moreover, the good for which all other goods are only means. Material prosperity, peace and civil order, justice and the moral virtues are means to the cultivation of the intellect. So Aristotle says in the *Politics:* "Now, in men reason and mind are the end towards which nature strives, so that the generation and moral discipline of the citizens ought to be ordered with a view to them." An education which served the means rather than their end would be misguided.

I agree, of course, that any plan of general education must be such as to educate the student for intelligent action. It must, therefore, start him on the road toward practical wisdom. But the question is what is the best way for education to start him and how far can it carry him. Prudence or practical wisdom selects the means toward the ends that we desire. It is acquired partly from intellectual operations and partly from experience. But the chief requirement for it is correctness in thinking. Since education cannot duplicate the experiences which the student will have when he graduates, it should devote itself to developing correctness in thinking as a means to practical wisdom, that is, to intelligent action. . . .

We have suggested that the curriculum should be composed principally of the permanent studies. We propose the permanent studies because these studies draw out the elements of our common human nature, because they connect man with man, because they connect us with the best that man has thought, because they are basic to any further study and to any understanding of the world. What are the permanent studies?

They are in the first place those books which have through the centuries attained to the dimensions of classics. Many such books, I am afraid, are in the ancient and medieval period. But even these are contemporary. A classic is a book that is contemporary in every age. That is why it is a classic. The conversations of Socrates raise questions that are as urgent today as they were when Plato wrote. In fact they are more so, because the society in which Plato lived did not need to have them raised as much as we do. We have forgotten how important they are.

Such books are then a part, and a large part, of the permanent studies. They are so in the first place because they are the best books we know. How can we call a man educated who has never read any of the great books in the western world? Yet today it is entirely possible for a student to graduate from the finest American colleges without having read any of them, except possibly Shakespeare. Of course, the student may have heard of these books, or at least of their authors. But this knowledge is gained in general through textbooks, and textbooks have probably done as much to degrade the American intelligence as any single force. If the student should know about Cicero, Milton, Galileo, or Adam Smith, why should he not read what they wrote? Ordinarily what he knows about them he learns from texts which must be at best second-hand versions of their thought.

In the second place these books are an essential part of general education because it is impossible to understand any subject or to comprehend the contemporary world without them. If we read Newton's *Principia*, we see a great genius in action; we make the acquaintance of a work of unexampled simplicity and elegance. We understand, too, the basis of modern science. The false starts, the backing and filling, the wildness, the hysteria, the confusion of modern thought and the modern world result from the loss of what has been thought and done by earlier ages. The Industrial Revolution begins our study of history and the social sciences. Philosphy begins with Descartes and Locke and psychology with Wundt and William James. Natural science originates with the great experimenters of the nineteenth century. If anything prior is mentioned, it is only as a reminder that our recent great achievements in these fields must, of course, have had some primitive beginnings in the dark earlier centuries. The classics, if presented at all, are offered in excerpts out of context, and for the most part for the sake of showing the student how far we have progressed beyond our primitive beginnings.

Yet we may with profit remember the words of Nicholas Murray Butler:

Only the scholar can realize how little that is being said and thought in the modern world is in any sense new. It was the colossal triumph of the Greeks and Romans and of the great thinkers of the Middle Ages to sound the depths of almost every problem which human nature has to offer, and to interpret human thought and human aspiration with astounding profundity and insight. Unhappily, these deep-lying facts which should be controlling in the life of a civilized people with a historical background, are known only to a few, while the many grasp, now at an ancient and well-demonstrated falsehood and now at an old and well-proved truth, as if each had all the attractions of novelty.

You will note that Mr. Butler says that only a scholar can realize these things. Why should this insight be confined to scholars? Every educated person should know the colossal triumph of the Greeks and Romans and the great thinkers of the Middle Ages. If every man were educated—and why should he not be?—our people would not fall so easily a prey to the latest nostrums in economics, in politics, and, I may add, in education.

You will observe that the great books of the western world cover every department of knowledge. The *Republic* of Plato is basic to an understanding of the law; it is equally important as education for what is known as citizenship. The *Physics* of Aristotle, which deals with change and motion in nature, is fundamental to the natural sciences and medicine, and is equally important to all those who confront change and motion in nature, that is, to everybody. Four years spent partly in reading, discussing, and digesting books of such importance would, therefore, contribute equally to preparation for specialized study and to general education of a terminal variety. Certainly four years is none too long for this experience. It is an experience which will, as I have said, serve as preparation for advanced study and as general education designed to help the student understand the world. It will also develop habits of reading and standards of taste and criticism that will enable the adult, after his formal education is over, to think and act intelligently about the thought and movements of contemporary life. It will help him to share in the intellectual activity of his time.

*   *   *

Jacques Maritain
Jacques Maritain was born in Paris on November 18, 1882, and was educated at the University of Paris. Growing dissatisfied with academic skepticism and materialistic science, he turned to the philosophy of Henri Bergson, which restored his faith in metaphysics. Although reared as a liberal Protestant, Maritain was converted to Roman Catholicism on July 11, 1906.

In 1913, Maritain was invited to lecture at the *Institut Catholique* in Paris on Bergsonian philosophy and was retained as a professor of philosophy. Gradually, he won recognition as a prominent member of the vanguard of the Catholic intellectual revival. As a leader of the neoscholastic movement, he urged a return to the harmony of faith and reason, as exemplified in the philosophy of Saint Thomas Aquinas.

In January 1940, Maritain came to the United States for a lecture and teaching tour. Because of the occupation of his native France by the Nazis, he remained in the United States and taught at Columbia and Princeton Universities. In 1953, he was made Professor Emeritus at Princeton University. Maritain has been a prolific author who has written on a variety of subjects as well as on philosophical issues. Among his books are: *Approaches to God* (1934), *Science as Wisdom* (1944), *Education at the Crossroads* (1943), *The Rights of Man and Natural Law* (1949), *Man and the State* (1951), *An Essay on Christian Philosophy* (1955), *Bergsonianism, Philosophy, and Thomism* (1955), *Truth and Human Fellowship* (1957), *On the Use of Philosophy* (1961), *Moral Philosophy* (1964), and *Integral Humanism* (1968). In the selection which follows, Maritain discusses the role of the humanities in the framework of liberal education.

* * *

A last observation must be made, that deals with the highest aim of liberal education which is to make youth possess the foundations of wisdom. At this point I need not dwell on the vindication of philosophy. It is enough to repeat a remark often made indeed, namely that nobody can do without philosophy, and that, after all, the only way of avoiding the damage wrought by an unconscious belief in a formless and prejudiced philosophy is to develop a philosophy consciously. Furthermore metaphysics is the only human knowledge which actually claims to be wisdom, and to have such penetration and universality that it can actually bring the realm of the sciences into unity, coöperation, and accord; and if anybody honestly wishes to dispute the validity of this claim, he must perforce begin by knowing the metaphysics that he challenges. In fine, education deals ultimately with the great achievements of the human mind; and without knowing philosophy and the achievements of the great thinkers it is utterly impossible for us to understand anything of the development of mankind, civilization, culture, and science.

There is, in this connection, a really difficult question. A good philosophy should be a true philosophy. Now the professors of philosophy are bound to hold philosophical positions which differ widely. And if one of these positions is grounded in true principles, apparently the others are not. The solution for this problem may take two forms. First, there is a common, though unformulated,

Jacques Maritain. *Education at the Crossroads*. New Haven: Yale University Press, 1943. pp. 71–75.

heritage of philosophical wisdom which passes through any real teaching of philosophy, whatever may be the system of the teacher. Reading Plato is ever a blessing, even if you disagree with the tenets of Platonism. Second, teachers in philosophy are not teaching to be believed but in order to awaken reason; and the students in philosophy owe it to their teacher to free themselves from him. There is indeed a third point, which is valid only for philosophers as hardened as myself: they may always hope, indeed, that by virtue of its very truth, the philosophy which they think to be true, as I do Aristotelian and Thomistic philosophy, will gain momentum among their fellow men, at least in the generation to come.

A further question may be posed concerning the ways of teaching philosophy. The difficulty, here, lies in the fact that philosophy starts from experience, and that there is in young men no experience, or very little, either in science or in life, fitted to provide a starting point. One remedy consists, to my mind, in beginning by giving historical enlightenment with regard to the great problems in philosophy: such a historical description, pointing less at history than at making clear the inner logic and development of the human awareness of these problems, is a kind of vicarious personal experience.

Now, those who share in the Christian creed know that another rational wisdom, which is rooted in faith, not in reason alone, is superior to the merely human wisdom of metaphysics. As a matter of fact, theological problems and controversies have permeated the whole development of Western culture and civilization, and are still at work in its depths, in such a way that the one who would ignore them would be fundamentally unable to grasp his own time and the meaning of its internal conflicts. Thus impaired, he would be like a barbarous and disarmed child walking amidst the queer and incomprehensible trees, fountains, statues, gardens, ruins, and buildings still under construction, of the old park of civilization. The intellectual and political history of the sixteenth, seventeenth and eighteenth centuries, the Reformation and the Counter Reformation, the internal state of British society after the Revolution in England, the achievements of the Pilgrim Fathers, the Rights of Man, and the further events in world history have their starting point in the great disputes on nature and grace of our classical age. Neither Dante nor Cervantes nor Rabelais nor Shakespeare nor John Donne nor William Blake, nor even Oscar Wilde or D. H. Lawrence, nor Giotto nor Michelangelo nor El Greco nor Zurbaran, nor Pascal nor Rousseau, nor Madison nor Jefferson nor Edgar Allan Poe nor

Baudelaire, nor Goethe nor Nietzsche nor even Karl Marx, nor Tolstoy nor Dostoevski is actually understandable without a serious theological background. Modern philosophy itself, from Descartes to Hegel, remains enigmatic without that, for in actual fact philosophy has burdened itself all through modern times with problems and anxieties taken over from theology, so that the cultural advent of a philosophy purely philosophical is still to be waited for. In the cultural life of the Middle Ages philosophy was subservient to theology or rather wrapped up in it; in that of modern times it was but secularized theology. Thus the considerations I have laid down regarding philosophy are still truer of theology. Nobody can do without theology, at least a concealed and unconscious theology, and the best way of avoiding the inconveniences of an insinuated theology is to deal with theology that is consciously aware of itself. And liberal education cannot complete its task without the knowledge of the specific realm and the concerns of theological wisdom.

As a result, a theological course should be given during the last two or three years of study of the humanities—a course which by its sharply intellectual and speculative nature is quite different from the religious training received by the youth in another connection.

The practical aspect of this question is of no difficulty for denominational colleges. With regard to nondenominational colleges, the practical solution would depend on the recognition of a pluralist principle in such matters. Theological teaching would be given, according to the diversity of creeds, by professors belonging to the main religious denominations, each one addressing the students of his own denomination. And of course, those students who nurture a bias against theology would be released from attending these courses and allowed to remain incomplete in wisdom at their own pleasure.

FURTHER READING

Hutchins, Robert Maynard. *Conflict in Education in a Democratic Society.* New York: Harper and Co., 1953.

_____. *A Conversation on Education.* Santa Barbara: Center for the Study of Democratic Institutions, 1963.

_____. *Education for Freedom.* Baton Rouge: Louisiana State University Press, 1943.

———. *Higher Learning in America.* New Haven: Yale University Press, 1936.

———. *The Learning Society.* New York: Praeger Publishers, Inc., 1968.

———. *Some Observations on American Education.* Cambridge, Eng.: Cambridge University Press, 1956.

———. *The University of Utopia.* Chicago: University of Chicago Press, 1953.

Maritain, Jacques. *Challenges and Renewals.* Notre Dame: Notre Dame University Press, 1966.

———. *Education at the Crossroads.* New Haven: Yale University Press, 1960.

———. *Integral Humanism.* New York: Charles Scribner's Sons, 1968.

———. *Man and the State.* Chicago: University of Chicago Press, 1951.

———. *On the Use of Philosophy.* Princeton, N.J.: Princeton University Press, 1961.

six

ESSENTIALISM

Essentialism is a convenient term which applies to positions asserting education properly involves the learning of those basic skills, arts, and sciences which have been useful to man in the past and are likely to be useful in the future. The Essentialist believes that there are some basic tool skills that have contributed to man's well being. Among these necessary skills are reading, writing, arithmetic, and desirable social behaviors. The tool skills are the appropriate and necessary elements that should be found in every sound elementary school curriculum. At the secondary level, the basic curriculum should consist of history, mathematics, science, language, and literature. It is through the mastery of these subjects, which deal with man's natural and social environment, that the student is prepared to function as a member of a civilized society. The learning of the tool skills and the arts and sciences requires effort and diligence on the part of the student. The teaching of these necessary skills and subjects calls for mature teachers who know their subjects and are able to transmit them to their students.

Among the advocates of Essentialism have been the group of educators who organized the Essentialist Movement at the convention of the National Education Association in 1938. Reacting against what they considered to be the excesses of Progressive education, the Essentialists argued that the basic function of formal education was to preserve and transmit the basic elements of human culture. Such Essentialists as Michael J. Demiashkevich and William Chandler Bagley raised the question: "Shouldn't our public schools prepare boys and girls for adult responsibility through systematic training in such subjects as reading, writing, arithmetic, history, and English, requiring mastery of such subjects, and, when necessary, stressing discipline and obedience?"[1] In presenting the case for intellectual discipline and basic education, Clifton Fadiman argues that the logic and experience of the human race demonstrate that some subjects have generative power while others do not. Subjects possessing generative power are basic to other subjects in that they enable the learner to master both minor subjects and those that are higher and more complex. Among the master or generative subjects are language, forms, figures, numbers, the laws of nature, the past, and the study of the earth.[2]

Although there are certain variations among the Essentialists, there are some common themes that can be identified with this position. Among them are: (1) the elementary curriculum should emphasize basic tool skills which contribute to literacy; (2) the secondary curriculum should consist of basic subject matters that must include history, mathematics, science, literature, and language; (3) discipline is necessary in school situations for systematic learning to take place; (4) respect for legitimate authority, in school and in society, is a valuable attitude to be cultivated in students; (5) the learning of a skill or a subject requires mastery on the part of the learner.

Perhaps the area of greatest disagreement among advocates of Essentialism lies in the question of vocational education. While some would reject vocational education as lacking the necessary generative power, others would see some vocational competency as necessary for social efficiency in an industrialized society.

The Essentialist educational philosophy can be made clear by examining the theories of two leading educators who have advocated a return to basic principles and subject matters. Henry Clinton Morrison is worth studying because his emphasis on the unit plan has had a significant impact on the organizing and teaching of subject matter in the secondary schools. Morrison recommended the contract method of instruction. There has been a recent resurgence of interest in the contract approach to instruction in which students agree to master certain materials, information, or skills. More recently, Arthur E. Bestor, Jr., an American historian and advocate of basic education, has argued that American education needs to return to an emphasis on education for intellectual discipline.

---

1. For a concise and clear discussion of Essentialism, see Adolphe E. Meyer, *The Development of Education in the Twentieth Century*. Englewood Cliffs, N.J.: Prentice-Hall, Inc., 1949. pp. 148–55.
2. Clifton Fadiman, "The Case for Basic Education," in James D. Koerner (ed.). *The Case for Basic Education*. Boston: Little, Brown and Company, 1959. pp. 5–6.

MORRISON AND EDUCATION

For Morrison, education is the transmission of the arts, sciences, and moral values which constitute the fabric of civilization. Through the educational processes, the immature individual learns to adjust to the conditions and requirements of the society in which he lives. The basic framework of formal instruction lies in the curriculum, which is constant and universal. The particular programming and patterns of instruction, however, vary according to the circumstances of particular school situations and the needs of individual students. For Morrison, the subject matter of the curriculum should be about the world. Since the world is common to all men, the curriculum is also common to all men. It should reflect the physical, biological, and sociological realities of the world and also those moral and aesthetic values which have endured over time. Since human nature is universally the same, the curriculum is also universally constant. According to Morrison:

We have seen that Education is a process of adjustment with the end of adaptability in a particular world. Now the world is common to all mankind. It is a world of physical and biological conditions, one of social conditions, one of moral and aesthetic values. Furthermore, so far as the anthropological disclosures tell us the story, human nature is at bottom the same the world over, however varied may be the cultural accumulations of different races and peoples, whatever may the spread in the extent to which different peoples have climbed the ladder of Civilization, and the differing extents to which Civilization may have been diffused among different populations. Hence the content of Education is at bottom the same the world over, and the framework upon which that content is hung, namely, the Curriculum, is the same in essentials. The pedagogical problems arise in the fields of programming and of teaching.[3]

For the Essentialist, as represented by Morrison, education is a means of introducing the young to the requirements of civilized life. Civilization is the art of community existence and associative life that has enabled man to conquer his environment. The art of civilized living is found in the universal institutions that man has created in the process of harnessing the environment. The general aspects, or essentials, of education should deal with those institutions that have advanced civilized life in all human societies. In the context of Morrison's argument, the basic institutions that have rendered such a contribution are the arts

---

3. Henry C. Morrison. *The Curriculum of the Common School.* Chicago: University of Chicago Press, 1940. p. 5. Copyright 1940 by the University of Chicago.

and sciences such as language, mathematics, natural sciences, humanities, commerce, and industry. By studying the basic curriculum, the student is led to educational maturity, the state from which a person is capable of directing his own further learning. Achieving educational maturity is not an easy task. It requires highly structured instruction and the expenditure of effort on the part of students.

Morrison and the Tool Skills Like other Essentialists, Morrison stressed that formal education leading to educational maturity was grounded on the basic tool skills which contribute to literacy and to mathematical computation. The Essentialists recognize that literacy is basic to success in the systematic subject-matter disciplines and to success in life in civilized and technological societies. In the elementary school, the student is to acquire the needed essential tool skills of reading, numbers, and handwriting.[4] In the primary years of formal schooling, the student is to learn to use these basic civilizational tools and to acquire the social skills needed for disciplined participation in group life.

Of the basic tool skills, reading is the basis of success in the systematic disciplines of the secondary school. To read means that the student has acquired the ability to penetrate the symbolic complexity of the printed page and is capable of comprehending the thought, the scene, or the action which is the subject of the narrative.

Skill in mathematical computation and processes is the second essential tool skill required of elementary education. Here the task is to acquire the elementary concepts of number and facility in dealing with mathematical relationships.

Handwriting is the tool needed to record learning and to express reactions to learning. Writing enables the student to commit his thoughts and insights to paper. Writing involves the clarification of thought and the organization of thinking in terms of logical coherency.

In addition to the tool skills of reading, number, and arithmetic, primary education properly involves the child in group situations. Children are egotistical upon entering the school. With practice in the amenities of group situations, the child acquires the necessary etiquette that facilitates group life. According to Morrison, the needed primary social adaptations include the following dispositions: (1) personal self-dependence; (2) acceptance of the teacher's authority in the classroom; (3) respect for property; (4) cultivation of the ability to work with others in group activities.

---

4. Henry C. Morrison. *The Practice of Teaching in the Secondary School.* Chicago: University of Chicago Press, 1931. pp. 3–15.

Secondary Education   After acquiring facility in the basic tool skills and in the processes of socialization, the student then enters the realm of secondary education. Here, Morrison has defined the aims of secondary education as: (1) the cultivation of a wide range of interests, one of which becomes dominant; (2) the development of a capacity for a self-dependent intellectual life. Again, educational maturity or self-dependence is the major goal. Educational maturity means that the student has grown to realize the meaning and purpose of study and has acquired the necessary internal discipline that frees him from dependence upon his teacher.

Morrison structured the activities of the secondary school into units of work. A unit is defined as the external material or skill to be learned by the student. A serviceable learning unit is a comprehensive and significant aspect of the environment, an organized science or art, a mode of conduct. When a student successfully acquires a unit of learning, he has mastered it. Here Morrison applies a stringent criterion. In mastering a unit, a student either learns it completely or he does not. The whole process of education is the mastery of unit learning.

The use of Morrison's mastery formula involves the teacher and the learner in well-defined stages of systematic instruction. Morrison's formula involves the following sequential steps: (1) pretest; (2) teaching; (3) testing the result of instruction; (4) adapting the instruction procedure; (5) teaching and testing again until the unit has been completely mastered by the student.

Values   For Morrison, formal education also involves the cultivation of proper ethical values which are conducive to civilized life. Among the values to be emphasized are the following: a willingness to defer satisfaction; a willingness to accept the consequences of one's actions; a sense of altruism and fair play; respect for property rights; a willingness to accept criticism; a recognition of the social values of cooperation; fidelity to promises; obedience to legitimate authority; sustained application; a capacity for hard work; a sense of duty, fortitude, and punctuality. These values are to be found in the abiding literature of the human race and in the biographies of men and women who could serve as models of conduct. The school is also to serve as a moral censor which provides moral sanitation by eliminating or correcting pernicious influences.

Mastery Learning and Education   The Morrisonian method of instruction is based, then, on those past and present human achievements and experiences which are regarded as indispensable to people living today. Such skills and knowledge are found in a subject-matter curriculum which stresses the mastery of bodies of knowledge through systematic and sequential instruction. Genuine freedom, through educational maturity, is attainable only through discipline, through effort, and through sustained application.

ARTHUR BESTOR AND INTELLECTUAL DISCIPLINE

Among the leading and most articulate critics of American education has been Arthur E. Bestor, who advocates a restoration of the intellectual disciplines in the American school. As a distinguished historian, Bestor represents the scholar who sees immense educational value in the pursuit of the liberal arts and sciences. Such intellectual disciplines should constitute the core of a general and liberal education for all men and women if they are to function intelligently as persons and citizens. Among Bestor's writings on education are two important books: *Educational Wastelands: Retreat from Learning in Our Public Schools,* 1953, and *The Restoration of Learning,* 1955. Bestor's books are highly critical of the educational establishment and were part of the movement to restore a basic subject-matter curriculum in the nation's schools.

In *The Restoration of Learning,* Bestor establishes a criterion of education based on intellectual disciplines and indicates that American education is failing to meet the criterion of disciplined intelligence. Strongly implied in Bestor's educational theory is a commitment to a conception of American democracy that is based on the rule of reasonable and intelligent citizens. An intelligently functioning democracy is a government of law, of orderly parliamentary processes, and of democratic guarantees for all citizens.

Bestor has a definite essentialist conception of a good education. It is that which provides:

... sound training in the fundamental ways of thinking represented by history, science, mathematics, literature, language, art and other disciplines evolved in the course of mankind's long quest for usable knowledge, cultural understanding, and intellectual power.[5]

These intellectual disciplines should be fundamental in the school curriculum since they are basic in modern life. In the elementary school, reading, writing, and arithmetic are the indispensable studies. The elementary school student should also be introduced to the information and methods of the natural sciences, geography, and history.[6]

5. Arthur E. Bestor, Jr. *The Restoration of Learning.* New York: Alfred A. Knopf, Inc., 1956. p. 7.
6. *Ibid.,* pp. 50–51.

Junior high school marks the beginning of organized and systematic study. A transition is made from arithmetic to the more abstract forms of mathematical reasoning, beginning with elementary algebra. History is to assume a recognized structure. From the generalized natural science studied earlier, a transition is made as the student is introduced to sciences such as biology, physics, and chemistry. Instruction in foreign languages moves forward to grammatical analysis. The five essentials of the secondary school curriculum are science, mathematics, history, English, and foreign languages. These intellectual disciplines are the instruments of a liberal education and are man's most reliable tools in solving his personal and social problems. Students in the senior high school are expected to have the ability to pursue a subject methodologically and to employ abstract reasoning. Specifically, the study of mathematics is continued through advanced algebra, plane geometry, trigonometry, analytical geometry, and calculus. Systematic work in chemistry, physics, and biology furnish the needed foundations of scientific knowledge. History's pattern and structure are emphasized. English is employed with accuracy, lucidity, and grace. One foreign language is mastered and another is begun.[7]

The function of the school is to channel the materials of man's undifferentiated experience into the organized, coherent, and differentiated unity of these five major disciplines. During the elementary, secondary, and through most of the collegiate educational period, the student has the experience of civilized man channeled to him, by the school, within a framework which is differentiated and structured. Only after the student has mastered the five essential disciplines can he be expected to use them to solve the problems that beset him as an individual and as a member of the human race.

Bestor's proposed curriculum is prescribed for all students. It is through this mastery of the intellectual disciplines that the student is prepared for life. Once he has mastered these essentials, the student can begin vocational or college education. Training in the liberating disciplines prepares a person for intellectual life, citizenship, and for a profession.

Bestor fears that American schools have failed to provide the needed intellectual discipline. They have been subjected to antiintellectual confusion. Bestor charges that some professional educators have postulated an erroneous view of a democratic education. Since the intellectual disciplines were once reserved to aristocratic elites, these educators fail to realize that the progress of the modern age has now made an intellectual education the prerogative of the many. Intellectual training is both

---

7. *Ibid.*

appropriate and valuable for the common man since the functions of the old elite have become the functions of the whole people.

Bestor also charges that professional educators, no longer content with methodological concerns, have usurped the function of curriculum-making. Curriculum construction is best exercised by the scholars and scientists who are expert in their disciplines. Some professional educators have distorted progressive education into what is a "regressive education." They have watered down the subject matters of the great disciplines and have introduced vocational and life adjustment courses into the general curriculum to the detriment of the academic disciplines. By weakening education in the disciplines, too much of public education has become both antidemocratic and antiintellectual.

Bestor's program of educational reform includes improving the professional competency of classroom teachers, inaugurating programs for slow learners, and revamping current conceptions of the graded school. To accomplish this educational reform, public education in the United States must be committed to two fundamental principles: (1) ensuring a minimum of disciplined intellectual training to every future citizen; (2) providing opportunity for advanced study to every young person who possesses genuine intellectual capacity and a willingness to exert himself in developing his own intellectual powers.[8]

These two principles serve as the basis for Bestor's enumeration of the school's primary responsibilities: (1) the school should provide a standard program of intellectual training in the fundamental disciplines geared to the needs of serious students and to the capacities of the upper two-thirds of the school population; (2) the school should provide special opportunities for exceptionally able students; (3) programs designed for the highest third of the school population should be balanced with adequate remedial programs for the lowest third, the slow learners; (4) a program of physical education for all children which is distinguished from interschool athletics should be provided; (5) the school should diversify its offerings to include certain areas of vocational training; (6) there should be certain extracurricular activities; (7) high ability students should continue in school; (8) life adjustment training should be provided only for the least able and least ambitious.[9]

Although it appears that the nonintellectual areas of vocational training, physical education, and even life adjustment have been included in the school's aims, in the overall context of Bestor's theory these areas would be greatly curtailed.

---

8. *Ibid.,* p. 358.
9. *Ibid.,* pp. 364–65.

Bestor's proposed reform runs counter to the progressive views of such educators as Kilpatrick. The chief point of contention is well evidenced in this quotation from *The Restoration of Learning:* "The school makes itself ridiculous whenever it undertakes to deal directly with 'real-life' problems, instead of indirectly through the development of generalized intellectual powers."[10]

Since the intellectual disciplines are to constitute the general education of every student, Bestor is concerned with the particular problems of the slow learner. Instead of using chronological age for class differentiation, Bestor relies on intellectual development and the mastery of the particular subject for promotion. In this way, the fundamental disciplines can be taught to all students, with each proceeding at his own individual pace. Both Morrison and Bestor postulate the mastery of subject matter as the basis for academic advancement.

Bestor is concerned with raising the professional competency of the classroom teacher. To accomplish this, he would limit the influence of colleges of education and would critically examine professional education requirements for state teacher certification. The role of the professional educator would be filled by a commission of scholars and scientists who would work closely with the classroom teacher. Courses in professional education would be replaced, to a large extent, by those in academic subject matter. He also introduced the idea of two new degrees for teachers: the Master of Education and the Doctorate of Education. These degrees parallel the present Master of Arts degree and Doctor of Philosophy degree, minus the dissertation requirements.

To a large degree, Bestor rejects the interdisciplinary approach in education. Synthesis is for those who have completed the requirements of the training specified in the intellectual disciplines. Social studies, language arts, and other core programs are rejected.

Some comparisons can be made between Bestor's theory and those of Hutchins and Morrison. Both Bestor and Hutchins are oriented in favor of the liberal arts and sciences. Hutchins builds his curriculum around the great books, the classics which embody the collected wisdom of Western civilization. Bestor builds his theory around the five intellectual disciplines. As the great books constitute a part of the subject matter of these disciplines, Bestor would utilize them. However, he objects to the strictly dialectical method of the great books program.

Morrison bases his educational theory on a curriculum founded upon the institutionalized mores and folkways of the culture. Bestor's social views are more liberal. Both Bestor and Morrison recommend a subject-matter curriculum.

---

10. *Ibid.,* p. 79.

CONCLUSION

Essentialism is, then, that educational philosophy which includes as the prime function of the school the preservation and transmission of the basic elements of human culture. Essentialists emphasize: (1) a return to systematic studies; (2) learning as the mastery of skills and knowledge; (3) the position of the teacher as mature director of learning activities; (4) education as a preparation for both work and citizenship. Above all, the Essentialists fear that modern schools may degenerate into mindless institutions that cater to transitory fads or to childish whims.

SELECTIONS

Henry C. Morrison

Henry Clinton Morrison, 1871–1945, who advocated mastery learning, was born in Maine. He received his Bachelor of Arts degree from Dartmouth in 1895, his Master of Science from New Hampshire College in 1906, and his doctorate from the University of Maine in 1914. From 1899 to 1904 he was State Superintendent of Public Instruction in New Hampshire. He later joined the faculty of the College of Education of the University of Chicago. Among his books are *The Practice of Teaching in the Secondary School* (1926), *Basic Principles in Education* (1934), *The Curriculum of the Common School* (1940), and *American Schools, A Critical Study of Our School System* (1943).

In the following selections, Morrison discusses: (1) education as the acquiring of the arts, sciences, and moral values that comprise a civilization; (2) adaptability as the capacity to deal with a wide range of adjustments; (3) instruction as the social process by which a society educates its young; (4) the curriculum as a constant and universal educational framework; (5) mastery as the acquisition of a unit of learning.

* * *

The title of the present work is *The Curriculum of the Common School.* In the interest of definiteness some introductory explanation is called for, in order that we may have at the outset some common understanding touching what it is that we are talking about.

Education The work apparently has to do with Education. The title chosen is meaningless, and the argument of the volume will not run,

---

From Henry C. Morrison, "Education in the Common School," *The Curriculum of the Common School,* pp. 1–5. Copyright © 1940 by The University of Chicago.

unless at the outset there is some clarity of ideas touching what is
meant by the term "education" itself.

In a previous work I have sought to find an answer to the
question, "What is Education?"—an answer based upon fact and
principle scientifically determined. The question posed was one
which might well stand in the place of the ever recurrent and
baseless query, "What ought Education to be?"

The conclusion of this earlier study was in substance that
Education is nothing else than taking on the arts and sciences and
moral attitudes which make up the fabric of Civilization. That it is
not erudition or information and not even enlightenment alone, or
mental training, or development of individual potentialities, or a
process of generating a new and better civilization.

Adjustment. Education is an organic or natural process, common
in the broadest sense to pretty much the whole animal kingdom. It
is a matter of individual learning how to get on in the world. It
arises in all creatures which exist in a changeable environment in
which there must be in the nature of the case solution of problems
of some sort. It contrasts with tropistic behavior in some of the
lower orders, where getting-on is a purely mechanical matter.
Nevertheless, education in humans is so fundamentally at a higher
level, owing to man's possession of organs which enable him to
produce a culture, chiefly exceedingly flexible hands and vocal
apparatus, that we rightly accord to human education a difference in
kind as well as in degree.

Learning how to get on in the world is *adjustment,* and so we
speak of the adjustment theory of Education as contrasted with the
eruditional theory or with theories in which it is held that Education
is a matter of organic development of some sort. It ought, however,
to be borne in mind that the adjustment theory is not to be
understood as meaning that the individual has literally to learn
somewhere every adjustment he must make. On the contrary, both
in the race and in the individual the prize is not adjustment but
adaptability, that is, the capacity to meet a very wide range of
adjustments as the need arises. Hence, it has been said, with great
penetration as I think, that "we do not learn what to do, but rather
become the kind of people who will know what to do."

It follows that as the individual learns out of his experience of life
he is always becoming something, in some way different from what
he was before learning took place. The result is what we call
personality, and every genuine learning product is an accretion to
personality. So far as we can make out, the infant starts life with no
personality and within a short space of time begins to learn—

something—and thus personality begins to be drawn together. Personality is not a material entity, it is not located anywhere, it does not have to be located. It is simply the quality found in the attitudes and acquired abilities which characterize a given individual. It is frequently, in many of the books, as well as in popular use, confounded with physiological and psychological temperament, which is quite a different thing. It is sometimes confounded with the metaphysical concept which we call "the soul."

Maleducation. Apart from effective upbringing and instruction, education is perhaps about as likely to go wrong as to go right. It must be borne in mind that Education is a natural process driven onward by natural laws, that those laws chiefly cluster about self-preservation and self-assertion, that the forces at work have nothing to do with ethics or right living in normal social relations. In simple terms the result of experience in the world, apart from upbringing and instruction, is in principle as likely to produce the worst of criminals as the best of citizens.

With this all in mind, we may practically dismiss the matter of maleducation, and when in this volume the term Education is used without qualifications, right or normal ethical education will be meant.

Instruction   We turn then to Instruction, or the social process by which the community seeks to guarantee that the education of the rising generation shall be right education, of which the citizen and not the criminal or insane is the outcome. We shall consistently use the term to mean the process as carried on in schools. The correlative is Upbringing, by which the Family seeks to guarantee in its children right education.

We must linger here to point out how misuse of words confuses thought, often with really disastrous consequences in the Community. English-speaking peoples, including most of their books, do not discriminate between Instruction, the process, and Education, the product. Not infrequently leaders fail to make the distinction and thus turn their leadership to bad account.

Not long ago a publicist attracted considerable attention by noting that calls for the support of education were becoming tiresome, for, said he in substance, the very period during which most money has been spent on education with the promise that social betterment would follow is the very one during which social disruption has been most pronounced. I entirely agree with what he probably meant but not with what he said. If he had stated his meaning accurately, his thought would have been diametrically opposite to what he had in mind. He would in that case have said something like this: We willingly have contributed great sums of money for the support of schools and colleges. The sponsors told us that the effect would be social betterment, but in actuality there has been social disruption. The school people should be told that their *instruction* is not producing *education*. Therefore, they should be told that they can have no more money until they can mend their ways and show educational results.

The school, college, and university people are constantly led into the same verbal fallacy until they imagine that even a better building will automatically produce better results in education. Indeed, I sometimes suspect that they confound the material equipment with education.

We are constantly reminded that education is of no certain value since highly educated men not infrequently find their way into the penitentiaries. Of course, the statement is false in its terms. The men are where they are because of the failure of their schools and colleges in generating education. The men may have been extensively schooled, may have brilliantly acquired advanced degrees, but so far we have instruction only, and an instruction which evidently failed.

The Curriculum   The basal framework of Instruction is the Curriculum. Without a curriculum, the school is in precisely the same situation as is a builder who bids on a project without plans and specifications and proceeds to erect with no better guidance. Evidently, if Instruction is to be systematically effective, the bedrock, the frame of reference, the plans and specification of the instruction provided, are in the Curriculum.

The term is an ancient one in pedagogy and originally it meant a race course, something to be "run through," a round of studies to be pursued and presumably learned. In our schools the term suffers from our habitual vagueness in matters of terminology. "Curriculum" is used when what is meant is "program of study" or "course of study" for a particular school.

Now the Curriculum is in its nature constant and universal. Programming, and especially teaching, are variable according to the circumstances of particular schools and individual pupils. Let us see.

We have seen that Education is a process of adjustment with the end of adaptability in a particular world. Now the world is common to all mankind. It is a world of physical and biological conditions, one of social conditions, one of moral and aesthetic values.

Furthermore, so far as the anthropological disclosures tell us the story, human nature is at bottom the same the world over, however varied may be the cultural accumulations of different races and peoples, whatever may the spread in the extent to which different peoples have climbed the ladder of Civilization, and the differing extents to which Civilization may have been diffused among different populations. Hence the content of Education is at bottom the same the world over, and the framework upon which that content is hung, namely, the Curriculum, is the same in essentials. The *pedagogical problems* arise in the fields of programming and of teaching.

*   *   *

Mastery   When a student has fully acquired a piece of learning, he has mastered it. Half-learning, or learning rather well, or being on the way to learning are none of them mastery. Mastery implies completeness; the thing is done; the student has arrived, as far as that particular learning is concerned. There is no question of how well the student has mastered it; he has either mastered or he has not mastered. It is as absurd to speak of degrees in mastery as to speak of degrees in the attainment of the second floor of a building or of degrees in being on the other side of the stream, or of degrees of completeness of any sort whatever. The traveler may indeed be part-way across the stream, he may be almost across, but he is not across until he gets there. Once across, he may continue his journey indefinitely, but he cannot continue his journey from midstream. The pupil may have begun to learn, we can see that he is making progress, he has almost learned; but he has not mastered until he has learned. He may continue to other masteries, and there will be all sorts of degrees in the number of masteries he attains. He may acquire skill in the application of his learning, and there may be an infinite number of degrees in his skill as he improves from no skill at all to expertness. There may be, and commonly are, degrees in the convincing character of the evidence from which we infer mastery. But in the unit learning itself there are no degrees; the pupil either has it or he has it not. We may then apply the term in substance to the true learning products which we have studied in the preceding chapter, and affirm that whenever the adaptation in the individual which corresponds to a given product in learning has taken place, the individual has arrived at the mastery level for that particular product. Thus, the child who has reached the primary reading

From Henry C. Morrison, *The Practice of Teaching in the Secondary School,* pp. 36–37. Copyright © 1926 and 1931 by the University of Chicago.

adaptation and can actually read may be said to have reached a mastery level. The pupil who has actually acquired that view of the material world which is implied in the atomic theory has attained a mastery level. He who has attained a new and better taste in the reading which he cultivates has attained a mastery. Similarly, the student who has reached the level of intellectual responsibility is a master at a vitally important stage in his intellectual and volitional development.

Now the whole process of education, of adjustment to the objective conditions of life is made up of unit learnings each of which must be mastered or else no adaptation is made. These unit learnings cannot be measured but they can all of them be evidenced by symptoms or signs revealed in the learner's behavior. Some symptoms are plainly manifest if we observe thoughtfully; others can be detected only by tests designed to bring them out; others still can be observed only by the methods, and it may be only with the help of the instruments, of the skilled psychologist. Whatever the test, its purpose is to throw light on the question, Has the pupil learned or has he not?

*   *   *

Arthur E. Bestor, Jr.

Arthur E. Bestor, Jr., was born in 1908 in Chautauqua, New York. He received his Ph.D. from Yale University in 1938. A distinguished American historian, he has held positions at Yale University, Columbia University, Stanford University, the University of Illinois, and the University of Washington. He also taught American studies at the University of Tokyo. From 1956 to 1957, Bestor was president of the Council for Basic Education. His books on American education, *Educational Wastelands: Retreat from Learning in Our Public Schools* (1953) and *Restoration of Learning: A Program for Redeeming the Unfulfilled Promise of American Education* (1955) generated a heated public debate over the aims of American education. Bestor is a staunch defender of basic education and intellectual discipline.

In the selection that follows, Bestor discusses the "ideal of disciplined intelligence"; and he argues for intellectual discipline as the aim of education on the grounds that: (1) American democracy and its representative institutions need literate, accurately informed, and rational citizens; (2) it will serve as an instrument of preserving the cultural values of the nation; (3) it is the deliberate cultivation of the ability to think which is necessary for all men.

*   *   *

As a people we believe that education is vital to our national welfare and to the security of our democratic institutions. But to believe this is not enough. We must understand why and in what way education is vital. Otherwise we cannot distinguish between the kind of schooling that truly protects and advances the well being of the country, and the kind that merely provides decorous amusements to while away the time of young men and women not yet ready to engage in the serious work of the world. Education is vital to American democracy for reasons that can be clearly specified. In the first place, a republican system of government requires citizens who are highly literate, accurately informed, and rigorously trained in the processes of rational and critical thought. If the schools fail to raise up a nation of men and women equipped with these qualities of mind, then self-government is in danger of collapse through the sheer inability of its electorate to grapple intelligently with the complex problems in science, economics, politics, and international relations which constantly come up for public decision.

In addition to this, the American public schools—working in close harmony with the colleges, universities, and professional schools—have the responsibility of training scientists, physicians, scholars, engineers, and other professional men equal in competence to the best that any educational system is capable of producing. If the schools fail to do their part in this, the nation is threatened with the loss of intellectual strength and, as a direct consequence, the loss of industrial prosperity and military security.

Less tangible, but no less real and significant, are the cultural values of a nation, which must likewise be safeguarded through intellectual training in its schools. With a decline of respect for cultural and intellectual values in and for themselves comes a decline of faith on the part of a people in its own higher purposes. Degradation of the spirit proceeds step by step: the undermining of genuine loyalty, the destruction of freedom of thought and of speech, and finally the loss of that self-respect which, to a man or a nation, is the ultimate source of courage and hope and virtue and will.

The economic, political, and spiritual health of a democratic state depends upon how successfully its educational system keeps pace

with the increasingly heavy intellectual demands of modern life.
Our civilization requires of *every* man and woman a variety of
complex skills that rest upon the ability to read, write, and calculate,
and upon sound knowledge of science, history, economics,
philosophy, and other fundamental disciplines. These forms of
knowledge are not a mere preparation for more advanced study.
They are invaluable in their own right. The student bound for
college must have them, of course. But so must the high-school
student who does not intend to enter college. Indeed, his is the
graver loss if the high school fails to give adequate training in these
fundamental ways of thinking, for he can scarcely hope to acquire
thereafter the intellectual skills of which he has been defrauded.

Throughout history these intellectual disciplines have rightly been
considered fundamental in education for practical life and for
citizenship, as well as in training for the professions. The modern
world has made them more vital than ever. Every vocation has
grown more complicated. The artisan of an earlier century might
make his way in the world even though illiterate and all but
unlearned in elementary arithmetic. Today even the simplest trades
require much more. The responsibilities of the citizen, too, have
grown more exacting year by year. Intelligent citizenship does not
mean merely a simple faith in American democracy. It calls for a
thorough knowledge of political principles and institutions, of
history, and of economics. It demands a clear understanding of the
various sciences, for the voter must help decide public policy on
such intricate matters as the development and control of atomic
energy. Above all, intelligent citizenship requires an ability to read,
to understand, and to test the logic of arguments far more
complicated than any hitherto addressed to the public at large.

The nation depends upon its schools and colleges to furnish this
intellectual training to its citizenry as a whole. Society has no other
institutions upon which it can rely in the matter. If schools and
colleges do not emphasize rigorous intellectual training, there will be
none. This is not true of the other services that educational agencies
may incidentally render. It is well for the schools to pay attention to
public health, for example, but if they are unable to do so, the
health of the nation will not go uncared for. The medical profession
and the existing welfare agencies remain unimpaired. But if the
schools neglect their vital function of intellectual training, the loss to
society is an irreparable one.

"Intellectual training" may seem a formidable phrase. But it means
nothing more than deliberate cultivation of the ability to think. It
implies no unnatural distinction between the mind and the

emotions, for men can think about emotional and aesthetic problems, and can be taught to think more clearly about them. It implies no opposition between the intellectual and the moral realm, for ethics is applicable to the thinking process itself, and rationality is a constituent of every valid ethical system. Morality enters the classroom and the study as it enters all the chambers of life. It assumes special form as intellectual honesty and as the species of reflectiveness which converts a mere taboo into an ethical imperative.

Least of all is there a sharp contrast between the intellectual and the practical. Knowledge does, of course, become more abstract and reasoning more intricate as one proceeds farther into each of the fields of science and learning. But this does not mean that knowledge becomes less practical or less applicable to human affairs as it advances. Quite the contrary. It becomes more practical because it becomes more powerful. A formula is abstract not because it has lost touch with facts but because it compresses so many facts into small compass that only an abstract statement can sum them up. Simple forms of knowledge can accomplish simple tasks; complex forms of knowledge can accomplish complex tasks. One does not need higher mathematics to build a workable waterwheel or an oxcart, but one does need it to build a dynamo or a jet-propelled plane.

The modern scientist or the modern scholar knows the delight of intellectual endeavor for its own sake, and he rightly resents the undervaluing of this motive. But when all is said and done, he knows that the principal value to society of a man's cultivating the power of abstract thought is that he is thereby enabled to deal more effectively with the insistent problems of modern life. If he prefers to work with differential equations instead of a screwdriver and a pair of pliers, it is not because he thinks the work of the hands ignoble, but because he thinks the work of the brain more powerful. The basic argument for the intellectual disciplines in education is not that they lift a man's spirit above the world, but that they equip his mind to enter the world and perform its tasks.

A school that sticks to its job of intellectual training is not thereby indifferent to the vocational needs of its students, to their physical development, to their moral conduct, or to their emotional and mental health. Such a school merely recognizes that it must deal with these matters within the context provided by its own characteristic activity. By knowing its capabilities and its limitations a school can make a more effective contribution to vocational training, to physical education, and to ethics than if it cherishes the delusion that it is home, church, workshop, and doctor's office rolled into one.

As a matter of fact, to define the school as an agency of intellectual training does not preclude the carrying out by the school of many ancillary tasks, important to the child and to society. The school does bring together almost all the children of the community. Consequently many health and welfare services can reach children and their families most conveniently through the school. Instructions concerning health and safety precautions, including emergency and civil-defense arrangements, can be disseminated most efficiently through the school. The school ordinarily conducts a program of social activities, and some of the niceties of social intercourse can receive unobtrusive attention in connection therewith. A pupil is better known to his teachers than to anyone else save his parents, hence the school can engage in certain kinds of counseling and can refer problems to agencies that might otherwise never learn of them.

So far as the school is able to do so without interfering with its essential programs of study, it should make its facilities available for these services. The list I have just given, however, indicates the variety of demands that can be made upon its time. It is all too easy for a school administrator to give in to the pressures that are brought upon him by well-meaning groups of various kinds, and to allow the school's own program to be engulfed by activities only distantly related to its central purpose. This has actually happened to an almost unbelievable extent in many American public schools. Only a firm conviction of the importance of fundamental intellectual training, and a stern insistence upon subordinating all other activities to this one, can enable teachers and administrators to preserve the educational system from utter chaos.

FURTHER READINGS

Bagley, William C. *Education and the Emergent Man.* New York: The Ronald Press, 1934.

Bestor, Arthur E. *Educational Wastelands: Retreat from Learning in Our Public Schools.* Urbana: University of Illinois Press, 1953.

————. *Restoration of Learning: A Program for Redeeming the Unfulfilled Promise of American Education.* New York: Alfred A. Knopf, Inc. 1955.

Council for Basic Education. *The Case for Basic Education: A Program of Aims for Public Schools.* Boston: Atlantic–Little, Brown and Company, 1959.

Demiashkevich, Michael. *An Introduction to the Philosophy of Education.* New York: American Book Company, 1935.

The Harvard Committee. *General Education in a Free Society.* Cambridge, Mass.: Harvard University Press, 1948.

Morrison, Henry C. *Basic Principles in Education.* Boston: Houghton Mifflin Company, 1934.

_____. *The Curriculum of the Common School.* Chicago: University of Chicago Press, 1940.

_____. *The Practice of Teaching in the Secondary School.* Chicago: University of Chicago Press, 1931.

Rafferty, Max. *Suffer, Little Children.* New York: The New American Library, Inc. 1963.

Rickover, Hyman. *Education and Freedom.* New York: E. P. Dutton & Co., Inc., 1959.

seven

JOHN DEWEY'S
EXPERIMENTALIST PRAGMATISM

John Dewey ranks foremost among the American philosophers who were concerned with problems of educational theory and practice. His pragmatic experimentalism, or instrumentalist, philosophy gave theoretical expression to the American frontier experience which was characterized by a mobile population migrating westward through a series of varying environments. In the light of the frontier experience, Americans came to measure success in terms of the consequences which accrued from harnessing the environment for human purposes. The openness of an expansive frontier was easily translated into a wider vision of an open universe, charged by the dynamics of constant flux, change, and movement. Dewey's pragmatic experimentalism boldly asserted the American propensity to discard purely speculative philosophy as a kind of empty metaphysical meandering. Philosophy's raw materials were social and educational rather than purely speculative or theoretical. Dewey's philosophy expressed his faith in man's capacity to create a progressive society. Experimentalism was the creed of the progressive social, political, and educational reformers who believed that the application of human intelligence could harness the environment and nourish both personal and social growth. Dewey's social philosophy became a theoretical rationale for social and political reformation. In particular, his educational philosophy contributed to the progressive education movement that sought to fashion the school as an educational community, an embryonic and miniature society, in which children shared experiences and solved mutual problems.

DEWEY'S LIFE AND WRITINGS

Since he is a major figure in American educational philosophy, a brief examination of Dewey's life and major writings is useful in establishing the context of his pragmatic experimentalism. Dewey was born in Burlington, Vermont, in 1859, the year in which Charles Darwin's *Origin of the Species* appeared. Dewey's father owned a general store, and his family was active in the social and political life of the small rural community which was characterized by the spirit of democratic neighborliness. When he developed his social philosophy, Dewey stressed the significance of the face-to-face community in which people shared common concerns and problems. His democratic vision was shaped by the New England town meeting, where people came together to solve their mutual problems through a peaceful process of discussion, debate, and decision making. In his later articulation of a social and educational philosophy, Dewey's concept of social control embraced both the spirit of the participatory community and the application of the scientific method.

Dewey attended the University of Vermont, from which he received his bachelor's degree. He then taught school in Oil City, Pennsylvania, and later in rural Vermont. He pursued graduate study in philosophy at Johns Hopkins University and received his doctorate in 1884. From 1884 to 1894, he taught philosophy at the University of Michigan.

Dewey spent a formative period of his life at the University of Chicago, where, from 1894 to 1904, he headed the Department of Philosophy, Psychology, and Education. From 1902 to 1904, he was director of the University's School of Education. It was here that he established his famous laboratory school, which enrolled children from ages four through fourteen and sought to provide experiences in cooperative and mutually useful living.[1] This aim was pursued through "activity method," which involved play, construction, nature study, and self-expression. These activities were designed to elicit the learner's active reconstruction of his own experience. Through such activities the spirit of the school was to be renewed, and it was to become a miniature community and an embryonic society.

In Dewey's school, the child's individual tendencies were to be organized and directed toward cooperative living in the school community. Dewey's work at the laboratory school further directed his attention to educational questions; and he later expressed his educational views in *The School and Society* (1923).

---

1. For a quite recent account of Dewey's laboratory school at Chicago, see Arthur G. Wirth, *John Dewey as Educator: His Design for Work in Education (1894–1904)*. New York: John Wiley & Sons, Inc., 1966.

In 1904, Dewey left Chicago to join the philosophy department at Columbia University, where he taught until 1930. During his tenure at Columbia, Dewey acquired an international reputation. He lectured in Japan, China, and Mexico. He visited schools in Turkey and in the Soviet Union. A prolific author, he wrote more than 1,000 books and articles that influenced the course of American educational and social philosophy.

In 1910 in *How We Think,* Dewey postulated the thesis that thinking is a series of problem-solving episodes that occur as man attempts to survive and grow within an environmental context. *Democracy and Education* (1916), Dewey's most complete statement of educational philosophy, argued that genuine education proceeded most effectively in an open or democratic environment where man was free of absolutes that blocked his freedom of inquiry. *Individualism, Old and New* (1929) rejected the inherited notion of rugged individualism as an archaic residue. In place of a competitive economy and society, Dewey urged men to deal with the problems of an emergent corporate and communal social order. In *Art as Experience* (1934), Dewey elaborated an aesthetic theory which asserted that art was properly a means of shared expression and communication between the artist and the perceiver of the art object.

Although he was often called the father of progressive education, Dewey's relationship to the progressive education movement must be carefully considered.[2] While many progressives accepted Dewey's experimentalist philosophy, other progressives did not. As a movement, the Progressive Education Association was an umbrella organization which covered a variety of people and groups, ranging from child-centered teachers to neo-Freudians. The publication of many of Dewey's educational writings coincided with the progressive education movement, and there were strong similarities between Dewey and the progressive reformers who opposed a static conception of learning and schooling. Although Dewey and many progressive educators agreed on the importance of experience, continuity, and the cultivation of the child's interests and needs, Dewey challenged the sentimental, romantic progressives who dogmatically asserted the doctrine of child-centered learning. Dewey's *Experience and Education* (1938) criticized progressive educators for failing to elaborate a positive educational philosophy based on experience. He challenged progressives to move beyond merely opposing the traditional school and urged them to develop a positive and affirmative educational posture.

2. See chapter eight, where Dewey's relationships to the progressive education movement are treated in detail.

Among Dewey's other major books were *Interest and Effort in Education* (1913), *Human Nature and Conduct* (1922), and *Freedom and Culture* (1939). Through his writing, lecturing, and presence on the American and world scene, Dewey contributed to the kind of political and social liberalism that urged social reform based on careful, pragmatic planning. His work stimulated the rise of an experimentalist philosophy which profoundly influenced American educational theory and practice. This chapter will examine the various components of his pragmatic experimentalist, or instrumentalist, educational philosophy.

The Uncertainty of Certainty Although *Democracy and Education* most completely stated his educational philosophy, the key to Dewey's system of thought is in *The Quest for Certainty.*[3] Throughout his philosophical and educational writings, Dewey argued against the dualistic conception of the universe, which he claimed man had created to postulate a theoretically unchanging realm of complete and perfect certitude. The more traditional Idealist, Realist, and Thomist philosophies were based on substantive metaphysical propositions that grounded reality in a world of unchanging ideas for the Idealist or structures for the Realist. Based upon these conceptions, Western man had devised a bipolar conception of reality. Traditional philosophers held a dualistic conception of reality in which there were the ideational, or theoretical, and the material worlds. While ideas, spirit, and thought were higher in the chain of being, work and action were located lower in the hierarchy. From this essential dualism, life and education were seen on two separate levels. Priority was given, however, to the immaterial and unchanging order. Thus, such classical dualisms as spirit–matter, mind–body and soul–body came to permeate Western thought. These metaphysical dualisms had an impact on life and education in that they created distinctions between theory and practice, liberal and vocational education, fine and applied art, and thought and action.

The bifurcation between theory and practice was not only a matter of philosophical speculation, but it also intruded into education. Philosophical dualism led to the principle of the hierarchy in curriculum in which those subjects which were strongly theoretical were given priority over those which were practical. Following the distinction between theory and practice, the traditional curriculum required that the learner should first master the symbolic and literary skills such as reading, writing, and arithmetic. The learning of these tool skills prepared the child to study systematically the subject matters of history, geogra-

3. John Dewey, *The Quest for Certainty: A Study of the Relation of Knowledge and Action.* New York: Minton, Balch and Co., 1929.

phy, mathematics, and science at the secondary and higher levels. In the traditional subject-matter curriculum, these disciplines were organized deductively as bodies of principles, theories, factual context, and examples. Formal education became excessively theoretical and bore little relationship to the learner's own personal and social experience. Furthermore, the subject-matter curriculum was geared to preparing students for future situations which were to occur after the completion of formal schooling. According to Dewey, the subject-matter curriculum was based upon the dualism between theory and practice. It created additional bifurcations that separated the child from the curriculum and the school from society.

Dewey's social conception of education was basic to his experimentalism, which saw thinking and doing as a unified flow of on-going experience. Thinking and acting were not separable; thinking was incomplete until tested in experience. To understand Dewey's pragmatic philosophy, it is necessary to examine his antagonism to the dualism which supported the belief in a higher, transcendent, unchanging reality.

According to Dewey, man lives in an uncertain world which is often hostile to his survival. In his mind, man seeks to create a concept of certainty which gives him a feeling of permanence and security. Since actual living is fraught with danger, man creates a distinction between the perils of everyday existence and the security of an unchanging reality. Early religious-philosophical systems created a world view which posited reality in a perfect, unchanging, and eternal universal. In this *Weltanchauung,* the inferior level of existence is the mundane, changing, and uncertain; and the superior order is that which is beyond the scope of the empirical, experiential, and work-a-day existence.

In contrast to dualistic conceptions of reality, Dewey emphasizes a changing and evolutionary universe where man's problem is not that of transcending experience but rather of using experience to direct and control his environmental interaction. The age-old quest for an unchanging order of Being distorted man's conception of reality and his attempt to direct his destiny in the real world of experience. Rather than seeking to escape experience, Dewey argues that philosophy should aid man in recognizing, reconstructing, and using experience to improve life conditions. In such a reconstruction of experience, theory and practice would be aspects of man's on-going activity. Derived from experience, theory is tested in experience. Instead of a dualism between the immutable and the changing, experience is a continuum in which man deals with a sequence of problems. In such a sequence, theory is derived from and tested in practice; mind is a social process of intelligently solving problems rather than an antecedent and transcendent category; education is liberal, as it frees man by giving him a methodology for dealing with all kinds of problems, including the social and vocational; the distinction between the fine and useful arts is to be disposed of by merging beauty and function. Dewey's thesis is that existence is uncertain. To exist means to be involved in a world of change. Man's quest is not for certainty but rather for a means, or a method, of controlling and directing the process of change insofar as this can be done in an imperfect world.

THE ORGANISM AND THE ENVIRONMENT

As mentioned earlier, Dewey's birth coincided with the publication of Darwin's *The Origin of the Species.* The shock of the full implications of Darwin's biological theory reverberated throughout the nineteenth and early twentieth centuries. At first glance, Darwin's theory seemed to challenge the traditional Judeo-Christian conception, based upon the book of Genesis, that God had created species in a fixed form. Those who literally accepted Genesis found themselves in conflict with Darwinian science. For some fundamentalist Protestant Americans, the impact of Darwin was shattering.

According to Darwin's thesis that species evolved slowly and gradually, the members of the species, or organisms, lived, adjusted, and adapted to the environment in order to survive. Those species which succeeded in surviving did so because they possessed favorable characteristics that enabled them to adjust satisfactorily to environmental changes. The transmission of these favorable characteristics to their offspring guaranteed the particular species' continuation. Darwin's theory emphasizes the competition of individuals for survival in a frequently hostile and challenging environment.

To appreciate Darwin's full impact upon Dewey, it is necessary to examine briefly the initial adaptation of evolutionary theory into a sociology of knowledge by such theorists as Herbert Spencer and William Graham Sumner, who sought to apply Darwinian principles to socioeconomic and political life.[4] These early sociologists viewed man as an individual social atom who is locked in a fiercely competitive struggle against other individuals. Through the motive force of individual competition and initiative, some individuals adjust to environment more readily than others. Such intelligent and strong competitors move upward in society to positions of social, economic, and political leader-

4. For a treatment of the impact of Social Darwinism and the rise of a pragmatic reformed Darwinism in American life, see Richard Hofstadter, *Social Darwinism in American Thought.* Boston: Beacon Press, 1958.

ship. Those who are unintelligent in their behavior, who can not compete effectively or efficiently, fall downward from the social ladder to become the dregs of society. For Spencer and Sumner, competition is the natural order of life, with the prize going to the fittest individuals. It is not difficult to extrapolate the social and educational implications of Social Darwinism. Both Spencer and Sumner regarded the *laissez-faire* economic and social order as the natural order and argued against tampering with the natural laws of competition. Society is composed of independent, autonomous, and competitive individuals, who, at the most direct level, struggle for economic survival. Schools best perform their social role when they prepare individuals for a competitive social order. Progress occurs as men discover and perfect new ways of competing against each other in exploiting the natural and social environment.

Both biological and social Darwinism had an impact upon Dewey's developing experimentalist philosophy. While accepting some of Darwin's basic biological conceptions, Dewey rejected Spencer and Sumner's attempt to apply competitive ethics to society. Darwin's notion of an evolutionary process was accepted by Dewey, who rejected his own earlier acceptance of the fixed, final, and transcendent Hegelian metaphysics. Dewey's educational philosophy, drawing upon an organismic psychology, uses the terms of organism and environment and applies them to life and to education. For Dewey, the human organism is a living and natural creature, physiologically composed of living tissue and possessing a set of impulses or drives designed to maintain life. Every organism lives within an environment which has elements that both nourish and threaten its life.

As the individual human being lives, he encounters problem situations which threaten his continued existence or experience. Upon encountering such a situation, the organism's activity is blocked. The successful person is able to solve these problems and to regain his activity. As a result of this network of interaction between the organism and its environment, the organism acquires experience. In Dewey's educational philosophy, the crucial concept of experience is best thought of as the interaction of an organism with its environment. Man knows through his experiences, or environmental interactions; each experiential episode adds to the individual's experience. When confronted by problems, the individual examines his experience for clues which might suggest the means for resolving the present difficulty.

At this point, several basic components of Dewey's educational philosophy can be asserted: (1) the learner is a living organism, a biological and sociological phenomenon, who possesses drives or impulses designed to keep him alive; (2) the learner lives in an environment which is both natural and social; (3) the learner, moved by his drives, is active and constantly interacts with his environment; (4) environmental interaction produces a series of problems which occur as the individual seeks to satisfy his needs; (5) learning, itself, is the process of solving problems arising in the environment.

As mentioned earlier, Dewey sought to establish the school as a miniature community or embryonic society. Although believing that society is made up of separate, discrete, individual human beings, he rejected the competitive ethic of social atomism advocated by Spencer and Sumner. For Dewey, man lives in a social as well as a purely physical environment. In striving to live, man comes to recognize that group life promotes the quest for survival by giving security. Associative living, or community, enriches human experience and adds to it as the group mutually engages in problem-solving activities. Man's collective experience provides the individual with a more complex set of experiences, or interactive episodes.

As used by Dewey, living involves the ability to solve problems and thus facilitate survival. If living is broadly construed as problem solving, then education involves learning the methodology of how to solve problems. Since interaction with environment is a transactive process that changes both the organism undergoing the experiences and the environment, education as problem solving can be defined broadly as any experience which alters beliefs or attitudes and makes a person different than he was prior to the experience.

THE CONSERVATIVE AND RECONSTRUCTIVE ASPECTS OF EDUCATION

In *Democracy and Education,* Dewey's primary concern is the relationship between society and education. The educative process occurs informally as the person matures within a cultural milieu and acquires the language, skills, and knowledge common to group life. In the more formal sense of schooling, education is a deliberate process of bringing the immature person into cultural participation by providing the necessary symbolic and linguistic tools needed for group interaction and communication.

Dewey conceived of education as having both a conservative and a reconstructive dimension. Education is preservative or conservative when it maintains cultural continuity by transmitting the heritage from adults to the immature members of the group, the children. In both its formal and informal aspects, education is always a value-laden process which involves cultural imposition, because it occurs within the context of a particular culture with its unique mores, folkways, and language. Although cultural imposition is always particular to a given time and place, it provides the means of communication and expression by which the individual liberates himself through group participation.

As transmission of the cultural heritage, education is the means by which the group reproduces the cultural type and thus perpetuates itself. For Dewey, the child is not born with distinctly human traits. Such human traits are acquired or learned as the child associates with the members of the group. Education is the instrument whereby the group transmits the cultural skills, knowledge, and values necessary to reproduce the desired cultural type and thus perpetuate the heritage.

Although clearly recognizing the conservative aspects of education which provides for cultural continuity, Dewey does not limit education to the preservation of the status quo. Education is a dynamic process. As the cultural heritage is imposed upon the young, the means of altering or changing that heritage are also provided. Dewey viewed the world as a universe in constant change. By using the scientific method, man possesses the possibility for directing the course of change. Culture is not conceived of as a static entity but rather in dynamic and process-oriented terms.

Formal Education   As a vast complex which includes the total experience of the human race and the particular experience of the group, the cultural heritage includes elements that are worthy and elements that are unworthy of perpetuation. Formal education is one of society's means of purifying and selecting those aspects of the cultural heritage that are worthy of perpetuation.

For Dewey, the school is a specialized environment established to enculturate the young by deliberately bringing them into cultural participation. As a social institution, the school is a selective agency which transmits part of the culture and seeks to reconstruct other aspects of the cultural heritage. The school's three-fold functions are those of simplifying, purifying, and balancing the cultural heritage.[5] To simplify the cultural heritage, the school selects elements of the heritage and reduces their complexity into appropriate units for learning, based on the learner's maturity and readiness. As a purifying agency, the school selects certain elements of the cultural heritage and eliminates unworthy aspects which limit human growth. Unworthy environmental aspects are not to be allowed to influence the formation of the character of the young. Balancing refers to the integration of the experiences which have been selected and purified into an harmonious totality. Many diverse groups live in society, and the children of one group need

---

5. John Dewey, *Democracy and Education: An Introduction to the Philosophy of Education.* New York: The Macmillan Company, 1916. pp. 22–26.

assistance in understanding the individuals from other groups. The genuinely democratic community is an integrated and balanced community based on mutually shared understanding. The school is a simplified, purified, and integrated (or balanced) community in which the immature human being deals with and solves problems and thus adds to his experience. While problem solving is individualized and personalized, it is also a social process. Group experience is a cooperative enterprise in which all the participants share their experiences. The more sharing that occurs, the greater are the possibilities for growth. Dewey recognized that the rise of an industrial, urban, and technological society had created a number of socio-educational problems. The more complex the society becomes, the greater is the gap or distance between the child's activities and the requirements of responsible adult life. Dewey's school society, based on mutually shared activities, is designed to be the embryo of an associative democracy. The problem-solving techniques used in solving problems in the school situation should transfer to the larger society.

DEMOCRATIC SOCIETY AND EDUCATION

Dewey rejected the Perennialist assumptions that education was everywhere the same or was intrinsically good. Rather, the quality of education varies as does the quality of life which is experienced by the group that sustains and supports the school. Dewey's conception of democratic social arrangements and democratic education are related to an experimenting society that possesses and uses a process-oriented philosophy. Dewey's conception of democratic education is not particular to the American form of government or to particular political institutions, but is rather an epistemological and sociological one that is characterized by the presence of an experimental temperament. In an experimenting society, the citizen is free from the impediments erected by absolutist governments or *a priori* philosophies. Since educational institutions socialize the young according to group values, genuinely democratic education occurs within the milieu of the experimental or inquiry-oriented school.

In a sociological context, Dewey's democratic society is one in which the members share the widest possible variety of interests. Any impediment or barrier to group interaction, such as racial, religious, or economic segregation, interfers with group sharing. Any form of human exploitation weakens the experimental temperament of a genuinely democratic society. Whenever individuals are involved in an exclusive activity without sharing, some form of exploitation is present. Exclusive, rather than shared, interests involve a narrow exploitation which harms both the exploiter and the exploited. A genuinely democratic society possesses a rich variety of shared activities, a concern based on mutuality of interests, and a willingness to experiment. Dewey emphasized the cooperative nature of shared human experience. The more sharing that occurs among individuals, the greater are the possibilities for human relationships and interactions. An examination of Dewey's emphasis on human association reveals three key elements: the common, communication, and community. The common, representing shared objects, instruments, values and ideas, arises in the context of group experience. Communication occurs when men frame and express their shared experiences in symbolic patterns. Community is the human association that results as individuals come together to discuss their common experience and problems through means of shared communication—a common, linking language. Although all human association is characterized by commonly shared social objects and instruments and by shared communication, Dewey prefers the free, open, and humane arrangements of the democratic community in which the experimental processes operate without the interference of absolutist or authoritarian structures. While Dewey emphasizes the importance of the like-minded community characterized by shared experience, such a community does not rest on conformity. A genuinely democratic community honors pluralism and diversity within a shared context. For Dewey, education is a builder of the sense of community.

Dewey placed crucial importance on the educative role that is exercised by the human group. Participation in group activities contributes to the developing of social intelligence. Dewey's school and classroom are an embryonic community in which learners work together, in common, to solve their mutually shared problems. As they discuss their common goals, aspirations, and projects, the students are transformed from a group of separate, disparate individuals into a community of shared concern and activity.

Dewey's conception of democracy was undoubtedly colored by his own experiences in rural Vermont. The vision of American life which Dewey and many of his associates shared rests on the town-meeting conception of face-to-face, shared democracy. Although the directly personal social experiences of small-town America had been eroded by the rise of a mass, industrialized technological society of impersonal relationships, Dewey envisioned an educational system which would cultivate the sense of community. As children cooperate in group projects, the socialized group problem-solving processes would transfer to the larger society.

In *Individualism: Old and New,* Dewey considers the problems created by the demise of the old, rural individualism and by the rise of the new technological and corporate society.[6] According to his analysis, the social course in a technological era is clearly corporate, as individuals unite to work in large industrial–technological–managerial aggregates. Dewey criticized *laissez-faire* capitalism which he believed had enabled a few individuals to profit by exploiting the majority of the population. A strictly *laissez-faire* economy makes it difficult for the majority to realize their personal capacities and to effect socio-political change. Although he recognized that industrial–technological change had altered the social fabric, Dewey believed that an intelligently controlled technology would benefit the entire society. An industrial and technological complex is capable of liberating man from the drudgery of a subsistence economy. If properly directed, it could free human energies to pursue the aesthetic and intellectual values.

The older, competitive education is patently obsolete and irrelevant to the problems of a corporate, urban, technological society. In the twentieth century, the ideologies of fascism, nazism, and communism arose as totalitarian responses to the organization of the corporate state and society. Rejecting these absolutist systems, Dewey hoped to formulate a social and educational philosophy that would be a viable instrument in enabling people to live in and contribute to a technological, but still democratic, corporate society.

INTELLIGENCE AND EXPERIMENTAL INQUIRY

Dewey's greatest philosophical concern was epistemological rather than metaphysical. He broke with the more traditional philosophies of Idealism and Realism which rested on metaphysical premises grounded in a conception of antecedent reality. Dewey believed that these more speculative philosophies had constructed a static theory of mind which is isolated from life's personal and social realities. Dewey proposed an active social conception of intelligence. While conditioned by societal institutions, human intelligence could exercise a dynamic influence on effecting social change.

For Dewey, intelligence is socially built through shared experience. Intelligence, the ability to define and solve problems, is acquired through the experience of persisting and working through problem-solving situations. The highest kind of qualitative intelligence is acquired as the individual works with others to solve mutual problems. Within the problem-solving context, intelligence results from shared activity in using instruments. The capacity for problem solving is a function of one's opportunity to learn as well as one's native ability. The

---

6. John Dewey, *Individualism: Old and New*. New York: Minton, Balch and Co., 1930.

more complex and sophisticated the society, the more instruments are present which can be used to solve problems. The savage or primitive society is characterized by an absence of instruments for solving problems. In contrast, the civilized society is one which possesses the instruments for use in group problem solving. Children in a civilized society are generally able to experience in a short time much of the funded experience of the human race. Dewey was not a materialist in the pejorative sense of the word since he did not value objects for their own sake. Rather, a civilized society uses material instruments for the social and personal growth of its members. The use of the material instruments of a particular culture involves the deliberate and intelligent control of these instruments.

For Dewey, thinking originates in the context of a problem or a conflict which exists because a need remains unsatisfied. In the quest to satisfy needs, thinking is an instrument to secure human satisfaction. According to experimental inquiry, ideas are tentative, instrumental plans of action designed to achieve human ends. Thinking involves the seeing of the relationships between action and the resulting consequences.

Complete Act of Thought   According to Dewey, genuine thought occurs as man encounters and solves problems according to the scientific method. Dewey's problem-solving method, the scientific method broadly conceived, consists of five clearly defined steps or phases: (1) In the *problematic situation,* the person is perplexed and confused because he is involved in an incomplete situation of indeterminate character. In the problematic situation, the individual's on-going activity is blocked by some situational element that is deviant from his past experience and is unique. (2) In *defining the problem,* the individual examines the problematic situation and locates that aspect of the situation which impedes his continuing activity. (3) *Clarification of the problem* involves a careful survey, examination, inspection, exploration, and analysis of the elements involved in the problematic situation. It is at this third stage that the individual does systematic and reflective research into the problem to locate the ideas and materials that could resolve the difficulty. (4) By *constructing tentative hypotheses,* the individual establishes a number of generalizations, "if–then" statements, that are possible means of solving the problem. This process involves mentally projecting oneself into the future and projecting the possible consequences of actions. As a result of hypothesizing and conjecturing, the individual frames tentative solutions which could resolve the difficulty and which have the greatest possibilities for securing the desired consequences. (5) The *crucial step* involves the testing of the preferred hypothesis into a plan of action which the individual applies to the existing state of affairs by acting to secure the anticipated result, thereby testing the hypothesis. If the hypothesis resolves the difficulty and effects the desired consequences, then the individual resumes activity until encountering another problem. If the problem remains, then another hypothesis is needed.[7] Dewey's experimental epistemology is directly translatable into the pedagogical methodology of problem solving. The learner, as an individual or as a group member, engages in problem-solving activities and uses the scientific method to resolve both personal and social problems. Each problem-solving episode is an experimental situation in which the learner applies the method of intelligence to real problems arising in his own experience. For Dewey and his followers, the problem-solving method can be encased into a flexible habit that is transferable to a variety of situations. Since the learner works to solve his own problems, he escapes the boring routine of the traditional school which stresses mastery of bodies of subject matters and the learning of verbal formulae.

Dewey's fifth step, the testing of the hypothesis, represents the greatest departure from the learning pattern found in the traditional subject-oriented school. While teachers and students in the more conventional schools might explore problems and frame tentative solutions, rarely do they attempt to solve these problems by acting on them directly. Although they might act upon problems encountered in their chemistry and mathematics lessons, the solutions to these problems have already been determined. It is most unlikely that students would be encouraged to act upon the pressing social, economic, and political problems of the day. Although such problems as war, peace, poverty, and pollution might be discussed in the conventional classroom, the students' active attempt to resolve these problems is likely to be deferred to times and situations outside of the formal institutions. They might, in fact, be deferred until the student reaches maturity and becomes a voter. In contrast, Dewey held that the validation of an idea occurs only as it is tested in experience. Thought is complete only when acted upon.

INTEREST AND EFFORT IN EDUCATION

Although he has been often associated with permissiveness in education, Dewey's conception of child freedom should be examined carefully. Freedom is not anarchy or doing as one pleases without regard to the consequences of action. Freedom, rather, calls for an open environ-

---

7. For Dewey's discussion of thinking, see *Democracy and Education,* pp. 163–78.

ment and attitude in which one can use experimental processes of inquiry to examine and test beliefs and values.

Dewey's group problem-solving method deviates from traditional classroom management in which the teacher's authority directs learning activities. Dewey rejected externally imposed classroom discipline and called for an internal discipline which would cultivate a self-directing and self-disciplining person. As proposed by Dewey, such discipline is task or problem centered and originates within the activity needed to solve the problem. Control or management comes from the cooperative context of shared activity, which involves the working with instruments and people. Rather than controlling the learning situation, the teacher guides the situation by acting as a resource person.

In Dewey's educational philosophy, the starting point of any activity is the felt needs of the learner. Such intrinsic interest, related to a real concern, is better designed to elicit the effort needed to satisfy the need and to solve the problem.

Educational aims are of two kinds: intrinsic and extrinsic. Arising inside of the experience and internal to the person, intrinsic aims are part of the problem or the task. In contrast, extrinsic aims are extraneous to the problem, task, or person's interest. For example, externally administered rewards or punishments which are used to motivate learning in many traditional school situations are extrinsic and often distort genuine learning. For Dewey, intrinsic aims are always superior to extrinsic ones, because they are personal, problematic, and related to the individual learner's own self-direction, self-control, and self-discipline. Intrinsic aims direct the activity. An educational aim, in Dewey's philosophy, arises in the context of the existing conditions of the learner's own experience. Such aims are flexible, capable of alteration, and lead to activity. An experimental aim is one that is a tentative sketch that is capable of being redirected.

In Dewey's context of task-centered discipline, the teacher's role is primarily that of guiding the learner who needs advice or assistance. Direction comes from the requirements of the particular task or problem to be solved. Educational aims are to be the learner's rather than the teacher's.

Dewey's conception of direction and guidance is based on his habit psychology or social behavioralism. While stimuli direct activity, a stimulus is a response and not a brute reaction. Responses can miscarry because of inadequate spatial and sequential definition. Problem solving is likely to miscarry when the problem has been incorrectly defined. Thus, the problem solver misses the scope of the problem. For a problem to be solved correctly, the student has to establish the proper relationships between the aim and the goal by creating an adequate sequence of procedures needed to solve the particular problem.

Teachers who use the problem-solving method need to be patient with their students. While coercion might stimulate students to obtain immediate results, it could impede the adequacy of future responses. The teacher's control of the learning situation is ideally indirect rather than direct. Direct control, coercion, or external discipline does not alter the internal dispositions of persons because it does not aid the learner in becoming a self-directed person. Many teachers err in that they are anxious to have their students get the right answer to a question in the shortest possible time. As resource persons, teachers are to allow students to make errors and to experience the consequences of their actions. In this way, students are more likely to become self-correcting. Dewey does not mean that childish whims or fancies should be permitted to dictate the curriculum, however. The teacher, as a mature person, is to exercise professional judgment and expertise so that the consequences of action do not become dangerous to the student or to his classmates.

GROWTH AS THE END OF EDUCATION

For Dewey, the sole end of education is growth, or that reconstruction of experience which leads to the direction and control of subsequent experience. Education is a process that has no end beyond itself. In establishing criteria to evaluate experiences, particular experiences will be judged on the basis of their contribution to growth or to the having of more experience. Desirable experiences contribute to additional experiences, while undesirable experiences inhibit and reduce the possibilities for subsequent experience. It might be recalled that intelligence involves the ability to solve problems and that problem solving involves the recognition of the connections and interrelationships between various experiences. Growth, in Dewey's context, means that the individual is gaining the ability to see the relationships and interconnections between various experiences, between one learning and another. Learning by experience, through problem solving, means that education, like life, is a process of continuously reconstructing experience.

Dewey's thesis that the desired kind of education contributes to growth for the purpose of directing subsequent experiences rejects the traditional school's emphasis on the doctrine of preparation. According to the theory of preparation, the student learns his lessons and masters subject matter to prepare for events or situations which are to occur after the completion of formal education. In contrast, Dewey conceives of life as taking place in a changing universe and society. To defer action until after schooling has been completed is to prepare the student for a world that is likely to be nonexistent when the student is ready to act. Instead of waiting for some remote future date, the learner is to act on his interests and needs as he seeks to resolve his problems. By using the method of intelligence, or problem solving, in his day-to-day affairs, the student can internalize a method which is applicable to all situations—present and future.

Dewey's critique of the doctrine of preparation is based on his concept of the child. As was true of such naturalistic reformers as Rousseau, Pestalozzi, and Francis Parker, Dewey rejected the view that the child is a miniature or unfinished adult. He also rejected the view that the child is depraved or deprived because of a flaw in human nature. While rejecting the archaic concept of childhood depravity, Dewey did not subscribe to Rousseau's romanticizing of the child as a being who is completely and innately good. For Dewey, childhood is a developmental phase of human life. The child who lives well at each stage of his development is likely to live an adequate and satisfying adult life. Dewey wanted the child to acquire a method for dealing with his environment that can enable him to achieve his purposes and aims.

THE EXPERIENTIAL CURRICULUM

Dewey challenged the traditional subject-matter curriculum which had long been associated with formal schooling. Critics of the subject-matter curriculum charge that the teaching of such separate bodies of information as history, geography, mathematics, science, and language tends to degenerate into past-centered, highly verbal bookishness and pedantry. Formal schooling is abstract in the sense that it is separated from the child's own interests, needs, and experiences. In contrast to the subject-matter curriculum, Dewey stressed a method of solving problems.

Dewey emphasized that methodology is intimately related to the curriculum when, in *Democracy and Education,* he recommended three levels of curricular organization: (1) making and doing; (2) history and geography; (3) organized sciences.[8] Making and doing, the first level of curriculum, engages the students in activities or projects based on their direct experience which require the using and manipulating of raw materials. These activities have intellectual possibilities within them and expose the child to the functional aspects of experience.

History and geography, the second curricular level, are regarded as two great educational resources for enlarging the significance of the child's direct personal experience. History and geography extend the child's temporal and spatial experience from the immediate home and school environments to the broader community and the world. For

---

8. For a discussion of curriculum, see *Democracy and Education,* pp. 228–70.

Dewey, history and geography are not properly taught as discretely organized bodies of information. Rather, the study of history and geography should begin with the child's immediate environment and then be extended so that the learner can gain perspective into time and place. Dewey recognized that all learning is particular and contextual to a given time, place, and circumstance. While cultural particularities impose themselves into learning, there is a distinction between imposition and indoctrination. While imposition reflects the concrete contingencies of living in a particular culture and environment with its unique heritage and values, indoctrination refers to the closing of the mind to alternatives and to divergent thinking. Dewey rejected the indoctrination of the young with ideological "isms." In contrast to indoctrination, the social studies are to be useful instruments designed to bring the child into gradual contact with the actual realities and needs of industrial and technological society.

Dewey's third stage of curriculum is the organized subjects, the various sciences, consisting of bodies of tested beliefs or warranted assertions. Students gain exposure to the various bodies of scientific information by mastering the processes of inquiry which are appropriate to these disciplines.

EXPERIMENTAL VALUATION

Dewey's experimentalism operated in his ideas on value as well as in matters of factual inquiry. Unlike the more traditional Idealist and Realist philosophers, who sought to discover the hierarchy of values inherent in the universe, Dewey was a moral relativist who believed that values are man-made responses to varying environmental situations. For Dewey, the major defect of hierarchical systems of value is that man is confronted by wide varieties of conflicting hierarchies. Each hierarchy rests on a basic assumption that is supposed to be self-evident, according to some principle of "right reason."

In addition to rejecting hierarchical arrangements of values, Dewey also turned from value theories which assert the primacy of tradition and custom as a determiner of values. The major weakness in the customary validation of values is that it justifies whatever exists at a particular time and place and becomes a rationale for preserving the status quo. In an interdependent modern world, it is necessary to have a methodology of valuation that could be used to adjudicate cross-cultural conflicts. In a technological society where the pace of social change is rapid, custom and tradition can not be relied upon to determine values.

In contrast to value systems founded upon universal hierarchies or tradition and custom, Dewey postulated criteria of valuation based on the relationships of aims, means, and ends. The basis of experimentalist valuation is found in human preferences, wishes, and needs. Evaluation occurs when there is a conflict in these raw materials of value. Since thinking occurs only within the context of the problematic situation, valuing occurs only when there is a conflict in wants. If a person has only a single desire, then he can act to satisfy that desire. In the case of value conflict, it is necessary to unify the apparently conflicting desires. If the desires can not be unified, then one has to choose between conflicting alternatives. Choice is made by evaluating the possible consequences to be experienced by acting upon the chosen preference.

Dewey's method of valuation is designed to unify aims, means, and ends. When an end is attained, it becomes a means for the satisfaction of still another end. If a person desires a given end, it is necessary to ask questions about the appropriate and efficient means of attaining that end.

RECONSTRUCTING EXPERIENCE

For Dewey, good education is that reconstruction of experience which adds to the meaning of experience and directs the course of future experiences. Dewey's conception of growth as the end of education relates to the intelligent and reflective direction of activity. As a broad concept, growth implies that the learner is aware of the interrelationships of experiences and the consequences which follow action. The insight to the relationships between experiences and actions and their consequences is transferred into meanings through the process of symbolization. Reasoning is thus construed as a process of combining meanings, or symbols, so as to draw conclusions from their manipulation. Reasoning is validated through a process of trial and error. One can never be sure that his reasoning is warranted until he has tested it by acting upon it. The test for thought is in its empirical verification. According to Dewey, cherished ideas and values, no matter how long they have been accepted, are always subjected to alteration when they are applied in particular situations.

The reconstruction of experience could be both personal and social. While each individual has private experience, the experience of the human race is public. It is in Dewey's notion of the experiential continuum that the private and the public modes of experience are blended. According to the experiential continuum, each man is what his past experiences have made him; the particular group is also the product of its history. For the individual and the group, the present moment is their personal and collective past. The future comes out of the present. Insofar as man can control his destiny by manipulating and altering the environment, he shapes his future. Thus, past, present, and future are one flow of on-going human experience. As man constructs his experience, it is impossible to state that unalterable conclusions have ever been reached. Rather than having absolute certitude, man has warranted generalizations which continue until a deviant particular is encountered which does not fit the rule prescribed by the generalization. Upon encountering the unique aspect in experience, it is necessary to reconstruct the experience and restructure the generalization. Such reconstruction of experience involves using those aspects of the generalization which fit the problematic situation created by the encounter with the unique element. As a result of reconstructing experience, the deviant particular is brought into the context of the experiential continuum.

Dewey rejected notions of absolute, unchanging, and eternal truth. All conclusions are tentative and subject to further evaluation and reconstruction. The purpose of human inquiry, or problem solving, is to reach the best possible conclusions on the basis of available evidence.

CONCLUSION

John Dewey's Experimentalist Pragmatism is based on an open conception of a universe that is constantly evolving and changing. Man is seen to be a complicated biological and sociological being who survives by his own functional intelligence which enables him to adapt and transform his ever-changing environment. It is the scientific method, the method of intelligence, which enhances man's ability to cope with the problems of the environment. Education is a process by which man adds to his personal and social intelligence by reconstructing his experience. The Deweyite teacher is one who manipulates the learning environment so that students encounter, deal with, and solve their personal and social problems through the disciplined use of the method of problem solving.

SELECTION

John Dewey

John Dewey (1859–1952) has been recognized as one of America's ablest educational philosophers. Expressed in more than 1,000 published articles and books, his view of Pragmatism, called Experimentalism or Instrumentalism, came to exert a profound influence over educational theory in the United States and throughout the world.

A prolific writer, Dewey examined themes in both general philosophy and educational theory. In 1899, his famous work *School and Society* was published. This was followed by such important books as *Democracy and Education* (1916), *Essays in Experimental Logic* (1916), *Reconstruction in Philosophy* (1920), *Human Nature and Conduct* (1922), *Experience and Nature* (1925), *The Public and its Problems* (1927), *The Quest for Certainty* (1929), *Art as Experience* (1934), *Logic: The Theory of Inquiry* (1938), *Experience and Education* (1938), and *Education Today* (1940).

Dewey rejected the notion of fixed or predetermined ends of education. In his classic work, *Democracy and Education,* he posited the concept of "growth" as both the aim and the end of the educative process. In the following selection, he defines growth and treats its educational implications.

* * *

1. *The Conditions of Growth.* In directing the activities of the young, society determines its own future in determining that of the young. Since the young at a given time will at some later date compose the society of that period, the latter's nature will largely turn upon the direction children's activities were given at an earlier period. This cumulative movement of action toward a later result is what is meant by growth.

The primary condition of growth is immaturity. This may seem to be a mere truism—saying that a being can develop only in some point in which he is undeveloped. But the prefix 'im' of the word immaturity means something positive, not a mere void or lack. It is noteworthy that the terms 'capacity' and 'potentiality' have a double meaning, one sense being negative, the other positive. Capacity may denote mere receptivity, like the capacity of a quart measure. We may mean by potentiality a merely dormant or quiescent state—a capacity to become something different under external influences. But we also mean by capacity an ability, a power; and by potentiality potency, force. Now when we say that immaturity means the possibility of growth, we are not referring to absence of powers which may exist at a later time; we express a force positively present—the *ability* to develop.

Our tendency to take immaturity as mere lack, and growth as something which fills up the gap between the immature and the mature is due to regarding childhood *comparatively,* instead of intrinsically. We treat it simply as a privation because we are measuring it by adulthood as a fixed standard. This fixes attention upon what the child has not, and will not have till he becomes a man. This comparative standpoint is legitimate enough for some purposes, but if we make it final, the question arises whether we are not guilty of an overweening presumption. Children, if they could express themselves articulately and sincerely, would tell a different tale; and there is excellent adult authority for the conviction that for certain moral and intellectual purposes adults must become as little children.

The seriousness of the assumption of the negative quality of the possibilities of immaturity is apparent when we reflect that it sets up as an ideal and standard a static end. The fulfillment of growing is taken to mean an *accomplished* growth: that is to say, an Ungrowth, something which is no longer growing. The futility of the assumption is seen in the fact that every adult resents the imputation of having no further possibilities of growth; and so far as he finds that they are closed to him mourns the fact as evidence of loss, instead of falling back on the achieved as adequate manifestation of power. Why an unequal measure for child and man?

Taken absolutely, instead of comparatively, immaturity designates a positive force or ability,—the *power* to grow. We do not have to draw out or educe positive activities from a child, as some educational doctrines would have it. Where there is life, there are already eager and impassioned activities. Growth is not something done to them; it is something they do. The positive and constructive aspect of possibility gives the key to understanding the two chief traits of immaturity, dependence and plasticity. (1) It sounds absurd to hear dependence spoken of as something positive, still more absurd as a power. Yet if helplessness were all there were in dependence, no development could ever take place. A merely impotent being has to be carried, forever, by others. The fact that dependence is accompanied by growth in ability, not by an ever increasing lapse into parasitism, suggests that it is already something constructive. Being merely sheltered by others would not promote growth. For (2) it would only build a wall around impotence. With reference to the physical world, the child is helpless. He lacks at birth and for a long time thereafter power to make his way physically, to make his own living. If he had to do that by himself, he would hardly survive an hour. On this side his helplessness is almost complete. The young of the brutes are immeasurably his superiors. He is physically weak and not able to turn the strength which he possesses to coping with the physical environment. 1. The thoroughgoing character of this helplessness suggests, however, some compensating power. The relative ability of the young of brute animals to adapt themselves fairly well to physical conditions from an early period suggests the fact that their life is not intimately bound up with the life of those about them. They are compelled, so to speak, to have physical gifts because they are lacking in social gifts. Human infants, on the other hand, can get along with physical incapacity just because of their social capacity. We sometimes talk and think as if they simply happened to be *physically* in a social environment; as if social forces exclusively existed in the adults who take care of them, they being passive recipients. If it were said that children are themselves marvelously endowed with *power* to enlist the coöperative attention of others, this would be thought to be a backhanded way of saying that others are marvelously attentive to the needs of children. But observation shows that children are gifted with an equipment of the first order for social intercourse. Few grown-up persons retain all of the flexible and sensitive ability of children to vibrate sympathetically with the attitudes and doings of those about them. Inattention to physical things (going with incapacity to control them) is accompanied by a corresponding intensification of interest and attention as to the doings of people. The native mechanism of the child and his impulses all tend to facile social responsiveness. The statement that children, before adolescence, are egotistically self-centered, even if it were true, would not contradict the truth of this statement. It would simply indicate that their social responsiveness is employed on their own behalf, not that it does not exist. But the statement is not true as matter of fact. The facts which are cited in support of the alleged pure egoism of children really show the intensity and directness with which they go to their mark. If the ends which form the mark seem narrow and selfish to adults, it is only because adults (by means of a similar engrossment in their day) have mastered these ends, which have consequently ceased to interest them. Most of the remainder of children's alleged native egoism is simply an egoism which runs counter to an adult's egoism. To a grown-up person who is too absorbed in his own affairs to take an interest in children's affairs, children doubtless seem unreasonably engrossed in *their* own affairs.

From a social standpoint, dependence denotes a power rather than a weakness; it involves interdependence. There is always a danger that increased personal independence will decrease the social capacity of an individual. In making him more self-reliant, it may make him more self-sufficient; it may lead to aloofness and indifference. It often makes an individual so insensitive in his relations to others as to develop an illusion of being really able to stand and act alone—an unnamed form of insanity which is responsible for a large part of the remediable suffering of the world.

2. The specific adaptability of an immature creature for growth constitutes his *plasticity.* This is something quite different from the plasticity of putty or wax. It is not a capacity to take on change of form in accord with external pressure. It lies near the pliable elasticity by which some persons take on the color of their surroundings while retaining their own bent. But it is something deeper than this. It is essentially the ability to learn from experience; the power to retain from one experience something which is of avail in coping with the difficulties of a later situation. This means power to modify actions on the basis of the results of prior experiences, the power to *develop dispositions.* Without it, the acquisition of habits is impossible.

It is a familiar fact that the young of the higher animals, and especially the human young, have to *learn* to utilize their instinctive reactions. The human being is born with a greater number of instinctive tendencies than other animals. But the instincts of the lower animals perfect themselves for appropriate action at an early period after birth, while most of those of the human infant are of little account just as they stand. An original specialized power of adjustment secures immediate efficiency, but, like a railway ticket, it is good for one route only. A being who, in order to use his eyes, ears, hands, and legs, has to experiment in making varied combinations of their reactions, achieves a control that is flexible and varied. A chick, for example, pecks accurately at a bit of food in a few hours after hatching. This means that definite coödinations of activities of the eyes in seeing and of the body and head in striking are perfected in a few trials. An infant requires about six months to be able to gauge with approximate accuracy the action in reaching which will coordinate with his visual activities; to be able, that is, to tell whether he can reach a seen object and just how to execute the reaching. As a result, the chick is limited by the relative perfection of its original endowment. The infant has the advantage of the *multitude* of instinctive tentative reactions and of the experiences that accompany them, even though he is at a temporary disadvantage because they cross one another. In learning an action, instead of having it given ready-made, one of necessity learns to vary its factors to make varied combinations of them, according to

change of circumstances. A possibility of continuing progress is
opened up by the fact that in learning one act, methods are
developed good for use in other situations. Still more important is
the fact that the human being acquires a habit of learning. He learns
to learn.

The importance for human life of the two facts of dependence
and variable control has been summed up in the doctrine of the
significance of prolonged infancy. This prolongation is significant
from the standpoint of the adult members of the group as well as
from that of the young. The presence of dependent and learning
beings is a stimulus to nurture and affection. The need for constant
continued care was probably a chief means in transforming
temporary cohabitations into permanent unions. It certainly was a
chief influence in forming habits of affectionate and sympathetic
watchfulness; that constructive interest in the well-being of others
which is essential to associated life. Intellectually, this moral
development meant the introduction of many new objects of
attention; it stimulated foresight and planning for the future. Thus
there is a reciprocal influence. Increasing complexity of social life
requires a longer period of infancy in which to acquire the needed
powers; this prolongation of dependence means prolongation of
plasticity, or power of acquiring variable and novel modes of
control. Hence it provides a further push to social progress.

2. *Habits as Expressions of Growth.* We have already noted that
plasticity is the capacity to retain and carry over from prior
experience factors which modify subsequent activities. This signifies
the capacity to acquire habits, or develop definite dispositions. We
have now to consider the salient features of habits. In the first place,
a habit is a form of executive skill, of efficiency in doing. A habit
means an ability to use natural conditions as means to ends. It is an
active control of the environment through control of the organs of
action. We are perhaps apt to emphasize the control of the body at
the expense of control of the environment. We think of walking,
talking, playing the piano, the specialized skills characteristic of the
etcher, the surgeon, the bridge-builder, as if they were simply ease,
deftness, and accuracy on the part of the organism. They are that, of
course; but the measure of the value of these qualities lies in the
economical and effective control of the environment which they
secure. To be able to walk is to have certain properties of nature at
our disposal—and so with all other habits.

Education is not infrequently defined as consisting in the
acquisition of those habits that effect an adjustment of an individual

and his environment. The definition expresses an essential phase of growth. But it is essential that adjustment be understood in its active sense of *control* of means for achieving ends. If we think of a habit simply as a change wrought in the organism, ignoring the fact that this change consists in ability to effect subsequent changes in the environment, we shall be lead to think of 'adjustment' as a conformity to environment as wax conforms to the seal which impresses it. The environment is thought of as something fixed, providing in its fixity the end and standard of changes taking place in the organism; adjustment is just fitting ourselves to this fixity of external conditions. Habit as *habituation* is indeed something *relatively* passive; we get used to our surroundings—to our clothing, our shoes, and gloves; to the atmosphere as long as it is fairly equable; to our daily associates, etc. Conformity to the environment, a change wrought in the organism without reference to ability to modify surroundings, is a marked trait of such habituations. Aside from the fact that we are not entitled to carry over the traits of such adjustments (which might well be called *accommodations*, to mark them off from active adjustments) into habits of active use of our surroundings, two features of habituations are worth notice. In the first place, we get used to things by *first* using them.

Consider getting used to a strange city. At first, there is excessive stimulation and excessive and ill-adapted response. Gradually certain stimuli are selected because of their relevancy, and others are degraded. We can say either that we do not respond to them any longer, or more truly that we have effected a persistent response to them—an equilibrium of adjustment. This means, in the second place, that this enduring adjustment supplies the background upon which are made specific adjustments, as occasion arises. We are never interested in changing the *whole* environment; there is much that we take for granted and accept just as it already is. Upon this background our activities focus at certain points in an endeavor to introduce needed changes. Habituation is thus our adjustment to an environment which at the time we are not concerned with modifying, and which supplies a leverage to our active habits.

Adaptation, in fine, is quite as much adaptation *of* the environment to our own activities as of our activities *to* the environment. A savage tribe manages to live on a desert plain. It adapts itself. But its adaptation involves a maximum of accepting, tolerating, putting up with things as they are, a maximum of passive acquiescence, and a minimum of active control, of subjection to use. A civilized people enters upon the scene. It also adapts itself. It introduces irrigation; it searches the world for plants and animals that will flourish under such conditions; it improves, by careful selection, those which are growing there. As a consequence, the wilderness blossoms as a rose. The savage is merely habituated; the civilized man has habits which transform the environment. The significance of habit is not exhausted, however, in its executive and motor phase. It means formation of intellectual and emotional disposition as well as an increase in ease, economy, and efficiency of action. Any habit marks an *inclination*—an active preference and choice for the conditions involved in its exercise. A habit does not wait, Micawber-like, for a stimulus to turn up so that it may get busy; it actively seeks for occasions to pass into full operation. If its expression is unduly blocked, inclination shows itself in uneasiness and intense craving. A habit also marks an intellectual disposition. Where there is a habit, there is acquaintance with the materials and equipment to which action is applied. There is a definite way of understanding the situations in which the habit operates. Modes of thought, of observation and reflection, enter as forms of skill and of desire into the habits that make a man an engineer, an architect, a physician, or a merchant. In unskilled forms of labor, the intellectual factors are at minimum precisely because the habits involved are not of a high grade. But there are habits of judging and reasoning as truly as of handling a tool, painting a picture, or conducting an experiment.

Such statements are, however, understatements. The habits of mind involved in habits of the eye and hand supply the latter with their significance. Above all, the intellectual element in a habit fixes the relation of the habit to varied and elastic use, and hence to continued growth. We speak of *fixed* habits. Well, the phrase may mean powers so well established that their possessor always has them as resources when needed. But the phrase is also used to mean ruts, routine ways, with loss of freshness, openmindedness, and originality. Fixity of habit may mean that something has a fixed hold upon us, instead of our having a free hold upon things. This fact explains two points in a common notion about habits: their identification with mechanical and external modes of action to the neglect of mental and moral attitudes, and the tendency to give them a bad meaning, an identification with "bad habits." Many a person would feel surprised to have his aptitude in his chosen profession called a habit, and would naturally think of his use of tobacco, liquor, or profane language as typical of the meaning of habit. A habit is to him something which has a hold on him, something not easily thrown off even though judgment condemn it.

Habits reduce themselves to routine ways of acting, or degenerate into ways of action to which we are enslaved just in the degree in which intelligence is disconnected from them. Routine habits are unthinking habits; "bad" habits are habits so severed from reason that they are opposed to the conclusions of conscious deliberation and decision. As we have seen, the acquiring of habits is due to an original plasticity of our natures: to our ability to vary responses till we find an appropriate and efficient way of acting. Routine habits, and habits that possess us instead of our possessing them, are habits which put an end to plasticity. They mark the close of power to vary. There can be no doubt of the tendency of organic plasticity, of the physiological basis, to lessen with growing years. The instinctively mobile and eagerly varying action of childhood, the love of new stimuli and new developments, too easily passes into a "settling down," which means aversion to change and a resting on past achievements. Only an environment which secures the full use of intelligence in the process of forming habits can counteract this tendency. Of course, the same hardening of the organic conditions affects the physiological structures which are involved in thinking. But this fact only indicates the need of persistent care to see to it that the function of intelligence is invoked to its maximum possibility. The short-sighted method which falls back on mechanical routine and repetition to secure external efficiency of habit, motor skill without accompanying thought, marks a deliberate closing in of surroundings upon growth.

3. *The Educational Bearings of the Conception of Development.* We have had so far but little to say in this chapter about education. We have been occupied with the conditions and implications of growth. If our conclusions are justified, they carry with them, however, definite educational consequences. When it is said that education is development, everything depends upon *how* development is conceived. Our net conclusion is that life is development, and that developing, growing, is life. Translated into its educational equivalents, this means (i) that the educational process has no end beyond itself; it is its own end; and that (ii) the educational process is one of continual reorganizing, reconstructing, transforming.

1. Development when it is interpreted in *comparative* terms, that is, with respect to the special traits of child and adult life, means the direction of power into special channels: the formation of habits involving executive skill, definiteness of interest, and specific objects of observation and thought. But the comparative view is not final.

The child has specific powers; to ignore that fact is to stunt or distort the organs upon which his growth depends. The adult uses his powers to transform his environment, thereby occasioning new stimuli which redirect his powers and keep them developing. Ignoring this fact means arrested development, a passive accommodation. Normal child and normal adult alike, in other words, are engaged in growing. The difference between them is not the difference between growth and no growth, but between the modes of growth appropriate to different conditions. With respect to the development of powers devoted to coping with specific scientific and economic problems we may say the child should be growing in manhood. With respect to sympathetic curiosity, unbiased responsiveness, and openness of mind, we may say that the adult should be growing in childlikeness. One statement is as true as the other.

Three ideas which have been criticized, namely, the merely privative nature of immaturity, static adjustment to a fixed environment, and rigidity of habit, are all connected with a false idea of growth or development,—that it is a movement toward a fixed goal. Growth is regarded as *having* an end, instead of *being* an end. The educational counterparts of the three fallacious ideas are first, failure to take account of the instinctive or native powers of the young; secondly, failure to develop initiative in coping with novel situations; thirdly, an undue emphasis upon drill and other devices which secure automatic skill at the expense of personal perception. In all cases, the adult environment is accepted as a standard for the child. He is to be brought up *to* it.

Natural instincts are either disregarded or treated as nuisances—as obnoxious traits to be suppressed, or at all events to be brought into conformity with external standards. Since conformity is the aim, what is distinctively individual in a young person is brushed aside, or regarded as a source of mischief or anarchy. Conformity is made equivalent to uniformity. Consequently, there are induced lack of interest in the novel, aversion to progress, and dread of the uncertain and the unknown. Since the end of growth is outside of and beyond the process of growing, external agents have to be resorted to to induce movement towards it. Whenever a method of education is stigmatized as mechanical, we may be sure that external pressure is brought to bear to reach an external end.

2. Since in reality there is nothing to which growth is relative save more growth, there is nothing to which education is subordinate save more education. It is a commonplace to say that education should not cease when one leaves school. The point of

this commonplace is that the purpose of school education is to insure the continuance of education by organizing the powers that insure growth. The inclination to learn from life itself and to make the conditions of life such that all will learn in the process of living is the finest product of schooling.

When we abandon the attempt to define immaturity by means of fixed comparison with adult accomplishments, we are compelled to give up thinking of it as denoting lack of desired traits. Abandoning this notion, we are also forced to surrender our habit of thinking of instruction as a method of supplying this lack by pouring knowledge into a mental and moral hole which awaits filling. Since life means growth, a living creature lives as truly and positively at one stage as at another, with the same intrinsic fullness and the same absolute claims. Hence education means the enterprise of supplying the conditions which insure growth, or adequacy of life, irrespective of age. We first look with impatience upon immaturity, regarding it as something to be got over as rapidly as possible. Then the adult formed by such educative methods looks back with impatient regret upon childhood and youth as a scene of lost opportunities and wasted powers. This ironical situation will endure till it is recognized that living has its own intrinsic quality and that the business of education is with that quality.

Realization that life is growth protects us from that so-called idealizing of childhood which in effect is nothing but lazy indulgence. Life is not to be identified with every superficial act and interest. Even though it is not always easy to tell whether what appears to be mere surface fooling is a sign of some nascent as yet untrained power, we must remember that manifestations are not to be accepted as ends in themselves. They are signs of possible growth. They are to be turned into means of development, of carrying power forward, not indulged or cultivated for their own sake. Excessive attention to surface phenomena (even in the way of rebuke as well as of encouragement) may lead to their fixation and thus to arrested development. What impulses are moving toward, not what they have been, is the important thing for parent and teacher. The true principle of respect for immaturity cannot be better put than in the words of Emerson: "Respect the child. Be not too much his parent. Trespass not on his solitude. But I hear the outcry which replies to this suggestion: Would you verily throw up the reins of public and private discipline; would you leave the young child to the mad career of his own passions and whimsies, and call this anarchy a respect for the child's nature? I answer,— Respect the child, respect him to the end, but also respect yourself.

... The two points in a boy's training are, to keep his *naturel* and train off all but that; to keep his *naturel,* but stop off his uproar, fooling, and horseplay; keep his nature *and arm it with knowledge in the very direction in which it points."* And as Emerson goes on to show this reverence for childhood and youth instead of opening up an easy and easy-going path to the instructors, "involves at once, immense claims on the time, the thought, on the life of the teacher. It requires time, use, insight, event, all the great lessons and assistances of God; and only to think of using it implies character and profoundness."

Summary. Power to grow depends upon need for others and plasticity. Both of these conditions are at their height in childhood and youth. Plasticity or the power to learn from experience means the formation of habits. Habits give control over the environment, power to utilize it for human purposes. Habits take the form both of habituation, or a general and persistent balance of organic activities with the surroundings, and of active capacities to readjust activity to meet new conditions. The former furnishes the background of growth; the latter constitute growing. Active habits involve thought, invention, and initiative in applying capacities to new aims. They are opposed to routine which marks an arrest of growth. Since growth is the characteristic of life, education is all one with growing; it has no end beyond itself. The criterion of the value of school education is the extent in which it creates a desire for continued growth and supplies means for making the desire effective in fact.

FURTHER READING

Bayles, Ernest E. *Pragmatism in Education.* New York: Harper & Row, Publishers, 1966.

Childs, John. *American Pragmatism and Education.* New York: Holt, Rinehart, & Winston, Inc., 1956.

_____. *Education and Morals.* New York: John Wiley & Sons, Inc., 1967.

_____. *Education and the Philosophy of Experimentalism.* New York: Appleton-Century-Crofts, 1950.

_____. *Education in the Age of Science.* New York: Basic Books, Inc., 1959.

Dewey, John. *Art as Experience.* New York: Minton, Balch and Co., 1934.

_____. *The Child and the Curriculum.* Chicago: University of Chicago Press, 1902.

————. *A Common Faith.* New Haven: Yale University Press, 1934.

————. *Democracy and Education.* New York: The Macmillan Company, 1916.

————. *The Educational Situation.* Chicago: University of Chicago Press, 1902.

————. *Essays in Experimental Logic.* Chicago: University of Chicago Press, 1916.

————. *Experience and Education.* New York: The Macmillan Company, 1938.

————. *Experience and Nature.* Chicago: Open Court Publishing Company, 1925.

————. *Freedom and Culture.* New York: G. P. Putnam's Sons, 1939.

————. *How We Think.* Boston: D. C. Heath and Co., 1910.

————. *Human Nature and Conduct.* New York: Holt, Rinehart, & Winston, 1922.

————. *Individualism: Old and New.* New York: G. P. Putnam's Sons, 1930.

————. *Interest and Effort in Education.* Boston: Houghton Mifflin Company, 1913.

————. *Moral Principles in Education.* Boston: Houghton Mifflin Company, 1909.

————. *Philosophy and Civilization.* New York: Minton, Balch and Co., 1931.

————. *The School and Society.* Chicago: University of Chicago Press, 1923.

———— and Evelyn Dewey. *Schools of Tomorrow.* New York: E. P. Dutton and Co., 1915.

Handlin, Oscar. *John Dewey's Challenge to Education.* New York: Harper & Row, Publishers, 1959.

Hofstadter, Richard. *Social Darwinism in American Thought.* Boston: Beacon Press, 1958.

Mayhew, Katherine C. and Anna C. Edwards. *The Dewey School.* New York: Appleton-Century-Crofts, 1936.

Wirth, Arthur G. *John Dewey as Educator: His Design for Work in Education (1894–1904).* New York: John Wiley & Sons, Inc., 1966.

eight

PROGRESSIVISM

Progressivism in American education began as a reaction against the formalism and verbalism of traditional schooling. The Progressive Education Association, organized in 1919, enlisted a variety of members from experimental private schools and colleges of education. While many of the initial participants in progressive education were individuals who were looking for innovative approaches to education that would liberate the child's energies, many of its later members were associated with John Dewey's Experimentalist philosophy.

SOURCES OF PROGRESSIVISM

Although the Progressive Education Association was formally established in the early twentieth century, its antecedents go back as far as the eighteenth century Enlightenment. Like the *philosophes* of the Age of Reason, modern progressives emphasized the concept of Progress; that is, they believed that man is capable of improving and perfecting his environment by applying human intelligence and the scientific method to the problems that arise in personal and social life. Like Rousseau, the progressives rejected notions of human depravity and believed that man is basically benevolent.

Progressivism was also rooted in the spirit of social reform which was part of the early twentieth century Progressive movement in American politics. As a socio-political movement, Progressivism held that human society could be refashioned by political means. Such American political programs as Woodrow Wilson's "New Freedom," Theodore Roosevelt's "New Nationalism," and Robert LaFollette's "Wisconsin Idea" varied in their particulars, but shared the common concern that the emerging corporate society should be ordered to function democratically for the benefit of all Americans. The leaders in progressive politics represented what was essentially the middle-class orientation to reform, characterized by gradual change through legislation and peaceful social innovation through education.

American educational progressives could also look to the major educational reformers of Western Europe for inspiration and stimulation. Jean Jacques Rousseau, author of *Emile,* had written about an education that proceeds along natural lines and is completely free of coercion. As an early rebel against traditional schooling and classical education, Rousseau argued that the child is naturally good and that learning is most effective when it follows the child's interests and needs.

Progressives could also feel an affinity for the work of Johann Heinrich Pestalozzi, a nineteenth century Swiss educational reformer, who, as a willing disciple of Rousseau, asserted that education should be more than book learning. It should embrace the whole child—his emotions, intellect, and body. Natural education, said Pestalozzi, should take place in an environment of emotional love and security. It should also begin in the child's immediate environment and involve the operations of the senses on the objects found in the environment.[1]

The work of Sigmund Freud was also useful to progressive educators. In examining cases of hysteria, Freud traced the origins of mental illnesses to early childhood. Authoritarian parents and home environments cause many children to repress their drives. This repression, especially in the case of sexual drives, can lead to neurotic behavior that has a deleterious effect upon the child and upon his adult life.

While the European educational reformers provided stimulus for progressive educators, it was John Dewey and his followers who came to exert a profound influence on progressive education. It should be noted, however, that not all progressives were Deweyites. Progressive education as a movement was a convenient platform, a rallying point, for those who opposed educational traditionalism; it was not a doctrinaire movement. It drew its inspiration from the European naturalist educators, such as Rousseau and Pestalozzi, from Freudian and neo-Freudian psychoanalytic theory, from currents of American political and social reformism, as well as from John Dewey's Pragmatic Instrumentalism.

The Progressive Educational Platform   Before commenting on John Dewey's reactions to progressive education as a movement, a short review of the history of the progressive education movement is useful for

---

1. For a discussion of Pestalozzi's educational theory and its significance for progressivism, see Gerald L. Gutek, *Pestalozzi and Education.* New York: Random House, Inc., 1968.

understanding the work of the progressive educators. Certain educators, such as Flora Cooke, principal of the Francis W. Parker School in Chicago, and Carleton Washburne of the Winnetka Schools, had in the early twentieth century developed innovative methods that stressed the child's own initiative in learning. Junius L. Meriam of the University of Missouri had developed an activity curriculum that was related to the child's life and included excursions, constructive work, observation, and discussion. Marietta Johnson had also established the School of Organic Education in 1907 in Fairhope, Alabama. Johnson's organic theory of education emphasized the child's needs, interests, and activities. Special attention was given to creative activity that included dancing, sketching, drawing, singing, weaving, and other expressive activities. Formal instruction in reading, writing, and arithmetic was reserved until the child was nine or ten years old. The general method of instruction was that of the free-flowing discussion.

In the winter of 1918–1919, a number of progressive educators met in Washington, D.C. and formed the Progressive Education Association, under the leadership of Standwood Cobb, head of the Chevy Chase Country Day School. To give cohesion to the progressive educational position, the Association stressed the following principles: (1) progressive education should provide the freedom that would encourage the child's natural development and growth through activities which cultivate his initiative, creativity, and self-expression; (2) all instruction should be guided by the child's own interest, stimulated by contact with the real world; (3) the progressive teacher is to guide the child's learning as a director of research activities, rather than a drill or task master; (4) student achievement is to be measured in terms of mental, physical, moral, and social development; (5) there should be greater cooperation between the teacher and school and the home and the family in meeting the child's needs for growth and development; (6) the truly progressive school should be a laboratory in innovative educational ideas and practices.[2]

At the onset, the Progressive Education Association was clearly a child-centered movement which was a reaction against the subject-matter orientation of traditional education. It attracted to its ranks teachers and parents associated with small private experimental schools. In the late 1920s and in the 1930s, the Progressive Education Association attracted profressional educators from colleges of education. Many of

---

2. For a clearly written exposition of the origins of the Progressive Education Association, see Adolph E. Meyer, *The Development of Education in the Twentieth Century*. Englewood Cliffs, N.J.: Prentice-Hall, Inc., 1949. pp. 64–74. A complete treatment of educational progressivism can be found in Lawrence A. Cremin, *The Transformation of the School: Progressivism in American Education*. New York: Alfred A. Knopf, Inc., 1961.

these educators were familiar with and had been influenced by John
Dewey's experimentalist philosophy of education.

DEWEY'S CRITIQUE OF PROGRESSIVE EDUCATION

Although the major ideas of John Dewey's experimentalism have already been treated, the progressive educational position can be made
clearer by a brief examination of the critique of the movement that was
contained in Dewey's *Experience and Education*.[3]

Dewey warned that the controversy between traditional and progressive educators tended to degenerate into an assertion of either–or positions. Although generally sympathetic to progressivism, he felt that
many progressives were merely reacting against traditional school practices and had failed to formulate an educational philosophy which was
capable of serving as a plan of pragmatic operations.

Dewey's analysis of the traditional and the progressive school is
useful in highlighting the contrasts between these two institutions. The
traditional school, he said, is a formal institution that emphasizes a
subject-matter curriculum, comprised of bodies of discretely organized
disciplines, such as language, history, mathematics, and science. The
traditionalists hold that the source of wisdom was located in man's
cultural heritage. Morals, standards, and conduct are derived from tradition and are not exposed to the test of contemporary requirements. The
traditional teacher regards the written word as the source of wisdom,
and relies on the textbook as the source of knowledge and the recitation
as the means of eliciting it from the students. Traditionalists attempt to
isolate the school from social controversies. In their belief that learning
is the transmission and mastery of bodies of knowledge inherited from
the past, the traditionalists ignore the learner's own needs and interests
and deliberately neglect pressing social and political issues. The products of conventional education are expected to be receptive of the traditional wisdom, to have habits and attitudes that are conducive to
conformity, and to be respectful and obedient to authority.

Although Dewey shared the Progressives' antagonism to the traditional school, he feared that many Progressives were merely reacting
against it. Too many Progressives ignored the past and were concerned
only with the present. In their opposition to the traditional school's
passivity, some progressives came to emphasize any kind of activity,
even purposeless activity. Many progressives became so antagonistic to
education which was imposed by adults on children that they began to

---

3. John Dewey. *Experience and Education*. 1938; New York: Collier Books, 1963.

cater to childish whims, many of which were devoid of social and intellectual purposes.

After urging that Progressive educators avoid entanglement in the polarization of an either–or educational position, Dewey outlined the philosophy which he believed was suited for the genuinely progressive school. In many ways, his message reiterates the basic premises that had been voiced in *Democracy and Education*. Progressive education needs a philosophy based upon experience, the interaction of the person with his environment. Such an experiential philosophy should have no set of external aims or goals. Rather, the end product of education is growth —that on-going experience which leads to the direction and control of subsequent experience.

Truly progressive education should not ignore the past but should rather use it as an instrument that would lead to the reconstruction of experience in the present and would direct the course of subsequent experiences. For Dewey, education should be based on a continuum of on-going experience that unites the past and the present and leads to the shaping of the future.

Dewey also warned that Progressive education should not become so absorbed in activity that it misconstrues the nature of activity. Mere movement is without value. Activity should be directed to the solution of problems; it should be purposeful and should contain social and intellectual possibilities that are contributory to the learner's growth.

The genuinely progressive educator is a teacher who is skilled in relating the learner's internal conditions of experience—his needs, interests, purposes, capacities, and desires—with the objective conditions of experience—the environmental factors that are historical, physical, economic, and sociological.

Above all, Dewey asserted progressivism should free itself from a blind and naive romanticization of the child's nature. While the child's interests and needs are always the initial points of learning, the child's impulses are the beginnings of intelligence and not its end. In the problematic situation, the child's impulses are blocked by obstacles that impede the satisfaction of his drive. Some impulses contain possibilities that would lead to the child's growth and development; other impulses have consequences that impede such growth. Impulse becomes reflective and intelligent when the learner is able to estimate the consequences of acting upon it. By developing an "end-in-view," the learner can conjecture the consequences that will result by acting in a given manner. The forming of purpose involves an estimation of consequences that have occurred from acting in similar situations in the past and a tentative judgment about the likely consequences of acting on impulse in the present situation. Progressive education should encourage the cultivation of purposeful, reflective habits of inquiry in the learner. As he concluded *Experience and Education,* Dewey wrote:

I see at bottom but two alternatives between which education must choose if it is not to drift aimlessly. One of them is expressed by the attempt to induce educators to return to the intellectual methods and ideals that arose centuries before scientific method was developed. The appeal may be temporarily successful in a period when general insecurity, emotional and intellectual as well as economic is rife. For under these conditions the desire to lean on fixed authority is active. Nevertheless, it is so out of touch with all the conditions of modern life that I believe it is folly to seek salvation in this direction. The other alternative is systematic utilization of scientific method as the pattern and ideal of intelligent exploration and exploitation of the potentialities inherent in experience.[4]

WILLIAM HEARD KILPATRICK AND THE PROJECT METHOD

Dewey's plea that progressive education develop a philosophy of education that would become a plan of purposeful activity to guide experience stimulated William Heard Kilpatrick, who was both an Experimentalist and a Progressive, to construct a methodology of instruction that unites activity and purpose. Kilpatrick, who was a popular lecturer at Teachers College of Columbia University, developed the project method, which came to characterize the best of progressive education for many American educators.

A brief discussion of Kilpatrick's route to the development of the project method is useful in understanding the progressive impulse among American educators. Kilpatrick was born in 1871 in White Plains, in rural Georgia, the son of a Baptist minister. He received a traditional education. After attending Mercer University, he taught algebra and geometry in the public schools of Blakely in his native state.[5]

As a mathematics teacher, Kilpatrick inaugurated a series of reforms in his classroom. For example, he believed that the practices associated with report cards and grades focused attention on extrinsic rewards that were not connected with the natural consequences of learning. He abolished the practice of external marks, which he felt encouraged egotism among the achievers and inflicted a sense of inferiority on the slower learners. In cultivating a sense of freedom in his classes, he encouraged his students to work cooperatively on their assignments. Early in his

---

4. *Ibid.,* pp. 85–86.
5. For a study of Kilpatrick's life, educational philosophy, and influence, see Samuel Tenenbaum, *William Heard Kilpatrick: Trail Blazer in Education.* New York: Harper and Brothers, 1951.

career as a classroom teacher, Kilpatrick revealed a liberal attitude to discipline which would later be more theoretically and systematically organized in the project method.

In 1907, Kilpatrick went to Teachers College, Columbia University, to continue his professional and academic preparation in education. Here he encountered and accepted John Dewey's pragmatic philosophical orientation. Later, as a professor of education at Teachers College, Kilpatrick became a noted interpreter of Dewey. His writing and lecturing, which exposited themes associated with experimentalist philosophy and the progressive educational posture, attracted a large and receptive audience. A gifted lecturer, Kilpatrick was able to clarify many of Dewey's more difficult theoretical concepts. He was not, however, only an interpreter but also advanced his own educational philosophy, which synthesized progressivism and experimentalism into what came to be referred to as the purposeful act, or the project method.[6] Because he reached such a large number of teachers in his classes, Kilpatrick came to exert a shaping influence over American educational theory and practice.

Kilpatrick's project method of education must be interpreted in terms of his rejection of traditional education's reliance on a book-centered learning program. Although he was not antiintellectual, Kilpatrick asserted that books are not a substitute for learning through living. The most pernicious form of bookishness is found in the textbook's domination of much conventional school practice. Too frequently teachers rely exclusively on the information contained in textbooks that are often mechanically organized, second-hand experiences. The student who succeeds in the traditional school situation is frequently one who is of a bookish inclination and successful in memorizing but not always in understanding the content which he reads. Because of its stress on bookishness and memorization, conventional schooling degenerated into a devitalized mechanical set of routines where teachers assign lessons from textbooks, drill their students on the assignments, hear recitations of memorized responses, and then evaluate them on the basis of their adherence to the predigested textbook formulae. Such schooling is dangerous, in Kilpatrick's view, because it fails to encourage individual creativity, it contributes to boredom, and it is devoid of cooperative social purposes.

In contrast to the authoritarianism and rote nature of traditional book-centered education, Kilpatrick devised the project method, which

---

6. William Heard Kilpatrick. "The Project Method," *Teachers College Record, 19* (1918). pp. 319–35; and *The Project Method*. New York: Teachers College Press, 1921.

was designed to elaborate a constructive progressivism along experimentalist lines. In the project method, students are encouraged to choose, plan, direct, and execute their work in activities, or projects, which can bring forth the student's purposeful efforts. In its theoretical formulation, the project is a mode of problem solving. Students, either as individuals or in groups, would define problems that arise in their own experience. The learning effort would be task-centered in that success would come by the resolution of the problem and the testing of the solution by acting upon it. Action that results from purposeful planning would meet the pragmatic test and would be judged by the consequences that it produces.

Kilpatrick recommended that the school curriculum be organized in terms of four major classes of projects: (1) The creative or construction project involves the concretizing of a theoretical plan in external form. For example, the students might decide to write and to present a drama. They would write the script, assign the roles, and actually present the play. Or the creative project might actually involve the design of a blueprint for a library. The test would come in the construction of the library from the plan devised by the students. (2) The appreciation or enjoyment project is designed to contribute to the cultivation of aesthetic experience. Reading a novel, seeing a film, or listening to a symphony are examples of projects that would lead to aesthetic enjoyment and appreciation. (3) The problem project is one in which the students would be involved in the resolving of an intellectual difficulty. Such problems as the resolution of racial discrimination, the improvement of the quality of the environment, or the organization of recreational facilities are social problems that call for disciplined intellectual inquiry. (4) The specific learning project involves acquiring a skill or an area of knowledge. Learning to type, to swim, to dance, to read, or to write are examples of the acquisition of a specific skill.

Kilpatrick's project method should be interpreted in terms of its suggested social consequences as well as its strictly educational aims. To be sure, the project method has educational objectives, such as improvement in creative, constructive, appreciative, intellectual, and skill competencies. However, the acquiring of these competencies is only a part of Kilpatrick's plan for educational reform. Kilpatrick believed, as did Dewey, that education as a social activity is a product of human association and sharing. In a free society, the democratic method of peaceful discussion, debate, decision, and action depends on the willingness of individuals to use the methods of open and uncoerced inquiry. Kilpatrick believed that the project method lends itself to group work, in which students could cooperatively pursue common problems and share in associative inquiry—the essence of the democratic processes. Even more important than the acquiring of specific skills, the student should acquire the dispositions that are appropriate to life in a democratic society.

The product that Kilpatrick envisioned as a result of the program of education based on purposeful activity is the democratic man or woman. Such a person would have an experimental attitude and would be willing to test inherited traditions, values, and beliefs. Through the mutual sharing and solving of problems in the project method, students would learn to use the democratic methods of open discussion, carefully reasoned deliberation, decision making that respects both the rights of the majority and the minority, and action that results in peaceful social change. Kilpatrick's model of the democratic citizen is much like that envisioned by the middle-class progressives in politics and in education. He would use a democratic methodology and would expect his opponents to use the same procedures. As a reconstructive person, the progressively educated man and woman would recognize that social institutions are creations of human intelligence and could be periodically renovated when the times require it. The democratic citizen would be open to the use of the scientific method and would discard theological, metaphysical, political, and economic absolutes as dogmatic impediments which block human inquiry into the conditions of life. Above all, Kilpatrick wanted to educate individuals who are sharers in a common framework of democratic values. Such men and women would be whole-hearted and willing participants in the democratic community.

THE PROGRESSIVE TEACHER

Progressive education calls for a teacher who is different in temperament, training, and techniques than the teachers associated with more traditional schools. Although the progressive teacher needs to be well grounded in the content and methods of inquiry associated with such academic disciplines as history, science, mathematics, and language, instruction in the progressive classroom requires more than a chronological or a systematic subject-matter presentation of the various learned disciplines. Kilpatrick's project method and the general progressive approach is interdisciplinary. Problems are not specifically located within the framework of various disciplines, but rather cut across them and borrow from several of them.

Since the progressive classroom is oriented to purposeful activity, the progressive teacher needs to know how to stimulate the students so that they initiate, plan, and carry on their project. Since the basic pattern of learning is centered in the participating group, the progressive teacher needs to know how to use group processes. Perhaps the most difficult thing for the teacher to do is to be able to act as a guide rather than the center of learning. The skilled teacher, in the progressive context, is not a person who dominates the classroom as its focal point. Rather, the progressive teacher makes the interests of the learner central. The teacher is properly a guide to discussing, planning, and executing learning.

CONCLUSION

Progressive Education is then both a particular movement within the broad framework of American education and also an attitude that calls for the liberation of the child from the bonds of a tradition which emphasizes rote learning, lesson recitations, and textbook authority. In opposition to the conventional subject-matter disciplines of the traditional curriculum, Progressives sought to develop an alternative mode of curricular organization. They experimented with such varied but related alternatives as activities, experiences, problem solving, and the project method. Progressive education has left a continuing legacy within the general patterns of American education which is characterized by: (1) a focus on the child as the learner rather than on the subject; (2) an emphasis on activities and experiences rather than an exclusive reliance on verbal and literary skills and knowledge; and (3) the encouragement of cooperative group learning activities rather than competitive individualized lesson learning. In its broad social directions, Progressivism in education encouraged the use of democratic procedures that were to effect community and civic reform. It also cultivated a cultural relativism which critically appraised and often rejected traditional beliefs and values.

SELECTION

William Heard Kilpatrick

William Heard Kilpatrick (1871–1965) was born in the small agricultural town of White Plains, Georgia. Kilpatrick first encountered John Dewey in 1898, while attending a summer session at the University of Chicago. At Columbia, Kilpatrick became an avid disciple of Dewey and sought to translate experimentalism into an educational method. A popular professor at Teachers College, Kilpatrick attracted thousands of classroom teachers and school administrators to his lectures on educational philosophy. Counted among the ranks of progressive educators, Kilpatrick developed the project method of teaching, which is associated with the activity curriculum.

Kilpatrick's books include: *Froebel's Kindergarten, Principles Critically Examined* (1916), *Foundations of Method* (1925), *Education for a Changing Civilization* (1926), *Education and the Social Crisis* (1932), *Educational Frontier* (1933), *Group Education for a Democracy* (1940), and *Philosophy of Education* (1951).

Throughout his long career, William Heard Kilpatrick ably defended progressive education. His project method and its supporting theory is a synthesis of both pragmatic philosophy and progressive practice. In the following selection, Kilpatrick explains the project method.

*   *   *

The Project Method   The word 'project' is perhaps the latest arrival to knock for admittance at the door of educational terminology. Shall we admit the stranger? Not wisely until two preliminary questions have first been answered in the affirmative: First, is there behind the proposed term and waiting even now to be christened a valid notion or concept which promises to render appreciable service in educational thinking? Second, if we grant the foregoing, does the term 'project' fitly designate the waiting concept? Because the question as to the concept and its worth is so much more significant than any matter of mere names, this discussion will deal almost exclusively with the first of the two inquiries. It is indeed entirely possible that some other term, as 'purposeful act,' for example, would call attention to a more important element in the concept, and, if so, might prove superior as a term to the word 'project.' At the outset it is probably wise to caution the reader against expecting any great amount of novelty in the idea here presented. The metaphor of christening is not be be taken too seriously; the concept to be considered is not in fact newly born. Not a few readers will be disappointed that after all so little new is presented.

A little of the personal may perhaps serve to introduce the more formal discussion. In attacking with successive classes in educational theory the problem of method, I had felt increasingly the need of unifying more completely a number of important related aspects of the educative process. I began to hope for some one concept which might serve this end. Such a concept, if found, must, so I thought, emphasize the factor of action, preferably wholehearted vigorous activity. It must at the same time provide a place for the adequate

---

utilization of the laws of learning, and no less for the essential elements of the ethical quality of conduct. The last named looks of course to the social situation as well as to the individual attitude. Along with these should go, as it seemed, the important generalization that education is life—so easy to say and so hard to delimit. Could now all of these be contemplated under one workable notion? If yes, a great gain. In proportion as such a unifying concept could be found in like proportion would the work of presenting educational theory be facilitated; in like proportion should be the rapid spread of a better practice.

But could this unifying idea be found? Here was in fact the age-old problem of effective logical organization. My whole philosophic outlook had made me suspicious of so-called 'fundamental principles.' Was there yet another way of attaining unity? I do not mean to say that I asked these questions, either in these words or in this order. Rather is this a retrospective ordering of the more important outcomes. As the desired unification lay specifically in the field of method, might not some typical unit of concrete procedure supply the need—some unit of conduct that should be, as it were, a sample of life, a fair sample of the worthy life and consequently of education? As these questionings rose more definitely to mind, there came increasingly a belief—corroborated on many sides—that the unifying idea I sought was to be found in the conception of wholehearted purposeful activity proceeding in a social environment, or more briefly, in the unit element of such activity, the hearty purposeful act.

It is to this purposeful act with the emphasis on the word purpose that I myself apply the term 'project.' I did not invent the term nor did I start it on its educational career. Indeed, I do not know how long it has already been in use. I did, however, consciously appropriate the word to designate the typical unit of the worthy life described above. Others who were using the term seemed to me either to use it in a mechanical and partial sense or to be intending in a general way what I tried to define more exactly. The purpose of this article is to attempt to clarify the concept underlying the term as much as it is to defend the claim of the concept to a place in our educational thinking. The actual terminology with which to designate the concept is, as was said before, to my mind a matter of relatively small moment. If, however, we think of a project as a pro-ject, something pro-jected, the reason for its adoption may better appear.

Postponing yet a little further the more systematic presentation of the matter, let us from some typical instances see more concretely what is contemplated under the term project or hearty purposeful act? Suppose a girl makes a dress. If she did in hearty fashion purpose to make the dress, if she planned it, if she made it herself, then I should say the instance is that of a typical project. We have a wholehearted purposeful act carried on amid social surroundings. That the dressmaking was purposeful is clear; the purpose once formed dominated each succeeding step in the process and gave unity to the whole. That the girl was wholehearted in the work was assured in the illustration. That the activity proceeded in a social environment is clear; other girls at least are to see the dress. As another instance, suppose a boy undertakes to get out a school newspaper. If he is in earnest about it, we again have the effective purpose being the essence of the project. So we may instance a pupil writing a letter (if the hearty purpose is present), a child listening absorbedly to a story, Newton explaining the motion of the moon on the principles of terrestrial dynamics, Demosthenes trying to arouse the Greeks against Philip, Da Vinci painting the *Last Supper,* my writing this article, a boy solving with felt purpose an 'original' in geometry. All of the foregoing have been acts of individual purposing, but this is not to rule out group projects: a class presents a play, a group of boys organize a base-ball nine, three pupils prepare to read a story to their comrades. It is clear then that projects may present every variety that purposes present in life. It is also clear that a mere description of outwardly observable facts might not disclose the essential factor, namely the presence of a dominating purpose. It is equally true that there can be every degree of approximation to full projects according as the animating purpose varies in clearness and strength. If we conceive activities as ranging on a scale from those performed under dire compulsion up to those into which one puts his 'whole heart,' the argument herein made restricts the term 'project' or purposeful act to the upper portions of the scale. An exact dividing line is hard to draw, and yields indeed in importance to the notion that psychological value increases with the degree of approximation to 'wholeheartedness.' As to the social environment element, some may feel that, however important this is to the fullest educative experience, it is still not essential to the conception of the purposeful act as here presented. These might therefore wish to leave this element out of the defining discussion. To this I should not object if it were clearly understood that the resulting concept—now essentially psychological in character— generally speaking, demands the social situation both for its practical working and for the comparative valuation of proffered projects.

With this general introduction, we may, in the first place, say that the purposeful act is the typical unit of the worthy life. Not that all purposes are good, but that the worthy life consists of purposive activity and not mere drifting. We scorn the man who passively accepts what fate or some other chance brings to him. We admire the man who is master of his fate, who with deliberate regard for a total situation forms clear and far-reaching purposes, who plans and executes with nice care the purposes so formed. A man who habitually so regulates his life with reference to worthy social aims meets at once the demands for practical efficiency and of moral responsibility. Such a one presents the ideal of democratic citizenship. It is equally true that the purposeful act is not the unit of life for the serf or the slave. These poor unfortunates must in the interest of the overmastering system be habituated to act with a minimum of their own purposing and with a maximum of servile acceptance of others' purposes. In important matters they merely follow plans handed down to them from above, and execute these according to prescribed directions. For them another carries responsibility and upon the results of their labor another passes judgment. No such plan as that here advocated would produce the kind of docility required for their hopeless fate. But it is a democracy which we contemplate and with which we are here concerned.

As the purposeful act is thus the typical unit of the worthy life in a democratic society, so also should it be made the typical unit of school procedure. We of America have for years increasingly desired that education be considered as life itself and not as a mere preparation for later living. The conception before us promises a definite step toward the attainment of this end. If the purposeful act be in reality the typical unit of the worthy life, then it follows that to base education on purposeful acts is exactly to identify the process of education with worthy living itself. The two become then the same. All the arguments for placing education on a life basis seem, to me at any rate, to concur in support of this thesis. On this basis education has become life. And if the purposeful act thus makes of education life itself, could we reasoning in advance expect to find a better preparation for later life than practice in living now? We have heard of old that "we learn to do by doing," and much wisdom resides in the saying. If the worthy life of the coming day is to consist of well-chosen purposeful acts, what preparation for that time could promise more than practice now, under discriminating guidance, in forming and executing worthy purposes? To this end must the child have within rather large limits the opportunity to purpose. For the issues of his act he must—in like limits—be held accountable. That the child may properly progress, the total situation—all the factors of life, including comrades—speaking, if need be through the teacher, must make clear its selective judgment upon what he does, approving the better, rejecting the worse. In a true sense the whole remaining discussion is but to support the contention here argued in advance that education based on the purposeful act prepares best for life while at the same time it constitutes the present worthy life itself.

A more explicit reason for making the purposeful act the typical unit of instruction is found in the utilization of the laws of learning which this plan affords. I am assuming that it is not necessary in this magazine to justify or even explain at length these laws. Any act of conduct consists of a response to the existing situation. That response and not some other followed the given situation because there existed in the nervous system a bond or connection joining the stimulus of that situation with that response. Some such bonds come with us into the world, as, for example, the infant cries (responds) when he is very hungry (situation acting as stimulus). Other bonds are acquired, as when the child later asks in words for food when he is hungry. The process of acquiring or otherwise changing bonds we call learning. The careful statements of the conditions under which bonds are built or changed are the laws of learning. Bonds are not always equally *ready* to act: when I am angry, the bonds that have to do with smiling are distinctly unready; other bonds controlling uglier behavior are quite ready. When a bond is ready to act, to act gives *satisfaction* and not to act gives *annoyance.* When a bond is not ready to act, to act gives annoyance and not to act gives satisfaction. These two statements constitute the Law of Readiness. The law that most concerns us in this discussion is that of Effect: when a modifiable bond acts, it is strengthened or weakened according as satisfaction or annoyance results. The ordinary psychology of common observation has not been so conscious of these two laws as it has of the third law, that of Exercise; but for our present purposes, repetition simply means the continued application of the law of Effect. There are yet other laws necessary for a full explanation of the facts of learning. Our available space allows for only one more, that of 'set' or attitude, the others we have to assume without explicit reference. When a person is very angry, he is sometimes colloquially said to be "mad all over." Such a phrase implies that many bonds are ready to act conjointly to an end, in this case, the end of overcoming or doing damage to the object of anger. Under such conditions there is (a) available and at work a stock of energy for attaining the end, (b) a state of readiness in the bonds pertaining to the activity at hand, and (c) a correlative unreadiness on the part of the bonds that might thwart the attainment of the end contemplated by the 'set.' The reader is asked to note (a) how a 'set' towards an end means readiness and action of pertinent bonds with reference to that end, (b) how this end defines success, (c) how readiness means satisfaction when success is attained, and (d) how satisfaction strengthens the bonds whose action brought success. These facts fit well with the generalization that man's mental powers and capacities came into being in connection with the continual attaining of ends demanded by the life of the organism. The capacity for 'set' means in the case of man the capacity for determined and directed action. Such action means for our discussion not only that (objective) success is more likely to result, but that learning better takes place. The bonds whose action brought success are by the resulting satisfaction more firmly fixed, both as distinct bonds separately considered and as a system of bonds working together under the 'set.' Set, readiness, determined action, success, satisfaction, and learning are inherently connected.

How then does the purposeful act utilize the laws of learning? A boy is intent upon making a kite that will fly. So far he has not succeeded. The purpose is clear. This purpose is but the 'set' consciously and volitionally bent on its end. As set the purpose is the inner urge that carries the boy on in the face of hindrance and difficulty. It brings 'readiness' to pertinent inner resources of knowledge and thought. Eye and hand are made alert. The purpose acting as aim guides the boy's thinking, directs his examination of plan and material, elicits from within appropriate suggestions, and tests these several suggestions by their pertinency to the end in view. The purpose in that it contemplates a specific end defines success: the kite must fly or he has failed. The progressive attaining of success with reference to subordinate aims brings satisfaction at the successive stages of completion. Satisfaction in detail and in respect of the whole by the automatic working of the second law of learning (Effect) fixes the several bonds which by their successive successes brought the finally successful kite. The purpose thus supplies the motive power, makes available inner resources, guides the process to its pre-conceived end, and by this satisfactory success fixes in the boy's mind and character the successful steps as part and parcel of one whole. The purposeful act does utilize the laws of learning.

But this account does not yet exhaust the influence of the purpose on the resulting learning. Suppose as extreme cases two boys making kites, the one with wholeheartedness of purpose, as we have just described, the other under direst compulsion as a most unwelcome task. For simplicity's sake suppose the latter under enforced directions makes a kite identical with the other. Call the identical movements in the two cases the 'primary' responses in kite-making. These furnish the kind of responses that we can and customarily do assign as tasks—the external irreducible minimum for the matter at hand. Upon such we can feasibly insist, even to the point of punishment if we so decide. Follow not the thinking of the two boys as they make their kites. Besides the thinking necessarily involved in the 'primary' responses, other thoughts, few or many, will come; some perhaps of materials or processes involved, penumbrae as it were of the primary responses; others more personal or by way of comment upon the process. The penumbrae of the primary we may call the 'accessory' or complementary responses; the others, the 'concomitants' or by-products of the activity. The terminology is not entirely happy, and exact lines of division are not easy to draw; but the distinctions may perhaps help us to see a further function of purpose.

As for the primary responses we need do little more than recall the discussion of the immediately preceding paragraphs. The factor of 'set' conditions the learning process. A strong set acting through the satisfaction which attends success fixes quickly and strongly the bonds which brought success. In the case of coercion, however, a different state of affairs holds. There are in effect two sets operating: one set kept in existence solely through coercion is concerned to make a kite that will pass muster; the other set has a different end and would pursue a different course were the coercion removed. Each set insofar as it actually exists means a possible satisfaction and in that degree a possible learning. But the two sets being opposed mean at times a confusion as to the object of success, and in every case each set destroys a part of the other's satisfaction and so hampers the primary learning. So far then as concerns even the barest mechanics of kite-making, the boy of wholehearted purpose will emerge with a higher degree of skill and knowledge and his learning will longer abide with him.

In the case of the accessory or complementary responses, the difference is equally noticeable. The unified set of wholeheartedness will render available all the pertinent connected inner resources. A wealth of marginal responses will be ready to come forward at every opportunity. Thoughts will be turned over and over, and each step will be connected in many ways with other experiences. Alluring leads in various allied directions will open before the boy, which only the dominant present purpose could suffice to postpone. The element of satisfaction will attend connections seen, so that the complex of allied thinking will the longer remain as a mental possession. All of this is exactly not so with the other boy. The forbidden 'set' so long as it persists will pretty effectually quench the glow of thought. Unreadiness will rather characterize his attitude. Responses accessory to the work at hand will be few in number, and the few that come will lack the element of satisfaction to fix them. Where the one boy has a wealth of accessory ideas, the other has poverty. What abides with the one, is fleeting with the other. Even more pronounced is the difference in the by-products or *concomitants* from these contrasted activities. The one boy looks upon his school activity with joy and confidence and plans yet other projects; the other counts his school a bore and begins to look elsewhere for the expression there denied. To the one the teacher is a friend and comrade; to the other, a taskmaster and enemy. The one easily feels himself on the side of the school and other social agencies, the other with equal ease considers them all instruments of suppression.

The contrasts here made are consciously of extremes. Most children live between the two. The question is whether we shall not consciously put before us as an ideal the one type of activity and approximate it as closely as we can rather than supinely rest content to live as close to the other type as do the general run of our American schools. Does not the ordinary school among us put its almost exclusive attention on the *primary* responses and the learning of these in the second fashion here described? Do we not too often reduce the subject matter of instruction to the level of this type alone? Does not our examination system—even our scientific tests at times—tend to carry us in the same direction? How many children at the close of a course decisively shut the book and say, "Thank gracious, I am through with that!" How many people 'get an education' and yet hate books and hate to think?

The thought suggested at the close of the preceding paragraph may be generalized into a criterion more widely applicable. The richness of life is seen upon reflection to depend, in large measure at least, upon the tendency of what one does to suggest and prepare for succeeding activities. Any activity—beyond the barest physical wants—which does not thus 'lead on' becomes in time stale and flat. Such 'leading on' means that the individual has been modified so that he sees what before he did not see or does what before he could not do. But this is exactly to say that the activity has had an educative effect. Not to elaborate the argument, we may assert that the richness of life depends exactly on its tendency to lead one on to other like fruitful activity; that the degree of this tendency consists exactly in the educative effect of the activity involved; and that we may therefore take as the criterion of the value of any activity—whether intentionally educative or not—its tendency directly or indirectly to lead the individual and others whom he touches on to other like fruitful activity. If we apply this criterion to the common run of American schools we get exactly the discouraging results indicated above. It is the thesis of this paper that these evil results must inevitably follow the effort to found our educational procedure on an unending round of set tasks in conscious disregard of the element of dominant purpose in those who perform the tasks. This again is not to say that every purpose is good nor that the child is a suitable judge as between purposes nor that he is never to be forced to act against a purpose which he entertains. We contemplate no scheme of subordination of teacher or school to childish whim; but we do mean that any plan of educational procedure which does not aim consciously and insistently at securing and utilizing vigorous purposing on the part of the pupils is founded essentially on an ineffective and unfruitful basis. Nor is the quest for desirable purposes hopeless. There is no necessary conflict in kind between the social demands and the child's interests. Our whole fabric of institutional life grew out of human interests. The path of the race is here a possible path for the individual. There is no normal boy but has already many socially desirable interests and is capable of many more. It is the special duty and opportunity of the teacher to guide the pupil through his present interests and achievement into the wider interests and achievement demanded by the wider social life of the older world.

The question of moral education was implicitly raised in the preceding paragraph. What is the effect on morals of the plan herein advocated? A full discussion is unfortunately impossible. Speaking for myself, however, I consider the possibilities for building moral character in a regime of purposeful activity one of the strongest points in its favor; and contrariwise the tendency toward a selfish individualism one of the strongest counts against our customary set-task sit-alone-at-your-own-desk procedure. Moral character is primarily an affair of shared social relationships, the disposition to determine one's conduct and attitudes with reference to the welfare of the group. This means, psychologically, building stimulus–response bonds such that when certain ideas are present as stimuli certain approved responses will follow. We are then concerned that children get a goodly stock of ideas to serve as stimuli for conduct, that they develop good judgment for selecting the idea appropriate in a given case, and that they have firmly built such response bonds as will bring—as inevitably as possible—the appropriate conduct once the proper idea has been chosen. In terms of this (necessarily simplified) analysis we wish such school procedure as will most probably result in the requisite body of ideas, in the needed skill in judging a moral situation, and in unfailing appropriate response bonds. To get these three can we conceive of a better way than by living in a social *milieu* which provides, under competent supervision, for shared coping with a variety of social situations? In the school procedure here advocated children are living together in the pursuit of a rich variety of purposes, some individually sought, many conjointly. As must happen in social commingling, occasions of moral stress will arise, but here—fortunately—under conditions that exclude extreme and especially harmful cases. Under the eye of the skillful teacher the children as an embryonic society will make increasingly finer discriminations as to what is right and proper. Ideas and judgment come thus. Motive and occasion arise together; the teacher has but to steer the process of evaluating the situation. The teacher's success —if we believe in democracy—will consist in gradually eliminating himself or herself from the success of the procedure.

Not only do defined ideas and skill in judging come from such a situation, but response bonds as well. The continual sharing of purposes in such a school offers ideal conditions for forming the necessary habits of give and take. The laws of learning hold here as elsewhere, especially the Law of Effect. If the child is to set up habits of acting, satisfaction must attend the doing or annoyance the failure. Now there are few satisfactions so gratifying and few annoyances so distressing as the approval and the disapproval of our comrades. Anticipated approval will care for most cases; but the positive social disapproval of one's fellows has peculiar potency. When the teacher merely coerces and the other pupils side with their comrade, a contrary 'set'—such as we earlier discussed—is almost inevitable, often so definite as to prevent the fixing in the child's character of the desired response. Conformity may be but outward. But when all concerned take part in deciding what is just —if the teacher act wisely—there is far less likelihood of an opposing 'set.' Somehow disapproval by those who understand from one's own point of view tends to dissolve an opposing 'set,' and one acts then more fully from his own decision. In such cases the

desired bond is better built in one's moral character. Conformity is
not merely outward. It is necessary to emphasize the part the
teacher plays in this group building of bonds. Left alone, as 'the
gentleman's grade' in college indicates, pupils may develop habits of
dawdling. Against this purposelessness the present thesis is
especially directed; but proper ideals must be built up in the school
group. As an ideal is but an idea joined with tendencies to act, the
procedure for building has been discussed; but the teacher is
responsible for the results. The pupils working under his guidance
must through the social experiences encountered build the ideals
necessary for approved social life. The regime of purposeful activity
offers then a wider variety of educative moral experiences more
nearly typical of life itself than does our usual school procedure,
lends itself better to the educative evaluation of these, and provides
better for the fixing of all as permanent acquisitions in the
intelligent moral character.

   The question of the growth or building of interests is important in
the theory of the plan here discussed. Many points still prove
difficult, but some things can be said. Most obvious is the fact of
'maturing' (itself a difficult topic). At first an infant responds
automatically to his environment. Only later, after many experiences
have been organized, can he, properly speaking, entertain purposes;
and in this there are many gradations. Similarly, the earliest steps
involved in working out a set are those that have been instinctively
joined with the process. Later on, steps may be taken by 'suggestion'
(the relatively automatic working of acquired associations). Only
comparatively late do we find true adaptation of means to end, the
conscious choice of steps to the attainment of deliberately formed
purposes. These considerations must qualify any statements made
regarding child purposes. In this connection a quotation from
Woodworth's new book is pertinent: "Almost any object, almost any
act, and particularly almost any process or change in objects that can
be directed by one's own activity toward some definite end, is
interesting on its own account, and furnishes its own drive, once it
is fairly initiated." (*Dynamic Psychology*, p. 202.) One result of the
growth here discussed is the 'leading on' it affords. A skill acquired
as end can be applied as means to new purposes. Skill or idea
arising first in connection with means may be singled out for special
consideration and so form new ends. This last is one of the most
fruitful sources of new interest, particularly of the intellectual kind.

   In connection with this 'maturing' goes a general increase in the
'interest span,' the length of time during which a set will remain
active, the time within which a child will—if allowed—work at any

given project. What part of this increase is due to nature and physical maturing, what part to nurture, why the span is long for some activities and short for others, how we can increase the span in any given cases, are questions of the greatest moment for the educator. It is a matter of common knowledge that within limits 'interests' may be built up, the correlative interest spans appreciably increased. Whatever else may be said, this must mean that stimulus-response bonds have been formed and this in accordance with the laws of learning. We have already seen the general part played by the factor of purpose in utilizing the laws of learning. There seems no reason to doubt that like considerations hold here. In particular the discussion of coercion with its two opposed sets holds almost unchanged. Since the 'set' of external origin has its correlative goal and its consequent possible success, there is a theoretical possibility of learning. In this way we may conceive a new interest built by coercion. Two factors, however, greatly affect the practical utilization of this possibility, the one inherently to hinder, the other possibly to help. The inherent hindrance is the opposed (internal) set, which in proportion to its intensity and persistence will confuse the definition of success and lessen the satisfaction of attainment. Acquiring a new interest is in this respect accordingly doubly and inherently hindered by coercion. The second factor, which may chance favorably, is the possibility that what (reduced) learning takes place may connect with some already potentially existent interest giving such expression to it that the inner opposition to the enforced activity is won over, and the opposing set dissolved. This second factor is of especial significance for the light it throws upon the relation of teacher and pupils in this matter of coercion. It seems from these considerations that if compulsion will result in such learning as sets free some self-continuing activity and these before harmful concomitants have been set up, we may approve such compulsion as a useful temporary device. Otherwise, so far as concerns the building of interests, the use of coercion seems a choice of evils with the general probabilities opposing.

It may be well to come closer to the customary subject matter of the school. Let us consider the classification of the different types of projects: Type 1, where the purpose is to embody some idea or plan in external form, as building a boat, writing a letter, presenting a play; type 2, where the purpose is to enjoy some (esthetic) experience, as listening to a story, hearing a symphony, appreciating a picture; type 3, where the purpose is to straighten out some intellectual difficulty, to solve some problem, as to find out whether or not dew falls, to ascertain how New York outgrew Philadelphia; type 4, where the purpose is to obtain some item or degree of skill or knowledge, as learning to write grade 14 on the Thorndike Scale, learning the irregular verbs in French. It is at once evident that these groupings more or less overlap and that one type may be used as means to another as end. It may be of interest to note that with these definitions the project method logically includes the problem method as a special case. The value of such a classification as that here given seems to me to lie in the light it should throw on the kind of projects teachers may expect and on the procedure that normally prevails in the several types. For type 1 the following steps have been suggested: purposing, planning, executing and judging. It is in accord with the general theory here advocated that the child as far as possible take each step himself. Total failure, however, may hurt more than assistance. The opposed dangers seem to be on the one hand that the child may not come out master of the process, on the other that he may waste time. The teacher must steer the child through these narrows, taking care meanwhile to avoid the other dangers previously discussed. The function of the purpose and the place of thinking in the process need but be mentioned. Attention may be called to the fourth step, that the child as he grows older may increasingly judge the result in terms of the aim and with increasing care and success draw from the process its lessons for the future.

Type 2, enjoying an esthetic experience, may seem to some hardly to belong in the list of projects. But the factor of purpose undoubtedly guides the process and—I must think—influences the growth of appreciation. I have, however, as yet no definite procedure steps to point out.

Type 3, that of the problem, is of all the best known, owing to the work of Professors Dewey and McMurry. The steps that have been used are those of the Dewey analysis of thought. This type lends itself, next to type 4, best of all to our ordinary school-room work. For this reason I have myself feared its over-emphasis. Our schools—at least in my judgment—do emphatically need a great increase in the social activity possible in type 1. Type 4, where the purpose has to do with specific items of knowledge or skill, would seem to call for the same steps as type 1, purposing, planning, executing, and judging. Only here, the planning had perhaps best come from the psychologist. In this type also there is danger of over-emphasis. Some teachers indeed may not closely discriminate between drill as a project and a drill as a set task, although the results will be markedly different.

The limits of the article forbid a discussion of other important aspects of the topic: the changes necessitated by this plan in room furniture and equipment, perhaps in school architecture, the new type of text-book, the new kind of curriculum and program, possibly new plans of grading and promotion, most of all a changed attitude as to what to wish for in the way of achievement. Nor can we consider what this type of procedure means for democracy in furnishing us better citizens, alert, able to think and act, too intelligently critical to be easily hoodwinked either by politicians or by patent-medicines, self-reliant, ready of adaptation to the new social conditions that impend. The question of difficulties would itself require a separate article: opposition of tradition, of taxpayers; unprepared and incompetent teachers; the absence of a worked-out procedure; problems of administration and supervision. All these and more would suffice to destroy the movement were it not deeply grounded.

In conclusion, then, we may say that the child is naturally active, especially along social lines. Heretofore a regime of coercion has only too often reduced our schools to aimless dawdling and our pupils to selfish individualists. Some in reaction have resorted to foolish humoring of childish whims. The contention of this paper is that wholehearted purposeful activity in a social situation as the typical unit of school procedure is the best guarantee of the utilization of the child's native capacities now too frequently wasted. Under proper guidance purpose means efficiency, not only in reaching the projected end of the activity immediately at hand, but even more in securing from the activity the learning which it potentially contains. Learning of all kinds and in its all desirable ramifications best proceeds in proportion as wholeheartedness of purpose is present. With the child naturally social and with the skillful teacher to stimulate and guide his purposing, we can especially expect that kind of learning we call character building. The necessary reconstruction consequent upon these considerations offers a most alluring 'project' to the teacher who but dares to purpose.

FURTHER READING

Cremin, Lawrence. *The Transformation of the School: Progressivism in American Education, 1876–1957.* New York: Alfred A. Knopf, Inc., 1961.

Collings, Ellsworth. *An Experiment with a Project Curriculum.* New York: The Macmillan Company, 1923.

Dewey, John. *Experience and Education.* 1938; New York: Collier Books, 1963.

Kilpatrick, William H. *Education for a Changing Civilization.* New York: The Macmillan Company, 1926.

_____. *The Foundations of Method.* New York: The Macmillan Company, 1925.

_____. *Philosophy of Education.* New York: The Macmillan Company, 1951.

_____. *The Project Method.* New York: Teachers College Press, 1921.

_____. *A Reconstructed Theory of the Educative Process.* New York: Bureau of Publications, Teachers College, Columbia University, 1935.

Rugg, Harold O. and Ann Shumaker. *The Child-Centered School.* New York: World Book Co., 1928.

Tenenbaum, Samuel. *William Heard Kilpatrick: Trail Blazer in Education.* New York: Harper and Brothers, 1951.

Washburne, Carleton. *What Is Progressive Education?* New York: The John Day Company, Inc., 1952.

nine

CULTURAL RECONSTRUCTIONISM

Cultural Reconstructionism, one of the more modern educational philosophies, sharply contrasts with the conservative positions of Essentialism and Perennialism, which are regarded by Reconstructionists as reflective theories that mirror inherited social patterns and values. The Reconstructionists assert that schools and educators should originate policies and programs which will bring about the reform of the social order. Teachers, they say, should deliberately use their power to lead the young in programs of social engineering and reformation.

Cultural, or Social, Reconstructionists claim to be the true successors of John Dewey's Experimentalism. While he never joined the Reconstructionist ranks, Dewey did emphasize the necessity of reconstructing both personal and social experience. He also stressed the social nature of education. Seizing upon Dewey's emphasis on the reconstruction of experience, Reconstructionists stress the social reconstruction of experience and apply it to the reconstruction of the cultural heritage.

Although Social Reconstructionists such as William O. Stanley and Theodore Brameld differ on certain aspects of their philosophical position, they and other Reconstructionists agree on such basic premises as: (1) all philosophies, including educational ones, are culturally based and grow out of specific cultural patterns which are conditioned by living at a given time in a particular place; (2) culture, as a dynamic process, is growing and changing; (3) man can shape and refashion his culture so that it promotes the optimum possibilities for human growth and development.[1]

---

1. Examples of Reconstructionist educational philosophy: Theodore Brameld, *Toward a Reconstructed Philosophy of Education*. New York: Holt, Rinehart & Winston, Inc., 1956; and William O. Stanley, *Education and Social Integration*. New York: Bureau of Publications, Teachers College, Columbia University, 1953.

For the Reconstructionists, educational philosophies are products of their age and are contextual to given cultural environments. Rather than being abstract or speculative exercises, philosophies are programs of life and of socializing that should guide human conduct. As a program of action, an educational philosophy should direct man to a better way of life.

Social Reconstructionists view the present age as one which is beset by a severe cultural crisis which is a consequence of man's inability to reconstruct his values in terms of the requirements of modern life. Man has entered the modern technological and scientific age with a set of values derived from the rural, pre-industrial past. To resolve the crisis, man needs to examine his culture and to find therein the viable elements that can be used as instruments to resolve the present crisis. If man examines his heritage, deliberately plans the direction of change, and carries out his plan, he will construct a new social order. It is the school's task to encourage the critical examination of the cultural heritage and find the elements that can be instrumental in the needed reconstruction.

CULTURAL CRISIS

As a philosophical position, Reconstructionism asserts that modern man is living in an age of profound and severe crisis engendered by his unwillingness to face the major task of cultural reconstruction. The symptoms of cultural crisis are many. For example, there are great variations in economic levels of life. While a few people live in wealth, the vast majority of people are doomed to struggle for survival at a level of subsistence that borders on dire poverty. In the United States, large numbers of people, especially Black, Spanish-speaking, and Appalachian Americans, have been victimized by decades of poverty. On the international scene, two-thirds of the world's people are barely surviving. While some feast, others starve. In an age of science, the Reconstructionist regards the contradiction between wealth and poverty to be a residue of the prescientific era.

The world is still plagued by war. The long war in Viet Nam, the continuing hostilities between Arab and Israeli, the tensions between the Soviets, the Chinese, and the Americans are symptomatic of a past which is archaic but still with us. In an age of thermonuclear destruction, military conflict with the threat of escalation into worldwide holocaust is an ever-present danger which jeopardizes man's continued existence on this planet.

Further, the Reconstructionist can point to a myriad of unresolved conflicts and tensions and to the waste of human talent. Such problems as the population explosion, environmental pollution, and the recurrence of violence are symptoms of the crisis of our age.

The root of the crisis lies in the fact that the theoretical, the religious, and the axiological dimensions of life are disconnected from the reality of life conditions. Man's own creative genius has developed scientific and technological instruments that are dynamic, liberating, and contributory to further change. At the same time that the dynamic forces of science and technology have changed man's material environment, we still cling to an idealized past that seeks to preserve the *status quo*.

CULTURAL RECONSTRUCTION

The Reconstructionists believe that modern society and modern man's survival are intimately related. To ensure human survival and to create a more satisfying corporate civilization, man must become a social engineer who is able to plan the course of change and direct the dynamic instruments of science and technology to achieve the desired goals. A Reconstructionist education is one that cultivates (1) a sense of conscious discrimination in the examination of the cultural heritage; (2) a commitment to work for deliberate social reformation; (3) a willingness to develop a planning mentality which is capable of plotting the course of cultural revision; (4) the testing of the cultural plan by enacting programs of deliberate social reform.

Reconstructionists believe that all social reform arises in existing life conditions. Students are expected to define the major problems facing mankind. A sense of conscious discrimination means that the student is capable of recognizing the dynamic forces of the present. It also means that he is equally able to detect the beliefs, customs, and institutions that impede cultural renewal. Those values that dominate merely because they are customary must be discarded. The moral and ideological culture is saturated with values that are residues of the prescientific and pretechnological age. Bigotry, hatreds, superstitions, and ignorance must be identified and discarded.

Although the Reconstructionists have not defined with precision the new society that they wish to create, some of its dimensions might be mentioned. It is likely to be one in which science will be used as a humane instrument; it is likely to be one which is corporate and in which all men equally share the good things of life; it is likely to be one that is international in scope.

COUNTS' *DARE THE SCHOOLS BUILD A NEW SOCIAL ORDER?*

A clear statement of the need for educational involvement in resolving social problems was made by George S. Counts in *Dare the Schools Build a New Social Order?*, which was published in 1932. Although Counts did not formally identify with those who called themselves Social Reconstructionists, an analysis of his educational theory is useful in clarifying some of the themes that are central concerns of contemporary Reconstructionist philosophers. George S. Counts has contributed greatly to American education. As a social and educational philosopher, as one-time Reconstructionist advocate, as expert on American and Russian education, as President of the American Federation of Teachers from 1939 to 1942, as member of the Educational Policies Commission from 1936 to 1942, and as teacher educator at the Universities of Washington, Chicago, Yale, and Teachers College of Columbia, his impact on American education has been that of a searching scholar and frequently fiery critic. Among his many books are *The Principles of Education, Secondary Education and Industrialism, The American Road to Culture, The Social Foundations of Education, The Prospects of American Democracy, Education and the Promise of America, Education and American Civilization,* and *Education and the Foundations of Human Freedom.* His message to American teachers during the Depression of the 1930s is frequently recounted in the history of American education. In 1932, he asked the teachers of the nation the still unanswered question, "Dare the Schools Build a New Social Order?" His question created a ferment which is still apparent for those committed to the theory and practice of education in the schools of the United States.

During the bleak Depression era of the 1930s many educators felt that American schools had failed to educate citizens who were prepared to understand and solve the problems of massive unemployment and economic dislocation. The Reconstructionist educators believed that the school should not only transmit the cultural heritage and develop intellectual habits, skills, and knowledge, but also should restructure the social order in light of the changing needs of modern life. Both podium and press resounded with the debate over the function of the schools. Traditionalists saw the school as an instrument of cultural preservation or as an institution which was purely intellectual. In contrast, the Reconstructionist held that educators were responsible for building new social patterns which would blend the new and the old into a viable cultural synthesis.

In the 1960s and continuing into the early 1970s, the currents of social discontent were directed with force against American public schools, their administrators, and their teachers. This discontent was not directed solely toward the educational system but was part of a larger dissatisfaction with the quality of American life. In particular, the perplexing problems of poverty, cultural deprivation, and racial discrimination that Counts talked about thirty years ago are still unresolved. Some of the problems of poverty and deprivation and some of the sources of discontent can be traced to America's social and economic situation. In many respects, President Johnson's War on Poverty was reminiscent of President Roosevelt's Second Inaugural Address of 1937 and the words:

In this nation I see tens of millions of its citizens—a substantial part of its whole population—who at this very moment are denied the greater part of what the very lowest standards of today call the necessities of life. I see millions of families trying to live on incomes so meager that the pall of family disaster hangs over them day by day. . . . I see one-third of a nation ill-housed, ill-clad, and ill-nourished.

The arguments of Counts have come alive again. The problems of poverty and discrimination have not been solved—at least not for all Americans. A large segment of the American population is culturally deprived—the inadequately educated, the poorly trained, and the un-skilled. For the culturally and technically disadvantaged, the problems of economic survival have never really been solved, despite suburban affluence, emphasis on programs for the gifted, and the space-age approach to education. The promise of American life is still blurred by the complexities, the confusions, and the disintegration of a society which, while massive, is not yet a "great society."

Contemporary discontent seems to have rekindled reconstructionism in education to the degree that the *Report to the Board of Education, City of Chicago, by the Advisory Panel on Integration of the Public Schools,* of March 31, 1964, read:

The individual does not live in isolation from society, and while the school ministers to his well-being it must contribute thereby to the strength and integrity of the social order—the neighborhood, the city, the state, and the nation. By its effect upon his attitudes and actions, the state of his knowledge, his rational capacities, and the level of his skills, it inevitably determines the character of society, its political integrity, its economic stability and prosperity, its solidarity of purpose, and its general moral strength. Not less important, the school is the chief determinant of the quality and character of the culture and the community. Upon it, more than any other institution or function of society, depends the character of the world in which the present generation must live and into which future generations will be born. What goes on in the schoolroom and laboratory profoundly affects the whole quality of personal and social life, the things men live by, the values they cherish, and the ends they seek. It can make the difference between a life that is full and meaningful and one that is empty and meaningless.[2]

---

2. The Advisory Panel on Integration of the Public Schools, *A Report to the Board of Education: Integration of the Public Schools—Chicago.* March 31, 1964. p. 25.

In much the same vein, the survey by Havighurst, *The Public Schools of Chicago,* states in regard to urban education:

The public school may be active or passive in this situation. They will be passive if the "four walls" school philosophy prevails. In this case the schools will do as good a job as possible for all kinds of students within the school, and will stay out of any direct involvement with community renewal programs. If they are passive, and follow the "four walls" principles, the effort at community renewal will probably fail.

If the public schools are active, they will adopt the "urban community" school philosophy. They will cooperate actively with the effort being made to achieve social and urban renewal in Chicago by the public and private agencies.[3]

These statements seem to be Reconstructionist and once again ask the question "Dare the Schools Build a New Social Order?"

Education For An Age of Crisis   For Counts, the great conflicts and crises of the twentieth century were symptomatic of an age of profound transition and rapid change. Acute cultural disintegration occurred as America moved between two very different social patterns. The older, agrarian, neighborhood community was displaced by a rapid rush into a mode of life which was highly complex, industrialized, scientific, and technological. From a loose aggregation of relatively self-contained rural households and neighborhoods, the nation, under the impetus of industrialization, evolved into a mass society characterized by minute structural and functional differentiations. While these rapid changes appeared to be primarily material; social, moral, political, economic, religious, and aesthetic life was also affected.

Change is not intrinsically crisis generating. Rather, crisis occurs when man is unprepared to cope with, order, and harmonize the processes of change. Counts feared that our educational systems, at all levels, fail to equip man, both cognitively and attitudinally, to deal with the changes occurring in the cultural or qualitative area of life. The crisis is further complicated because changes occur multilaterally. Alterations in one area accelerate changes and compound crises in other dimensions. Because of man's difficulty in reconstructing his environment rationally and efficiently, turmoil and maladjustment characterizes periods of profound adjustment.

---

3. Robert J. Havighurst, The Public Schools of Chicago, *A Survey For the Board of Education of the City of Chicago.* Chicago, The Board of Education of the City of Chicago, 1964. p. 370.

Counts' analysis draws heavily on the cultural lag theory. Cultural lag occurs when man's practical inventiveness outdistances his moral consciousness and social organization. The crisis in institutional arrangements results from a whole series of maladjustments between inherited ideas and customs, on the one hand, and material–technological innovations on the other.

One of the most serious dislocations is economic, where inherited values associated with economic individualism impede the development of a planning, cooperating, and coordinating socioeconomic order. The Reconstructionist distinguishes a planning society from a planned society. In a planning society, the social design is never really completed but is continually refashioned by man's creative intelligence. Today efforts at urban community renewal and an integrated society are often blocked by reluctance to reconstruct inherited institutional forms and ideas, such as the neighborhood school pattern or the very concept of the urban community itself. In the international realm, the invention and development of thermonuclear weapons have affected military, economic, political, and even psychological behavior. However, inherited concepts of national sovereignty have inhibited development of controls over these new instruments of power. Even though nuclear weapons systems possess the capability of massive destruction, adequate controls remain to be developed.

To Counts, the crucial educational problem is the need to formulate a philosophy of education that can prepare educators to deal with social crisis and cultural lag by reconstructing ideas, beliefs, and values in light of changing conditions. In *Dare the Schools Build A New Social Order?,* Counts challenged:

I would consequently like to see our profession come to grips with the problem of creating a tradition that has roots in American soil, is in harmony with the spirit of the age, recognizes the facts of industrialism, appeals to the most profound impulses of our people, and takes into account the emergence of a world society.[4]

American education's task is two-fold: (1) reconstruction of the theoretical foundations based upon the American cultural heritage; (2) the experimental development of school practices which would enable man to deal with problems of acute cultural crisis and social disintegration.

Since education is always relative and particular to a given society, American education is a product of its unique heritage. For American

---

4. George S. Counts, *Dare the Schools Build A New Social Order?* New York: The John Day Company, Inc., 1932. pp. 17–18.

education to serve broad social needs, these needs must be examined in the light of inherited traditions. Then these traditions can be reconstructed in view of social problems. In *The Social Foundations of Education,* Counts began with the statement:

The historical record shows that education is always a function of time, place, and circumstances. In its basic philosophy, its social objectives, and its program of instruction, it inevitably reflects in varying proportions, the experiences, the conditions, and the hopes, fears, and aspirations of a particular people or cultural group at a particular time in history. . . . Education as a whole is always relative, at least in its fundamental parts, to some concrete and evolving social situation.[5]

A viable conception of the American cultural heritage in the twentieth century would have to rest on two necessary conditions: (1) affirmation of the values embodied in the democratic tradition; and (2) recognition of the dominant reality of contemporary society—the emergence of industrial civilization. Upon these two conditions, American educators might fashion an educational philosophy that exalts socially useful labor and might attempt fundamental social reconstruction. This philosophy would have to be based on a rational concept of cooperative behavior in an essentially cooperative society. A cultural synthesis of the viable elements of the democratic heritage and the requirements of scientific technology would harness scientific and technological powers for the realization of democratic ends that would preserve individual integrity and achieve efficient and popular control of social and economic mechanisms. The reconstruction of a comprehensive educational theory encompasses the entire range of human activities. Labor, income, property, leisure, recreation, sex, family, government, public opinion, race, nationality, war, peace, art, and aesthetics are subjects appropriate to educational theory and practice.

When he challenged educators to fashion a cultural philosophy of education suited to modern American life, Counts was also urging them to assume the responsibilities and burdens of "educational statesmanship." Counts defined the statesman as a civilizational leader, a proponent of vital ways and means, a man of ideas, and an initiator of broad policy. For too long a time, teacher education has concentrated on mechanics and has neglected the major social and economic problems facing modern society. As public servants, educators are obliged to foster the greatest possible development of the capacities of citizens. In assuming the responsibilities for formulating educational philosophies

---

5. George S. Counts, *The Social Foundations of Education.* New York: Charles Scribner & Sons, 1934. p. 1.

and programs, the educational statesman is providing national leadership. This responsibility involves the making of policy determinations based upon emergent ethical and aesthetic values in light of natural endowments, technological resources, the cultural heritage, and great social trends.

Counts' educational statesman is to assume the task of reconstructing the heritage; upon this reconstructed heritage he is to fashion the philosophy and program of American education. Such a reconstructed heritage would encompass two basic themes: the democratic ethic and emergent technology. Counts' conception of the democratic ethic is definitely and uniquely associated with the American experience. It exalts the frontier and the popular democracy associated with Jackson, the progressivism of Wilson, the liberalism of Roosevelt, and the attempts of a planning society as found in the New Freedom, the New Deal, the experimentalism of John Dewey, and the historical relativism and economic interpretations of Charles Beard. In emphasizing the progressive–liberal side of the American tradition, Counts rejected the more conservative ideas of Hamilton, Social Darwinism, economic individualism, and rugged competitive capitalism. American democracy is not only a political expression but is and should continue to be a product of the combined economic, social, moral, and aesthetic forces operating within the heritage. Democracy must penetrate all areas of life; it rests on an egalitarian social base. Only in a society of equals can democracy develop and flourish. Any economic, social, or political attempt to subvert the egalitarian foundations of American democracy should elicit vigorous opposition from the proponents of the democratic heritage. Inequalities of opportunity caused by wealth, race, color, or religion are subversive to the democratic ethic. Since the social life of industrialized society is highly organized, the preservation of democracy rests on the American community's capacity to reconstruct institutional life in harmony with the emergent technological civilization. In *Dare the Schools Build A New Social Order?* Counts said the reconstructed democracy should:

manifest a tender regard for the weak, the ignorant, and the unfortunate; place the heavier and more onerous social burdens on the backs of the strong; glory in every triumph of man in his timeless urge to express himself and to make the world more habitable; exalt human labor of hand and brain as the creator of all wealth and culture.[6]

A reconstructed philosophy and program of American education directly relates to the rise of industrial civilization, a product of science

6. Counts, *Dare the Schools Build A New Social Order?* pp. 42–43.

and technology. The application of science to the modes and techniques of life created a new cultural force—technology, which is "the art of applying science and mechanics to the various departments of human economy." Technology is a practical and purposeful instrument, a creative factor in cultural evolution, marked by emphasis on precise, orderly, and defined relationships. While its experimental methods concern the practical application of knowledge, technology is not confined solely to material products, discoveries, and inventions. It is also a process, a method, of solving problems and of viewing the world. Since technology applies science to life, the role of science in a reconstructed educational philosophy should be examined. Counts saw science as man's most accurate instrument and method of problem solving. As the method of intelligence, science produces ordered and precise knowledge. Giving man power, control, and freedom, science is the greatest single force moving and shaping man's environment. Defining science as "a method of organized and critical common sense," Counts elaborated on this method: (1) the scientific method begins with a hypothesis growing out of previous experience, knowledge, and thought; (2) the hypothesis is tested by a process of accurate and adequate observation employing the most precise instruments; (3) data are compiled and the hypothesis proved or rejected on the basis of empirical and public verification.[7]

In commenting on science's potential as a cultural instrument, Counts examined the characteristics of technology—the application of science to the modes and techniques of life. Technology is rational, functional, planful, centripetal, dynamic, and efficient. Technological rationality rests on its freedom from tradition. When given free rein, it destroys traditional barriers to thought. Embracing a complex of immediately relevant ideas and methods that serve human purposes, technology observes, inquires, and accurately and mathematically describes. As quantitative reasoning tests the outcomes of technology and predicts their consequences, man's freedom of action increases. As it occupies larger areas of life, the inherent rationality of science will make deep operational inroads into other social functions.

Since it is functional rather than purely abstract, technology's basically utilitarian nature is demonstrated in the application of its findings to man's physical world. Since it is planful, technology requires carefully formulated purposes, determination of directions, and conception of plans of action prior to their undertaking. The operational plans have to be definite and based on positive knowledge of the ends to be real-

---

7. George S. Counts, *Education and the Promise of America.* New York: The Macmillan Company, 1946. pp. 87–88.

ized. The technological mode opposes an impulsive and capricious subjectivism. The technological age requires a planning and cooperating society. Technology is centripetal. Dominated by necessities of rational design, it enters into adjoining areas of life once ruled by haphazard and chance operation. Drawing chaotic procedures within its ordered embrace, technology unites and arranges adjacent operations around a core of rational planning. By its action and exploration, technology is dynamic. One invention or discovery initiates an ever-greater unending cluster of new inventions and discoveries. The acceleration of change initiated by inventions and discoveries is not solely material; it has spread into nonmaterial culture and caused subsequent economic, political, moral, and social alterations. The dynamic character of technology has accelerated social change.

Efficiency is technology's most pervasive characteristic. Technological processes achieve the greatest possible end with the least expenditure of material and energy. Originating in the machine, the ideal of efficiency extends first to human labor and then throughout the entire community. Technology places a premium on professional competence; for without the expert knowledge of the specialist, the entire productive mechanism might fall into disorder. As technology advances, inexpert opinion yields to trained intelligence.

Technology places great power in human hands. Like science, technology is a neutral instrument that can serve humane and enriching purposes or be an instrument of ruthless exploitation. In a nuclear age, it is an instrument of liberation or of destruction. This powerful instrument is not a mere additive to civilization. A culture is not an aggregation of discrete, separate items; it is rather a system of relationships which responds to interior and exterior stresses and strains and continually alters social patterns. The technological age requires continual reconstructions of the economy, society, education, government, and morals or civilization.[8]

Counts' examination of American civilization affirmed two essential strains: an equalitarian democratic ethic and the emergence of a scientific–industrial–technological society. These two strains are elements in a reconstructive synthesis that has become the basis of a civilizational philosophy for American education. Counts refused to predetermine the contours of the needed new social order. Rather than rigidly formulate the desired shape of the future democracy, he preferred that social planning be open-ended and experimental. The American people would shape their own destiny, using their own elastic democratic tempera-

---

8. Counts, *Social Foundations of Education.* pp. 70–73.

ment. Impatient with customary authority, Americans in their westward movement have transformed a hostile wilderness into an
hospitable environment. Americans are ready to experiment, to judge
by consequences, and to compromise. Counts wrote that the course of
American democracy depends on the ability of the people:

To learn from experience, to define the problem, to formulate a program of
action, to discover, appraise, and marshall the apparent and latent, the
actual and potential resources of American democracy.[9]

THE SCHOOL AND CULTURAL RECONSTRUCTION

In formulating a viable educational philosophy, the Reconstructionist
philosopher gives careful attention to the school as a cultural agency.
However, caution is exercised so that the school's potentiality as an
instrument of reconstruction is not exaggerated. It is necessary to distinguish between education and schooling. Education is more informal and
refers to the total process of enculturation. The school is a specialized
social agency which was established to bring children into group life
through the deliberate cultivation of certain socially preferred skills,
knowledge, and values.

Counts believed that Americans have not recognized the differences
between education and schooling. They have identified the school with
progress and regarded schooling as an unfailing solution to all problems.
However, world crises multiplied during the period of the greatest expansion of schooling. Instead of directing social change, the school was
driven aimlessly by external forces. The immature American faith in the
power of schooling derived from a notion of education as a pure and
independent quality isolated from social, political, and economic conflicts. This uncritical attitude inhibits the serious examination of education's moral and social foundations. Although Americans associate
education solely with democracy, history has demonstrated that an
appropriate education exists for every society or civilization. In the
twentieth century, totalitarians have proved extremely adept at using
education to promote their particular ideologies. German education under the Nazis and Soviet education under the Communists demonstrate
that the school can serve many masters.

Some educators, including many progressives, erroneously believe
that the school is capable of reconstructing society without the support
of other social institutions. Since the school is only one of several

9. George S. Counts, *The Prospects of American Democracy.* New York: The John Day
Company, Inc., 1938. pp. 350–51.

educative social institutions, educators have to be constantly aware of the changing functions and structures of the society which determines its task. An educational theory based solely upon schooling lacks reality and vitality.[10] Counts felt that the school, while important, is only one of many cultural agencies. When he asked educators to "build a new social order," Counts was urging educators to examine the culture and ally with those social forces and groups which exemplify the democratic ethic in the light of emergent technological trends. Although educators can not reform society without the support of others, "educational statesmen" can provide leadership in building a new society. While this is a limited type of educational origination, it differs from the reflective theory which holds that the school should merely mirror society. Mere reflection means that powerful economic and pressure groups can dominate the school for their own special interests. Counts' educational theory also opposes the "four walls philosophy of the school," which asserts that educators should be concerned only with schooling and should ignore social issues.

In outlining a democratic educational program, Counts emphasized two major objectives: (1) development of democratic habits, dispositions, and loyalties; (2) acquisition of knowledge and insight for intelligent participation in democratic society. Public education is to develop a feeling of competency and adequacy in the individual; allegiance to human equality; brotherhood, dignity, and worth; loyalty to the democratic methodology of discussion, criticism, and decision; integrity and scientific spirit; and respect for talent, training, and character.[11]

Counts attacked the doctrines of educational impartiality and neutrality which demand the teacher's complete objectivity. All education is committed to certain beliefs and values. Some criteria are necessary to guide the selection or rejection of educational goals, subjects, materials, and methods. At no point can the school assume complete neutrality and at the same time be a concrete functioning reality. Counts emphasized that every educational program is biased because it has form and substance, pattern and value, aversion and loyalty. For every society, there is an appropriate and distinctive education. The primary obligation of American educators is to clarify the underlying assumptions and guiding principles which give commitment and direction to the school.

As each new generation is brought into social participation, it masters society's skills, knowledge, and attitudes. Without this transmission and perpetuation, the particular society perishes. The release of human

---

10. George S. Counts, *The American Road to Culture.* New York: The John Day Company, Inc., 1930. p. 18.
11. George S. Counts, *The Schools Can Teach Democracy.* New York: The John Day Company, Inc., 1939. pp. 16–17.

energy occurs, not by freeing the individual from tradition, but by introducing him to a vital and growing tradition. Counts said:

The real question, therefore, is not whether some tradition will be imposed by intent or circumstance upon the coming generation (we may rest assured that this will be done), but rather what particular tradition will be imposed. To refuse to face the task of selection or the fashioning of this tradition is to evade the most crucial, difficult, and important educational responsibility.[12]

In affirming the democratic and equalitarian values, Counts urged educators to emphasize the areas of the heritage which foster shared experience or cooperative activities. The curriculum should include broad areas of social and technological knowledge and should investigate the real problems of modern life. A generation of Americans who can actively seek to solve the problems of reconstructing democracy in light of the needs of a technological society is needed.

In urging the commitment of educators to the fostering of democratic values, Counts challenges both the traditionalists and the child-centered progressives. The traditionalists stress education as purely intellectual and untouched by social problems. For them, the school is to cultivate intellectual habits, skills, and knowledge. In the pure pursuit of pure knowledge, the school is not to engage in economic, political, and social controversy.

In addition to opposing educational traditionalism, Counts takes issue with the child-centered progressive educators. He attacks the notions of some progressives who encourage the possibility of a completely neutral school in which the child is never imposed upon but is completely free to develop according to his own nature and interests. Counts held that only as a member of society, participating in a culture through use of cultural instruments, can the child grow through experience. As a cultural participant, the child is imposed upon by the culture and in turn imposes upon the culture.

CONCLUSION

Counts considered education to be the highest form of statesmanship. The process of education requires the transmission of a viable cultural heritage to the immature members of society. Educational statesmanship involves the formulation of such a heritage in terms of philosophy and program. Such a philosophy of education of necessity has to be

---

12. George S. Counts, "Theses on Freedom, Culture, and Social Planning and Leadership," *National Education Association Proceedings. 70* (1932), p. 249.

composed of the elements of democracy and technology. These cultural elements have to be deliberately imposed by the school. As education is a process of reconstruction, the task of formulation is never finished and never completed, but is a part of an open-ended experimental process which continues as long as change in man's environment continues. Since human history is the record of change over time, man's life on this planet is the record of on-going reconstruction of experience. As such, the task of the school is always the building of a new social order.

SELECTIONS

George S. Counts

George S. Counts was born on December 9, 1889, near the town of Baldwin, Kansas, where he attended the local public schools. He received his undergraduate education at Baker University, in Baldwin, and received the Bachelor of Arts degree in 1911. He began graduate work at the University of Chicago in 1913 and was awarded a Ph.D. in Education in 1916.

Counts began his teaching career in 1911 as a teacher of science and mathematics in the Sumner County High School in Wellington, Kansas. From 1912 to 1913 he served as principal of the public high school in Peabody, Kansas. After receiving his doctorate, Counts served as head of the education department of Delaware College in Newark, Delaware. In 1918 he taught at Harris Teachers College in St. Louis; in 1919, at the University of Washington; and then joined the faculty of Yale University in 1920. He became a member of the faculty of Teachers College, Columbia University, in 1927, and taught there until retiring in 1955. After his retirement from Teachers College, he taught at the University of Pittsburgh, the University of Colorado, Michigan State University, Northwestern University, and Southern Illinois University.

Professor Counts has concentrated his scholarly efforts and teaching in the social, cultural, and comparative foundations of education. In 1925 he was a member of the Philippine Educational Survey Commission. In 1927 and again in 1929 he visited the Soviet Union to study educational and social change. In 1946 he was a member of the Educational Mission to Japan to advise on the reconstruction of Japanese education after World War II.

Among Professor Counts' numerous works on social and educational theory are: *The Selective Character of American Secondary Education* (1924), *The Social Composition of Boards of Education* (1927), *School and Society in Chicago* (1928), *The American Road to Culture* (1930), *The Soviet Challenge to America* (1931), *Dare the Schools Build A New Social Order?* (1932), *The*

Social Foundations of Education (1934), The Prospects of American Democracy (1938), The Schools Can Teach Democracy (1939), The Education of Free Men in American Democracy (1939), Education and the Promise of America (1946), Education and American Civilization (1952), The Challenge of Soviet Education (1957), and Education and the Foundations of Human Freedom (1962).

In Dare the Schools Build A New Social Order? Counts urged educators to devote their energies to formulating a philosophy and program of education that is adequate to the needs of a technological civilization. Counts' greatest contribution to philosophy of education is his concept that education arises in the context of particular civilizations. In the selection that follows, Counts writes that American education is a product of its own unique cultural context. After examining the traditional American faith in the power of education, he calls for the development of a great conception of civilization and of education.

* * *

Our great interest in education has stimulated a vast amount of discussion, research, and experimentation throughout the period of our history as a nation. But because of our general and persistent failure to probe deeply into the nature of education as a moral and social undertaking, much of this activity has been relatively futile. Although we have developed a good education, an education of which we may be rightly proud, we have not developed a truly great education, an education which confronts the realities of the age, expresses the best in our heritage, and takes full advantage of our prospects. In education we have lived below the possibilities of our civilization.

During the current century, with the establishment of numerous teachers colleges and departments of education in our universities, we have devoted an enormous amount of energy to the improvement of education. Our literature, both lay and professional, is full of discussions of what is wrong with the school and of proposals to correct its weaknesses. The shelves of our libraries groan under the weight of educational reports, surveys, and studies. New theories and experiments follow one another in an endless stream. This activity is by no means all lost motion; it has undoubtedly resulted in very considerable improvement in the conduct of the school. Yet most of it deals with either the surface or

Reprinted by permission of the publisher from George S. Counts, Education and American Civilization. (New York: Teachers College Press, © 1952, by Teachers College, Columbia University), pp. 29–40.

the mechanics of the problem. Indeed, some of the most widely and hotly discussed proposals for reform during our generation are little more than nostrums which largely ignore the basic problem of all educational thought—the problem of the relation of education to the nature and fortunes of our civilization in its historical and world setting. Three such proposals have been prominently before us for some time.

The first proposal accepts the substance of the traditional program and concentrates on the concept of mechanical efficiency. The principles and philosophy of mass production, one of the truly magnificent products of American genius in the field of industry, are applied to the rearing of the young. The school system is regarded as a gigantic automobile assembly line which at the upper levels divides and subdivides in terms of desired models. It takes in the children as raw material at one end, passes them on from one teacher or workman to another, and finally turns them out as finished products, each leaving the school or factory freshly painted, under his own power, and hitting on all cylinders. Vast attention is of course given to the perfection of the machinery of education, to the integration of parts, and to the elimination of friction, to the improvement of buildings and equipment, to the standardization of procedures, to the invention of pedagogical gadgets, to the construction of tests and rating scales for both pupils and teachers, and to the keeping of records of all actions and transactions. Never in the history of education has so much paper been used to so little purpose.

This drive for mechanical efficiency has been unfortunate, not because efficiency is not desirable. The contrary is clearly the case. But efficiency is secondary to the ends that are to be served. It seems probable that the transference to education of a conception of operation developed in relation to the production of material things is a fundamental mistake. Unfortunately, moreover, many of the best minds of the profession have been engaged in the study of the mechanics of education at a time when the consideration of its substance has been imperative. Primary concentration on school efficiency during a period of cultural crisis and transformation is both a form of escape and a way of compounding the troubles of the age.

The second proposal seeks guidance in the interests and problems of children. The presumption here seems to be that the child achieves maturity through a process of spontaneous generation or unfoldment which the adult world through its educational agencies should merely guard and nourish. According to this view the child, and not the teacher or the school, should play the decisive role in shaping both the processes and the ends of education. The interests and problems of boys and girls are assumed to constitute a more trustworthy guide than the experience and wisdom of their elders. It is argued, moreover, that any positive interference by members of the older generation is a form of imposition or indoctrination and is certain to lead to frustration. Here undoubtedly is the most romantic interpretation of human nature since Rousseau.

In the proposal, however, there is an important insight. It recognizes the psychological truth that interest is a condition of effective and economical learning. The immediate concerns of the young therefore should always play a large role in education. Like the learning process and the "laws of the organism" generally, they provide the limits within which the teacher must operate. But those limits are known to be extremely wide. We must assume, if we are faithful to the findings of science, that children in their biological inheritance are essentially the same in all times and places, among all races and peoples, among all groups and classes. Yet their interests vary greatly from epoch to epoch and from society to society. Also they are extraordinarily fluid. The interest that a child brings to school in the morning may be the result of the casual conversation of parents at home, of a radio program devised to sell a hair tonic, of a moving picture produced with an eye on the box office, or of some incident observed in the street or on the highway. The responsibility of the school is, not to follow the interests of the young, but rather to assist in arousing and building worthy and fruitful interests.

It should be recognized also that this proposal contains a great moral affirmation. In conformity with the democratic ethic, it affirms that the child is a person and that his personality should always be treated with respect and regarded as precious. The historical record of the treatment of the young by their elders is full of horrors. The liberation of boys and girls from the reign of adult tyranny and ignorance is one of the marks of a high civilization. Yet respect for the personality of the child is expressed more fully in an educational program designed to develop a mature personality deserving respect. "We see quite clearly," writes Bronislaw Malinowski, "why the freedom of the child, in the sense of letting him do what he wishes and as he likes, is unreal. In the interest of his own organism he has constantly to be trammeled in education from acts which are biologically dangerous, or which are culturally useless. His whims, his fits of idleness or disobedience must be gradually curtailed, formed, and translated into culturally relevant choices. There is also no freedom in action except within the context of organized human groups."

The third proposal finds the solution of the educational problem in the study of the "one hundred great books" at the college level and in preparation for their study in the lower schools. It must be admitted at once that from the standpoint of the teacher this is the most attractive proposal now current. It is the ideal answer of the pedagogue to the truly vexing problems confronting education. In the first place, it would give him a virtual monopoly over a special body of knowledge. He would have no competitors. If he could only convince the other members of society of the worth of this knowledge, he would be in the enviable position of a long line of ancestors reaching back to the shaman and the medicine man of primitive society. In the second place, once having mastered the "great books" he could pursue his calling for the rest of his life without being disturbed by the issues of depression and prosperity, of war and peace, of tyranny and freedom, of the future of civilization. He could withdraw from the world and dwell all his years in a scholastic paradise. He could be fairly sure, moreover, that only two or three books would be added in his lifetime, that their status would be uncertain for at least a century, and that anyway they could not equal those written by the "ancients" long ago.

The basic argument of the proposal seems to be that education is essentially a process of mental training, that the great literary classics are the finest product of the human mind, and that therefore they are the best tools for the development of the mind. As a matter of fact, education is far more than mental training: it is first of all a process of inducting the young into the ways, privileges, and responsibilities of a given society. Also, these classics, precious as they are, cannot be said without qualification to be the finest products of the human mind: they scarcely rank above a great living civilization, a system of democratic government, or even a fine person who possibly never read a single one of them. Likewise, that they are the best tools for the development of the mind is hardly supported either by the history of education or by psychological investigation. Experience suggests rather that this is the surest road man has yet discovered to formalism, sterility, and death in education. Although the proposal properly directs attention to certain sublime achievements of the mind of man, emphasizes the processes of thought and reflection, and stresses enduring and universal elements in the human heritage, it is fundamentally a

manifestation of academic nostalgia. It constitutes an attempt to
retire, without sacrifice of glory, from the present troubled age.

Education Always Expresses a Conception of Civilization. Education can
never be a purely autonomous process, independent of time and
place and conducted according to its own laws. It is as much an
integral part of a civilization as an economic or a political system.
The very way in which education is conceived, whether its purpose
is to free or enslave the mind, is an expression of the civilization
which it serves. The great differences in educational philosophy and
practice from society to society are due primarily to differences in
culture and civilization. Although all educational programs in the
world today, including our own, should embrace the conception of a
common humanity, no such program as a whole should be regarded
as an article of export either with or without the support of dollars
or machine guns.

Our American education has always expressed an interpretation of
our civilization. Many foreign visitors from Alexis de Tocqueville to
D. W. Brogan have dwelt at length on this fact. "There is probably
no better place than a school-room," wrote Francis J. Grund more
than a century ago, "to judge of the character of a people." He then
proceeded to contrast American and German education as follows:
"Who, upon entering an American school-room, and witnessing the
continual exercises in reading and speaking, or listening to the
subject of their discourses, and watching the behavior of the pupils
towards each other and their teacher, could, for a moment, doubt his
being amongst a congregation of young republicans? And who, on
entering a German academy, would not be struck with the principle
of authority and silence, which reflects the history of Germany for
the last half dozen centuries? What difficulty has not an American
teacher to maintain order amongst a dozen unruly little urchins;
while a German rules over two hundred pupils in a class with all
the ease and tranquillity of an Eastern monarch?" He concludes his
discussion with the warning directed beyond the Atlantic that "it
would only be necessary to conduct some doubting European
politician to an American school-room, to convince him at once that
there is no immediate prospect of transferring royalty to the shores
of the New World."

Sir Charles Lyell, lamenting the undisciplined character of
American children, made a like observation: "Many young
Americans have been sent to school in Switzerland, and I have heard
their teachers, who found them less manageable than English or
Swiss boys, maintain that they must all of them have some dash of

wild Indian blood in their veins. Englishmen, on the other hand, sometimes attribute the same character to republican institutions." Our education today expresses a conception of our civilization. This it does in spite of our heavy borrowing from other times and places, in spite of the lag behind the movement of events and conditions. It expresses a conception of our civilization, however partial or limited, in every part of its program—in its controlling purposes and in the extension or limitation of opportunities, in the architecture of the school and in the subjects of study, in the methods of instruction and in the forms of motivation, in the activities of the pupils and in their social relations, in the status of the teacher, in the patterns of administration, and in the relations of the school to the local community and the state. In similar fashion the education of every other country is seen to be a creature of its civilization. The more the civilization differs from our own the more obvious is this relationship.

It must be emphasized, however, that organized and deliberate education does not reflect a civilization. Nor is it derived automatically through a process of assembling and analyzing data. Always at the point where an educational program comes into being definite choices are made among many possibilities. And these choices are made, not by the gods or the laws of nature, but by men and women working both individually and collectively—by men and women who often do not quite know what they are doing—by men and women who are moved by all of those forces and considerations that move them in other realms of conduct, by their knowledge and understanding, their hopes and fears, their purposes and loyalties, their views of the world and human destiny. Presumably a given society at any time, therefore, might formulate and adopt any one of a number of educational conceptions or programs, each of which would obviously be an expression of a conception of its civilization. But each would also be stamped by the special qualities of the men and women who framed it. These men and women in turn would be authentic, though not exclusively authentic, products of their civilization.

The formulation of an educational program is thus a creative act, or rather a long series of complex creative acts. It is a threefold process embracing analysis, selection, and synthesis. It always involves choice among possibilities, and even decision as to what is possible. It likewise involves the affirmation of values and the framing of both individual and social purposes. Inevitably education conveys to the young responses to the most profound questions of life—questions of truth and falsehood, of beauty and ugliness, of good and evil. These affirmations may be expressed in what an education fails to do as well as in what it does, in what it rejects as well as in what it adopts. In its organized phases it is deliberately designed to make of both individual and society something which otherwise they would not and could not become. The launching of an educational undertaking is therefore a very serious business. It is one of the most vital and responsible forms of statesmanship. It throws whatever power it represents to the support of one rather than another conception of civilization. And in so doing it supports one rather than another conception of man.

A Great Education Always Expresses a Great Conception of Civilization. There is no quick and easy road to a great education. There is no simple device or formula for the achievement of this goal. Such an education cannot be derived from a study of the process itself, nor can it be found in the interests of children or in any number of "great books." It can come only from a bold and creative confronting of the nature, the values, the conditions, and the potentialities of a civilization. An education can rise no higher than the conception of civilization that pervades it, gives it substance, and determines its purpose and direction.

At this point the democracies are challenged by the totalitarian states and movements of our time. In each case the leadership has formulated a conception of life and destiny of great power and appeal. That the champions of human freedom cannot accept any one of them and must in fact repudiate them all is of course taken for granted. The Fascist conception of a master race or people destined to rule the world under a divinely appointed leader is too horrifying to contemplate. Likewise the Communist conception of a revolutionary elite dedicated to the task of liberating all oppressed peoples, through the medium of dictatorship and violence, terror and fraud, cannot satisfy us. But we should realize before it is too late that the totalitarian conceptions have shown themselves in our time to possess vast power to arouse and enlist the energies and loyalties of the young. If the democracies are to triumph in this struggle for the minds and hearts of men, they will be compelled to derive from their civilizations conceptions of equal power.

At no time in our history have we as a people recognized clearly the obvious and fundamental truth that a great education for America must express a great and authentic conception of our civilization. Individuals now and then, to be sure, have caught a glimpse of this truth. It was grasped most generally perhaps in the heroic period of our national history, in the later years of the eighteenth century that marked the launching of the Republic. The American Philosophical Society, founded in 1743 and led successively by Benjamin Franklin, David Rittenhouse, and Thomas Jefferson, offered a prize of one hundred dollars in 1796 for the best essay outlining a "System of liberal Education and literary instruction, adapted to the genius of the Government of the United States." Some of the best minds in the country took part in the contest. The essays presented were fresh and original, obviously reflecting a consciousness of the historical significance of our bold venture in popular government. Unfortunately, though they constituted one of the high points in the history of educational thought in America, they seem to have had little effect on the practices of the period.

During the nineteenth century the idea of the development of an education expressing a great conception of our civilization appeared from time to time. But curiously enough, except for an occasional native social radical, the proposals came generally either from foreign travelers or from naturalized American citizens, probably because they could see the novel and challenging features of our institutions more clearly than those who were familiar with them from birth. Of the visitors from abroad, as we have noted, George Combe was most articulate. Of American citizens by choice Francis J. Grund and Francis Lieber, both of German origin, were outstanding. But in the middle of the century a Connecticut-born educator, Edward D. Mansfield, author and public servant, in his *American Education* advanced something of the argument of the present volume. Here is the substance of his thought:

If America has presented any thing new to the world, it is a new form of society; if she has any thing worthy to preserve, it is the principles upon which that society is instituted: hence it is not a Grecian or a Roman education we need—it is not one conceived in China, Persia, or France. On the contrary, it must have all the characteristics of the American mind, fresh, original, vigorous, enterprising; embarrassed by no artificial barriers, and looking to a final conquest over the last obstacles to the progress of human improvement.

In the present century, amidst a vast amount of irrelevant, superficial, and escapist educational discussion, research, and experimentation, the question of the relation of education to civilization has slowly forced its way into the arena. More than a generation ago, in 1899, John Dewey published his *School and Society*. From this volume and subsequent works by the same author and from the studies of American civilization by Charles A. Beard and others, there stems a vigorous movement for educational reform and reconstruction. Increasingly attention has been given to the role of the community and the culture in the educational process, to the importance of relating the school and all educational agencies to the ongoing life of society. And in more recent years, probably because of the crisis facing mankind and free institutions, we have become more and more conscious of the value and meaning of democracy for education. But unfortunately much of our discussion has tended either toward the abstract and the universal or toward the immediate and the local. At its best our approach has been incomplete and partial. The time has arrived to relate our thought about education to the whole sweep and substance of our American civilization—its history, its finest traditions, its present condition, and its promise.

We Must Proceed Without Delay to Develop a Great Conception of Our Civilization.   The age now unfolding, to repeat, is the most critical age of our history. We face deep troubles at home, powerful revolutions and counterrevolutions abroad, unprecedented responsibilities in the world, a future of almost limitless possibilities for good and evil. In the decades ahead our democracy may be transformed into some form of totalitarian despotism or it may march from triumph to triumph and fulfill gloriously and nobly the historic promise of America.

Our first responsibility as educators is to formulate on the foundations of fact a living and challenging conception of American civilization. We must ask ourselves in all soberness what is to be the course of our democracy. Only when we have answered this question, and answered it magnificently and powerfully, will we be in a position to draw the broad outlines of a great education for our people in the coming years. If we can find no answer, or if we find a mean and feeble answer, our education, however efficiently it may be conducted, will at best be mediocre and uninspired. And if we find a narrow, exclusive, and bigoted answer, the people of the world may come to regard the development of America into the mightiest power of the earth as one of the foremost tragedies of history. We must fashion a conception of civilization that will respect the rights of all nations and champion the cause of human liberty at home and before the world. Such a conception should provide the source of an education for the American people that would prepare them to discharge with honor and strength the heavy responsibilities which history has placed firmly on their shoulders.

We shall begin this task in the present volume with a broad inquiry into the historical and geographical bases of our civilization. Without getting lost in details, we shall strive to set forth the great and profoundly characteristic strands of our heritage which seem to have meaning for the emerging age. The resulting synthesis will of course embrace elements of faith and affirmation as well as elements of fact.

* * *

William O. Stanley

William O. Stanley, who was born in Sedalia, Missouri, in 1902, received the bachelor's degree from Baker University in 1936 and the Doctorate of Philosophy from Columbia University in 1951. He taught at Columbia University and the University of Illinois. During his career, Professor Stanley has been a consistent proponent of the Social Reconstructionist philosophy of education. In the following selection, Stanley examines the theme of educational confusion and crisis.

* * *

Nevertheless, no thoughtful educator can deny the patent truth of the most serious, if not the most vociferous, criticism that has been urged against American education—that it is a patchwork of unrelated subjects containing within itself neither a unified intellectual outlook nor a consistent system of moral values. It must be admitted that a candid examination of educational practices will reveal with startling clarity that the public school has no unifying purpose or objective, and that it rarely, except in an isolated course here and there, makes any attempt to develop in its students either a social or personal philosophy. Instead, it is marked by a bewildering variety of more or less unrelated, and often conflicting, objectives operating through a multitude of discrete courses or subjects.

Despite the severity of this indictment of American education, it is merely the expression of the common judgment. From the layman's point of view, Dorothy Thompson asserts that education is characterized by "too little intellectual discipline and too much information about too many things, wholly outside the frame of any standards or point of reference." "Student thought," she continues, "is for the most part of an ephemeral and superficial nature. They

Reprinted by permission of the publisher from William O. Stanley, *Education and Social Integration.* (New York: Teachers College Press, © 1953, by Teachers College, Columbia University), pp. 19–25.

know a great deal about a great many things. But their education
has given them neither a personal nor a social philosophy."
Miss Thompson's strictures are confirmed by the sober judgment
of able students of American life. A great American president and
scholar, Woodrow Wilson, observed as early as 1907 that "with all
our teaching we train nobody . . . with all our instructing we educate
nobody;" and James Truslow Adams, easily one of America's most
distinguished historians, has recorded as an obvious historical fact:

Education, by which we had thought to keep the electorate competent for
self-government, was breaking down because we had no scale of values and
no real objective in our educational system. For the masses, at best, it had
become a confused jumble of "book learning" that gave them neither values
to strive for nor that knowledge and intellectual training which might have
been of help in understanding the complexity of the forces with which they
had to deal intelligently.

The professional educator is, if anything, even more caustic. One
may read from the pen of able scholars, who have devoted their
lives to the cause of education, that the school displays "a sorry
confusion of purposes;" that it "undertakes to provide a 'good'
education, without any clear notion of what such education would
be like if it could be had;" that the "most striking fact about the
higher learning in America is the confusion that besets it;" that
"everywhere in Western civilization education is in a state of
confusion;" that "no sound or consistent philosophy, thesis, or
principle lies beneath the American university today;" that "by any
reasonable audit secondary education for the masses is bankrupt;"
and that "the outstanding characteristics of educational philosophy
in the present generation have been superficiality, fickleness, and
instability." Clearly, as Professor Dewey has said, "the problem as
to the direction in which we shall seek for order and clarity in
education" has now become "the most important question facing
education and educators today."
Not unnaturally, the public and even some professional
educators have become impatient with this state of affairs. But the
achievement of order and clarity in education, as an able observer of
the contemporary educational scene has wisely suggested, will not
be materially advanced by mere indictments unless the indictment
penetrates to the heart of the condition responsible for the confusion
in thought and in practice which characterizes American education.
It would be easy, as it is natural, to place the primary blame upon
"the mediocrity of educational leadership," "the incompetency, the

inertia, and timidity of the educational profession," or the "pernicious influence" of some philosophical or educational theory with which we do not agree. But to yield to this impulse is to obscure both the extent and the gravity of the crisis which confronts American education and to conceal the basic causes that have created it.

One fact is clear. The present condition in education is not due to lack of discipline in the public school, to the inadequacies of any educational method, or to the complacency, ignorance or incompetence of the educational profession. Nor can it be cured simply by more subject matter or by greater emphasis upon the mastery of subject matter. The confusion in American education, as the previous discussion has revealed, is not a confusion in the methods or procedures of teaching but of the fundamental purposes of education. The heart of the complaint against the public school is that it does not embody a way of life, that its activities are not guided by any consistent system of intellectual and moral values, and that it does not instill in its students an abiding faith in any social or personal philosophy.

The record, moreover, clearly demonstrates that educators have for some time been fully aware of the gravity of this criticism, and that they have made persistent effort to deal with the situation which evoked it. Rarely, if ever, in the history of education has there been a greater interest in the social purposes and function of education. For considerably more than a decade a flood of educational criticism, diagnosis, and prescription has poured in an ever-increasing volume from the printing presses of the nation. No significant aspect of educational theory or practice has been ignored but even a cursory review of this vast literature will reveal that the greater part of it has been primarily concerned with the social ends of education. "It has been scarcely possible," writes one student, "to pick up a professional journal of education without finding some reference to, if not a feature article on, the relation of the schools to society and the processes of social change."

Unfortunately, this prolonged and intense discussion, while it has undoubtedly served to reveal significant differences and to clarify important issues, has not culminated, as yet, in a formulation of the social purposes of education which has either commanded general consent or released concerted action. On the contrary, it has been characterized by a flock of divergent proposals and by a multitude of claims and counter claims which have exposed deep cleavages of opinion, in the public and in the profession, respecting both the basic moral and intellectual principles which should underlie educational order and the social ends which that order should serve. It is, of course, precisely this failure to achieve substantial consensus that has prevented significant educational reform. The urgent necessity for such reform is clearly understood by a large proportion of American teachers and school administrators; what is not clear is the nature of the reform required and the direction which it should take. Under such circumstances there is but little cause for surprise, however much there may be for regret, that both teachers and administrators, confronted as they are with a multitude of conflicting philosophies and a host of divergent proposals, have tended to seek a degree of order and security in the traditional routines of school life.

The crux of the problem raised by the persistent criticisms of American education, therefore, is to be found in conflicting conceptions of the type of character that the school should seek to develop and of the kind of personal and social philosophy that it should undertake to encourage. This fact is highly significant, for it indicates that the primary educational problem of our times is the confusion and conflict with respect to the basic intellectual and moral norms of public education. It indicates, also, that the first task of the student of educational philosophy is to discover the cause of this deep-seated cleavage in the very foundation of educational thought.

A pregnant clue to the source of this crisis in educational theory is to be found in the fact that ultimately, as Professor Benne has brilliantly argued, the bearer of educational authority is not the schoolmaster, but the community. The contours of education are inevitably molded by the culture of the community which it serves; its philosophy and objectives are invariably framed with reference to the ideals, the aspirations, and the needs embedded in the culture. Nor is it necessary to seek very far to find the reasons for this fact. To educate is to act, and to act involves both preferences and consequences. Since the preferences which it embodies and the consequences which it entails are necessarily reflected in the character of those subjected to its discipline, education (whatever else it may be) is inescapably a moral undertaking. It is, moreover, a political as well as a moral affair. For the public school is a social institution not only in the sense that it is supported and maintained by the state but also in the more forcible sense that the moral and intellectual choices inherent in education are inevitably social choices which necessarily entail significant social and political consequences. Ultimately, the foundations of the state rest upon the character of its citizens; and to mold the character of the young, by the very nature of the case, is to shape the ideals, the aspirations, and the conceptions which underlie social and political action. All education, therefore, consciously or unconsciously, implies some social philosophy, and promotes in effect, if not in intent, one political ideal rather than another. To say that deliberate education does, and of necessity must, embody within it some conception of public welfare and that it invariably induces far-reaching social and political consequences is not to assert that the public school is, or should be, controlled for narrow political ends. In a democracy, at least, the exact reverse is true. But it does imply that fundamental questions as to the purposes which the school shall serve and the kind of character which it seeks to build cannot be wholly separated from the major problems of social policy which dominate the society in which the school exists.

Hence, the definition of the ends of education is not merely an intellectual and a moral problem; but in its widest and most inclusive sense it is also a social and a political problem. More than two thousand years ago Plato and Aristotle recognized, as a fundamental principle of statecraft, that the adaptation of education to the form of government is everywhere the best guarantee of the permanence of constitutions. This principle has subsequently been fully confirmed by the great masters of education and political science alike, including that remarkable generation of political philosophers and statesmen that laid the foundation of our nation.

Consequently, no society will be, nor can any society afford to be, indifferent about the underlying and controlling conceptions which determine the education of its children. The definition of the final objectives of education in any society, therefore, is not, and will not be, left to the exclusive determination of professional educators.

Further, the educator is himself the product of a culture, typically of the society in which he functions as educator. No more than other men has he escaped its pervasive and molding influence. Undoubtedly, as with other men, the cultural pattern is, in detail, reflected through the glasses of his personal and occupational experience, but he shares in common with all other members of his society the aspirations and ideals, the standards of judgment and methods of thought, and the ways of thinking, acting, and feeling which form the core of the culture that has nourished him. His conceptions of the nature of education and of the purposes which it should serve, therefore, while undoubtedly conditioned by the history and tradition of his profession and by his personal and occupational experience, are shaped by the common standards and conceptions of his culture. Indeed, since these standards and conceptions necessarily form the basic structure of his mind, he will almost invariably interpret both the educational tradition and his personal experience in terms of his culture inheritance. In the last analysis, as noted above, the controlling ends of education are not determined by professional educators. But if the educational profession were granted unlimited freedom to shape the objectives of education, their formulation would reflect the basic conception of standards, and values of their society.

Hence, it may be confidently asserted, as a necessary corollary of the principle that educational philosophies are rooted in the culture of a particular people, that there will be little doubt or confusion about the fundamental purposes of education in a society that possesses a clearly defined and commonly accepted standard of public welfare. In such societies, the basic objectives of education are assumed and taken for granted, not debated and questioned. There may, indeed, be no dearth of educational problems and controversies but these controversies will rarely, if ever, centrally involve the underlying and controlling ends of education.

A babble of voices concerning the fundamental purposes of education, therefore, is an almost certain indication of deep-seated social confusion and conflict. The implication is clear. The root cause of the patent confusion in American education, in all probability, must be sought in a wider and deeper confusion in the social, moral, and intellectual perspectives of the American people.

This hypothesis is reinforced by another consideration. For it must be admitted that the American public school, except possibly for the nineteenth century liberal arts college with its ideal of the Christian gentleman, has never consciously inculcated a way of life.* But that is simply to say that the American public school, until recently, has been primarily a peripheral institution concerned with the imparting of special knowledges and skills, leaving fundamental education in the hands of the community, the church, and the home. This arrangement, while probably never wholly satisfactory, undoubtedly functioned reasonably well as long as the American community embodied a unified and consistent social and personal outlook. The very fact that the public school is now persistently criticized on every hand because it has failed to develop in its students a consistent personal and social philosophy is, in itself, powerful evidence that the community, church, and home are no longer successfully performing this essential task. This conclusion, in its turn, is confirmed by the fact, cited elsewhere in this text, that

---

*Except incidentally, as in the case of the moral content of the McGuffey reader.

competing group interests and perspectives have in large measure replaced the unity of persuasion and outlook characteristic of the nineteenth-century local community. It may be readily admitted that these arguments do not conclusively demonstrate the existence of widespread confusion and conflict in the basic normatives of the American people. They do, however, suggest that the educational philosopher or statesman interested in the establishment of an integrated and consistent system of educational objectives must seriously explore the hypothesis that the present confusion in education is the reflection of confusion and conflict in the intellectual and moral foundations of public policy. They suggest, also, that if the hypothesis is confirmed, order and clarity in education, pending the development of a new social consensus, can be obtained in our time only as the school undertakes to deal, in some way, with the major confusions and conflicts in the basic normatives of the American people.

FURTHER READING

Brameld, Theodore. *Toward a Reconstructed Philosophy of Education.* New York: Holt, Rinehart, & Winston, Inc., 1956.

Counts, George S. *The American Road to Culture: A Social Interpretation of Education in the United States.* New York: The John Day Company, Inc., 1930.

_____. *Dare the Schools Build A New Social Order?* New York: The John Day Company, Inc., 1932.

_____. *Education and American Civilization.* New York: Bureau of Publications, Teachers College, Columbia University, 1952.

_____. *Education and the Foundations of Human Freedom.* Pittsburgh: University of Pittsburgh Press, 1962.

_____. *The Prospects of American Democracy.* New York: The John Day Company, Inc., 1938.

_____. *The Schools Can Teach Democracy.* New York: The John Day Company, Inc., 1939.

_____. *The Social Foundations of Education.* New York: Charles Scribner's Sons, 1934.

Gutek, Gerald L. *The Educational Theory of George S. Counts.* Columbus, Ohio: Ohio State University Press, 1970.

Stanley, William O. *Education and Social Integration.* New York: Bureau of Publications, Teachers College, Columbia University, 1953.

ten

EXISTENTIALISM

Since World War II, there has been a pronounced interest in Existentialist philosophy. This interest has extended into educational philosophy, where a number of theorists, such as Harold Soderquist, Van Cleve Morris, and George Kneller, have elaborated the educational implications of Existentialism.

EXISTENTIALIST PHILOSOPHIZING

Philosophers who have attempted to extrapolate the educational implications of Existentialism have encountered serious difficulties. Kneller has indicated that Existentialism, embracing a number of differing views, is not a systematic philosophy in the traditional sense.[1] It is rather an act of philosophizing that permeates various philosophies.

In its simplest terms, Existentialism is a way of viewing and thinking about life in the world so that priority is given to individualism and subjectivity. It is not concerned with the problems of constructing an architectonic or systematic philosophy. In abandoning building a metaphysical system, the Existentialist seeks to examine man's persistent doubts and problems from the perspective of the individual human being. Existentialist involvement calls for individual philosophizing about the persistent human concerns of death, life, love, and meaning. Existentialists accept the premise that man lives in a world which exists

---

1. George F. Kneller. *Existentialism and Education.* New York: John Wiley & Sons, Inc., 1966. p. 19.

as a brute fact of life. This world which man inhabits is really an indifferent world. While it may not be antagonistic to human purposes, it is nonetheless devoid of meaning. In this world, each man is born, lives, chooses his course, and establishes the meaning of his own existence. Among the key sentiments which can be found in Existentialist philosophizing are: (1) man's existence is taken for granted as a given condition of experience; (2) individual self-definition or authenticity is asserted by making those choices which create a meaningful life; (3) the basic educational task is that of stimulating each man to become aware that he alone is responsible for creating his own meaning and self-definition.

THE CRISIS OF TWENTIETH CENTURY MASS SOCIETY

Existentialism's rise to popularity coincided with the evaporation of nineteenth century positive optimism. Since the world wars, there has been evidence of a profound malaise in the western world. Although defining and isolating the causes of western anxiety are beyond the scope of this book, some comments might be made about certain trends in mass society which work to depersonalize and dehumanize the individual. Although incoherence and conflict have plagued man throughout his history, the rise of technological society has aggravated the feeling of alienation. A crisis attitude has been induced partially by man's attempt to deal with the consequences of mass production and mass consumption produced by the industrial and technological revolutions. The industrial revolution introduced innovative mechanisms which facilitated efficient production and supply and demand. The logic of the machine age and the efficiency of the assembly line require that machine parts be both standardized and interchangeable. When a machine part wears out, it can be replaced by an identical part which fits the machine and allows it to function properly. The logic of interchangeable machine parts was gradually extended to individuals in society. The individuals associated with the corporate and productive industrial –technological complex have become functioning parts of the corporate mechanism rather than persons. In a massive but efficient corporate society, individuals are designated by the roles which they exercise. When such functioning individuals wear out or become obsolete, they can be discarded and replaced by other standardized individuals who have been trained to perform the same function.

Although the industrial revolution and the resultant rise of an industrial–technological society have reduced scarcity at the subsistence level in terms of quantitative goods and services, there have been debilitating effects on the qualitative or humane dimension of life. While life has become materially more secure, the rise of a massive industrial technology has contributed to the feeling of anxiety because the person is not really necessary to the process. The end result of the rise of industrial–scientific–technological society is to minimize the individual's significance as a person.

The rise of mass production–consumption systems, technological society, and scientific engineering attitudes has produced an urban, corporate, and mass society. At the root of the mass society is mass production, which creates mass housing, communications, media, and entertainment. The thrust of the corporate structure and its subsidiaries is to either ascertain and to satisfy the average man or to persuade him to prefer certain goods. In gearing its energies to satisfying the needs of the average man, the corporate structure caters to the needs of a standardized human being. The capacities of the technological complex are geared to standardizing production. As a consumer and as a citizen, the private man is rendered into a standardized public man whose needs, desires, and wishes can be measured and quantified. While the industrial –technological processes have liberated man from the perils of a subsistence economy, they have also forced him to conform to a standardized life.

The public life has been extended into what was once the private preserve of man's life, where as a person he could create a unique life style. As the impersonal forces of industrialization and standardization work, they isolate the unique elements in man's life and detach them from the realm of meaningful activity. Uniqueness is then labelled as eccentricity rather than as the means of achieving self-definition. Success is measured quantitatively in terms of power or possession. Standardization objectifies, quantifies, and reduces man to an object or a functional adjunct of the corporate mechanism.

The corporate and standardized features of mass society are not restricted to economic, political, and social life, but have also been extended into education. The larger technology of corporate industry and advertising has encouraged an educational technology and technocracy which seek to emulate the efficiency of the business world. The engines of mass production based on the factory system and the assembly line caused the demise of the entrepreneur and craftsman. Assembly line logic has extended into the educational complex, as schools attempt to apply the logic and techniques of mass production to education. Although the urban and corporative society educates greater numbers of students than ever before, it does so in large buildings which resemble educational factories, producing a standardized product. The maintainance of a massive and corporate structure requires managerial and engineering elites who apply their planning and administrative expertise to the problem of efficient production. The managerial cadres of administrators found in corporate industry also have their counterparts in the educational administrators who form the bureaucracies of school systems. In seeking to educate or to train large numbers of students in massive educational complexes, educators have sought to devise methods designed to render the learning process more efficient. Educational technology, or innovative media, has entered the school. Teaching machines, televised instruction, multimedia instructional packages, and standardized tests are only a few of the various aspects of educational technology that have been introduced to make instruction efficient in the vast educational complexes of the mass society. Large class sizes, impersonal bureaucracies, and little student–teacher contact have resulted from the extension of impersonality into education. However, it should be emphasized that neither the industrial–technological corporate society nor its educational counterpart is the product of sinister conspiracy. They arose as a consequence of social change and altered lifestyle caused by a transformation in basic economic activities from a rural to an urban society. In education, the advocate of Existentialism seeks to reduce the impersonalization that has affected schooling in the twentieth century and to assert an "I–Thou" relationship between the teacher and the learner. Although disagreeing on particulars, Existentialists share a common commitment to reshaping the human situation to encourage the highest, freest, and most genuine assertion of human personality.

REJECTION OF PHILOSOPHICAL SYSTEMS

As a philosophy, Existentialism rejects not only the architectonic metaphysical systems associated with such traditional philosophies as Realism and Idealism, but it also denies the Experimentalist's exclusive reliance on the scientific method. Denying universals, absolutes, and categories, Existentialists distrust the philosophic systems which seek to construct an all-encompassing world view which categorizes human experience according to conceptions of antecedent reality. Such philosophical systems are based on affirmations of an antecedent reality which exists prior to man's entry on the world scene. According to the traditional views, man enters, is assigned a place in the world, and is expected to conform to reality. In such systems, man is defined or catalogued as having a role or place in reality. For example, Aristotelian natural realists assert the existence of an objective order of reality which is independent of human plans and purposes. Man, as a part of this reality, has an assigned place in it. Man, a rational being, possesses an intellect and naturally seeks to know. The descriptive assertion of man's rationality leads to a prescription according to which man ought to act or behave rationally. The Existentialist objection to the Aristotelian premise says that if reason is asserted as the primary element in the definition of man, then there is no genuine freedom in the human condition. If reason is a constituent and determining part of human nature, then man cannot really choose reason as a value. In contrast, Existentialists assert that man is a choosing and valuing animal who can reason if he so chooses. The Existentialist sees life as too varied, complex, confused, and unpredictable to be arranged in neatly structured philosophical categories.

Dewey's Experimentalist educational philosophy emphasizes both the scientific method and shared human association. It stresses the individual's ability to use the empirical procedures of science as the exclusive means of establishing tentative truths. Experimentalism also asserts the individual's ability to participate in meaningful group interaction. Although Dewey believes that the individual gains freedom through group association, some Existentialists find the "like-minded" group to be a coercive agency in which the individual is subordinated to the group will. The group can overwhelm the individual who is forced to comply with the group's decisions and dictates.

Anti-Scientific Reaction   The era of modern society was made possible by the application of science to industrial processes. The modern era is characterized by an emphasis on science as the means of attaining truth and of solving problems. The scientific method deliberately minimizes the subjective and the value-laden. Personal wishes, preferences, and prejudices are not allowed to interfere with scientific objectivity. The demand for scientific objectivity has led to the quantification of human experience. But while quantities are measurable, qualities are not. Social science, sociology, social psychology, and behavioralism, which seek to examine man in objective terms, are derivatives from science. The result of science has been the objectification of man, and his reduction to an object that can be weighed, measured, and evaluated. In its behavioral aspects, the scientific method has had the impact of a reductionism which seeks to analyze man by breaking down the quality of human experience into a number of measurable and quantified responses.

EXISTENTIALIST ASSERTIONS
Existentialism's basic premise that "Existence precedes Essence" asserts the primacy of human subjectivity.[2]   Man first arrives on the world

2. For a clear and very readable treatment of Existentialism's educational implications, see Van Cleve Morris, *Existentialism in Education*. New York: Harper & Row, Publishers, 1966. My treatment of the basic assertions of Existentialism relies heavily on Morris' excellent book.

scene and then begins to define himself. Any and all philosophizing begins with an existing being who is aware of his own existence. Man's awareness of his own existence puts him in a position of being his own "essence-maker." Through individual, personal, and subjective choice making, man defines himself. Man, however, finds that he is a victim of a paradox. Since he is an individual, he is unique. His uniqueness is of value in the world. However, at the same time, each man lives in a universe which is indifferent to his existence. Man's awareness of his own existence also implies a coordinate awareness of nonexistence. The possibility of his own nonexistence is the source of profound anxiety. Despite the fact that his existing carries with it the ever present threat of nonexistence, man must work out his own definition in a meaningless universe.

Thus the basic thrust of Existentialist philosophizing is to portray man's struggle to define himself through choice. Traditional philosophies, theologies, and group-centered sociology have all looked to the world to provide man's reason-for-being. These views, which see man as some part of a system, have defined him as a constituent element in a structure which gives him his purpose for existing. In contrast, Existentialism asserts that man's purpose is not found in the metaphysical, theological, or sociological structure of the Universe. Man is responsible for making his own values.

For the Existentialist, the basic philosophic issue is that of valuing and choosing. Values are not posited in some conception of a metaphysical or sociological antecedent reality. Values result from personal choices. Man, a baseless chooser of values, creates and frames his own values. In a purposeless universe, only man can have purposes. There is no universal criterion that can be used to measure values. Man has to choose and cannot escape from choice.[3]

The quest of an Existentialist life and education is for an authentic man who is free and is aware of his freedom. He is aware that every choice made is an act of personal value creation. The authentic man knows that his own definition can never be determined by anyone or anything that is outside of the self. The struggle for authenticity involves being aware of the personal responsibility for choice, of creating alternatives, and of choosing without the intervention of a moral arbiter that is external to the self.

A basic problem for the Existentialist is posed by the relationship of the individual self to other persons and agencies. In experience, the person encounters other persons that seem to be like him. The encounter between the self and the other person leads to a fear that the other will objectify and threaten his freedom. Or the other person might

---

3. Morris. *Existentialism in Education*. pp. 31–53.

"functionalize" or "instrumentalize" him by using him as an instrument to accomplish his purposes. Functionalization is a special threat in the context of the industrialized mass society. The productive processes of a technological society, dependent on mass production and mass consumption, are highly organized according to the logic of interchangeable, standardized, and specialized functioning parts. When the premise of interchangeability is extended to social organization, it leads to the construction of a society that is planned and organized according to some pattern of social engineering.

The mode of organization and decision making in a mass society is beyond the control of the individual, and the person becomes lost in intricate networks of organization and managerial bureaucracy. Thus, the society itself can exercise a limiting influence on a person's search for authenticity. The person can choose to accept or conform to social norms and patterns, or he can reject and revolt against these patterns. The crucial question for the individual's authenticity is his free choice of either conforming or rebelling. The inner-directed, authentic man seeks to make his choice upon his own baselessness as a value creator. The other-directed man allows other persons to make choices for him and seeks to escape the reality of recognizing that choice is still his own responsibility.

The era of mass society has been criticized as being an age in which people are reluctant to become personally involved with other people. The tendency to be aloof personally stems from a fear that the encounter with another person will lead to the objectification of the self. Although such objectification is a risk that accompanies encounters with others, it does not necessarily follow that the other person will objectify the one who is encountered. The I–Thou relationship is fragile and delicate; there is the constant risk that the Thou may be made into an object or a function. Morris refers to friendship as meaning that one has encountered another person and has not treated his subjectivity as a function or as an object.[4] Friendship refers to a subject-to-subject, or an I–Thou relationship.

COERCIVENESS OF MODERN EDUCATION

The American educational tradition, based on the common school conception of Horace Mann and Henry Barnard, conceived of schooling as an instrument in building an American community in which common knowledge, values, and loyalties were fostered. The public school idea

4. *Ibid.,* pp. 69–78.

was designed as an instrument to fuse varied racial, social, ethnic, religious, and economic groups into a common national identity. The common language and curriculum, associated with public school education, was a means of achieving national integration. While it served the aims of nation building, the public school was often coercive of individuality and of diversity.

It has already been mentioned that educational systems in mass society tend to emulate the larger corporate structures and in so doing depersonalize the teaching–learning relationship. There is also another sense in which formal education can impede personal authenticity. The various subdivisions of professional education, such as educational psychology, methodology, measurement, and evaluation, draw heavily from the social sciences of psychology, sociology, and political science. Emulating the physical sciences, these various social sciences seek to predict behavior. Instruction is structured according to behavioral objectives so the degree that behavior has changed can be measured. Such a conception of learning views the learner as a social object or phenomenon and elicits responses which are quantified and rendered into measurable statistical and otherwise standardized responses.

Contemporary American education has become highly group-centered as a result of the progressive educator's stress on shared activity in learning situations and because of the dominance of educational psychology theories that emphasize social acceptance and adjustment. The aims of socialized education are such objectives as learning to cooperate with others, functioning successfully in group situations, and working as a learning team or committee. According to group-centered educational theories, the individual becomes more effective and efficient as he identifies with and participates in group activity.

Existentialist educators are critical of overemphasizing the group. In the midst of crowds, man is still lonely and anxiety-ridden. Indeed, some group-centered learning situations may become so coercive of the individual that personal authenticity may be sacrificed to the pressures of like-minded consensus. When a person freely chooses to join and to participate in a group, then there are still opportunities for authentic choice. However, most group-centered situations in schools are not freely chosen. Learning situations organized around groups should be such that they permit and encourage the opportunities for individuals to assert the unique aspects of their personalities.

TOWARD AN EXISTENTIALIST PEDAGOGY

While not specifically defining an Existentialist education, Morris does assert that education should cultivate an "intensity of awareness" in the learner. This means that students should recognize that as individuals they are constantly, freely, baselessly, and creatively choosing. A student who is aware would recognize his responsibility for determining how he wants to live his own life and for creating his own self-definition. According to Morris, "If education is to be truly human, it must somehow awaken awareness in the learner—existential awareness of himself as a single subjectivity present in the world."[5]

In developing the outlines of an Existentialist educational psychology, Morris has referred to a "pre-Existential" period of human growth and development and to the "Existential Moment."[6] During the pre-Existential period of early childhood (prior to puberty), the child is not really aware of his human condition; he is not yet really conscious of a personal identity and destiny. The pre-Existentialist school years are the time of elementary education when the child acquires the tool skills of reading, writing, arithmetic, and communication. He also learns some physical, recreational, and social skills. Dependent upon the particular mode of curricular organization, the child learns some subject matter and problem-solving skills.

Morris uses the term *Existential Moment* to refer to the situation that arises when the individual is conscious of his presence as a self in the world. As an Existentialist educator, Morris is most concerned with education during and after the Existential Moment. Although the experiencing of the Existential Moment varies with the individual, most people experience it around the time of puberty. The Existentialist Moment is characterized by an insight into one's own consciousness and an awareness of one's presence in the world and the responsibility for conduct. For some, the Existential Moment is a period of great power and thrust; for others, it is a time when one seeks to escape adult responsibilities and return to childhood's innocence.

Existentialist education would begin in the years of the junior high school and continue onward through the senior high school and the undergraduate college. The thrust of such an education would be to awaken and to intensify self-awareness. It would be most concerned with affective experience, with those elements of experience which are subjective and personal. It would encourage involvement in situations that are conducive to the knowledge that one is involved in questions of good or bad and right or wrong.

EXISTENTIALIST EPISTEMOLOGY

Existentialist philosophy asserts that the individual is responsible for defining his own life. In much the same manner, Existentialist epis-

---

5. *Ibid.,* p. 110.
6. *Ibid.,* pp. 111–16.

temology assumes that the individual is responsible for his own knowledge. Knowledge originates in and is composed of what exists in the individual's consciousness and feelings as a result of his experiences and projects. Human situations are comprised of both rational and irrational components. The validity of knowledge is determined by its value and meaning to the particular individual. An Existentialist epistemology emerges from the recognition that human experience and knowledge are subjective, personal, rational, and irrational. While the Experimentalist emphasizes the exclusive use of the scientific method of problem solving, the Existentialist prefers to probe man's aesthetic, moral, and emotional concerns as well as his cognitive ones.

Morris has described Existentialist epistemology as being "appropriation."[7] Knowledge about the world is always partly subjective in that the knower must choose to know and decide to do something with his knowledge. Appropriation is a personal choosing, taking, and adopting of something that is available to all. Any truth must first be seized and appropriated by a learner.

The concept of the epistemology of appropriation might be made clear by using an example from a class in history. Suppose, for example, that a history teacher makes the simple factual statement that the Republican Party nominated Abraham Lincoln for President in 1860. Such a statement is based on data present in the historical record, which includes primary and secondary sources. There have been historical interpretations of the impact of Lincoln's nomination on the course of American history. Some historians have alleged that Lincoln's nomination and subsequent election caused the southern states to secede from the Union, led to the Civil War, produced the Emancipation Proclamation, and indeed, led to Lincoln's assassination. Nevertheless, it is possible to state that an event occurred, that Lincoln was nominated for President in 1860. There appears to be a subject matter which is objective and external to both the teacher and the student. Certainly, neither the teacher nor the student was responsible for Lincoln's nomination.

The important aspect of the fact of Lincoln's nomination lies in the meaning that the student wishes to give to this historical event by appropriating it into his own consciousness. Each student creates and becomes personally responsible for giving meaning to the event. It might be worthwhile to consider a few of the possibilities for meaning that such a simple historical event might have for students. Lincoln's nomination might be seen as a personal victory for a self-made man who was able to overcome the hardships of his frontier youth to become the nation's leader. In contrast, it might be seen as a result of Lincoln's expediency in dealing with the issue of Negro slavery in his earlier

---

7. *Ibid.*, pp. 120–22.

election campaigns for Senator from Illinois. In the case of such an historical event, the past takes on the meaning that is determined by the learner's present choosing and project.

The learning which flows from an epistemology of appropriation is very different from the conception of learning which an Essentialist might hold. An Essentialist teacher would probably assert that the important thing is to master the facts and the authoritative historical interpretations that are based on them. The learner's own personal interpretation would be valuable only insofar as it agrees with the facts and the interpretations of learned historians. In contrast, the Existentialist would see the historical event as a springboard for the students to examine their own lives in the light of history.

AN EXISTENTIALIST CURRICULUM

Such school subjects as history, literature, language, mathematics, and science are taken for granted as existent or "given" bodies of knowledge and sources of information. School subjects are merely tools for the realization of subjectivity. The crucial learning phase is not found in the structure of knowledge or in the organization of the learned disciplines, but rather in the student's appropriation of the subject—his willingness to choose and give meaning to that subject. In the "Existentialist" curriculum situation, the student is an actor who gives meaning to that subject which he appropriates, as he incorporates it into his own being and interprets it according to his own project. As Morris says, "Whatever experiences in the school are most likely to arouse the individual's own private way of looking at life will be elevated to first position in anything that might some day be called an Existentialist school."[8]

The curriculum, actually the script which the student uses as the vehicle of interpretation, contains both cognitive and normative elements. The factual, descriptive, and scientific bodies of knowledge of the cognitive dimension represent the givens of the phenomenological order. The normative or attitudinal dimension is comprised of those curricular areas which are primarily ethical. Such humanistic studies as history, the arts, literature, philosophy, and religion are especially rich sources of ethical values.

The arts, the areas designed to cultivate aesthetic experience, include such forms as music, drama, dance, creative writing, painting, and the film. The aim of aesthetic education, according to the Existentialist, is not to imitate the style of selected model artists, although these might be studied, but rather to stimulate aesthetic expression. In the aesthetic

---

8. *Ibid.*, pp. 124–25.

dimension of education, the teacher's role is to evoke and to stimulate the learner's sense and desire for aesthetic expression. Although not knowing what the learner will create, the teacher provides a variety of creative media so that the learner will have the raw materials from which to create his own art object. The learner uses the various media to portray the world as he views it in his own consciousness and to produce the art work that comes from the center of his private experience. Literature and the humanities would occupy a major area in an existentialist curriculum. Literature is useful and relevant for awakening the learner to the significance of choice making; it reveals the various strategies for choice making that have been used in literature to portray basic human concerns. By using literature, the drama, and film, the learner places his capacities for feeling at the disposal of the author. The vicarious involvement of the learner in the basic human questions of love, death, suffering, guilt, and freedom are excellent means for portraying the human condition and for finding personal meaning in an apparently indifferent world.

Like literature and the other humanities, history is a forceful vehicle for examining how men in the past have faced and answered the recurrent human concerns. Historical study, as viewed by the Existentialist, is not so much a matter of establishing cause–effect relationships or examining the origin and development of particular civilizations. Indeed, no universal or enduring generalizations can be deduced from historical study. History's use is in illuminating man's past and in presenting contemporary men with alternative hypotheses as to how life might be lived in the present. Kneller dramatically states, "The student should therefore learn to handle his history with passion, personal thrust, and in the manner of a stage director, talentedly manipulating the human scene, with all its heroes, villains, and plots."[9]

EXISTENTIALIST TEACHING AND LEARNING

Although the Existentialist educator may choose to use a variety of educational methods, none of these methods should be permitted to obscure the basic personal I–Thou relationship that ought to exist between the teacher and the learner. The Socratic dialogue is an appropriate method for those following an Existentialist perspective in education. The dialogue questions the learner so that he becomes conscious of the condition of his life. Unlike the Idealist's use of the Socratic

9. Kneller. *Existentialism and Education.* p. 130.

dialogue, the Existentialist teacher does not know the answers to the questions which he poses. Indeed, the best kind of question would be that which could be answered only in the student's own subjectivity. In an Existentialist methodology, the teacher is to stimulate an "intensity of awareness" in the learner by encouraging the quest for a personal truth by asking questions that concern life's meaning. It is the teacher's task to provide the climate and the situation for the expression of the student's subjectivity. It is only the learner who can come face to face with his responsibility for self-definition. The creation of the "intensity of awareness" is as much the learner's own responsibility as it is the teacher's. Such an awareness involves the sense of being personally involved in the ethical and aesthetic dimension of existence.

CONCLUSION

Unlike the systematic world views presented by the more traditional philosophies, Existentialism seeks to free man from the fetters of a categorized and systematized universe. Emphasizing human subjectivity, personal freedom, and individual responsibility, Existentialism boldly portrays man as a being who exists in a world in which he alone is responsible for his self-definition. In the quest for authenticity, each man must become aware that he makes his own values and creates his own essence without recourse to an external criterion.

An Existentialist education would be one which holds human freedom as its paramount concern. Stressing individual subjectivity, the Existentialist educator seeks to cultivate a sense of self-awareness and responsibility in students. By making significant personal choices, it is the student alone who can forge his self-definition. The goals of such an education cannot be specified in advance nor can they be imposed by the teacher or the school system. Each man has the responsibility for his own education.

SELECTIONS

Van Cleve Morris

Professor Van Cleve Morris was born in Kalamazoo, Michigan, on June 28, 1921, and was educated in the local public schools. He did his undergraduate work at Oberlin College in Oberlin, Ohio. He attended Teachers College, Columbia University, where he received the M.A. degree in 1947 and a doctorate of education in 1949. He has taught philosophy of education as a member of the college of education of the University of Georgia and as a member of the staff of the graduate school of education at Rutgers University. He is now Dean of the college of education of the University of Illinois at Chicago Circle.

Among Professor Morris' writings are such books as *Philosophy and the American School* (1961), *Existentialism in Education* (1966), *Modern Movements in Educational Philosophy* (1969), and *The Anti-Man Culture* (1971), written with Charles Tesconi. In the following selection, Professor Morris discusses the question of baseless choice.

*   *   *

To return to the basic problem of the search for values by which a life can be lived, it is clear that this search must be undertaken not in the outside world of "moral advisers"—philosophical, ecclesiastical, or conventional—but rather in the phenomenon of my own choosing. I may discover in the choices I make—in the things I do, in the attitudes I hold, in the goals I set for myself—I may find in these seemingly prosaic phenomena the values I have been trying to identify. In this sense, my problem turns out to be deceptively simple. Whereas I have been instructed in the past to look for values outside my choices, I discover under the aegis of Existentialism that the whole problem lies much closer at hand, i.e., in the way I individually live my life. My values turn out to be nothing more or less than my choices.

And the point of the argument is just this: that in living my life I simultaneously identify those values on behalf of which I am living it. In the act of existing, I choose every day what I am going to do, what I am going to say, what goals I am going to pursue. To choose is, by definition, to set one alternative ahead of another; to choose therefore is by definition an exercise in valuing, an exercise in favoring this over that. It is in the very act of choosing that I point to those values which I wish to have listed on my "eligibility application" for recognition. But the difficulty is that I never know whether this or that choice is the one I should have made because there are no "advisers"—other than those I myself *choose*—to justify my choices. I am ultimately the author of all my choices, and since I can turn to no certifying agency to finally justify me in my choices, I discover that my choices are without base. They cannot be justified. I am a baseless base of values.

I therefore find myself in an odd position: I am the starter of the value-making process, but as such I myself have no base to stand on that can tell me which values I should start making. In this role,

From pp. 39–41 and 46–53 in EXISTENTIALISM IN EDUCATION by Van Cleve Morris.
Copyright © 1966 by Van Cleve Morris. By permission of Harper & Row, Publishers, Inc.

then, I discover that I am the originator, the inventor, the *creator* of values. And the oddness of my position is that I cannot help it; I cannot escape being the creator of values, for I cannot escape choosing in the world. Even to choose not to choose is a choice. I am therefore "condemned," as it were, to the peculiar role of being a chooser and therefore a value creator in the world.

In Chapter 1, you will recall, we had occasion to note that man is the being by whom "existence" and "nothingness" come into the world. We have now advanced to a point in our argument where we can see the practical meaning of this assertion, namely, that man, as existential chooser, is the being by whom values come into the world. *In the act of choosing, man brings values into being.*

In this sense, then, we may say that man creates something out of nothing. Consider a man in a situation. Before he chooses a course of action, there are no values in that situation; there is merely a value-free set of circumstances, a region of "pure phenomena." Once he chooses, he brings something new into existence: a "way of responding" to that situation. It does not matter what advice he got antecedent to his responding. In the final act he was the one who either accepted or rejected the advice, he was the one who responded, and he therefore was the one who brought a value into being in that situation. The value was not there before; now it is. And he is responsible for its being there.

Many people, even sophisticated intellectuals, somehow find the idea that man is the creator of values too extreme to believe. But is it really so bizarre? We may find anticipations of it in certain forms of the philosophy of Pragmatism. Listen, for instance, to William James. In the chapter on religion in his *Pragmatism—A New Name for Some Old Ways of Thinking* he says that theologians and philosophers like to think of themselves as supremely rational; they like to insist that there must be reasons for contending that this or that object really exists in the universe. Then he says,

But if one talks of rationality—and of reasons for things, and insists that they can't just come in spots, what kind of reason can there ultimately be why anything should come at all? Talk of logic and necessity and categories and the absolute and the contents of the whole philosophical machine-shop as you will, the only real reason I can think of why anything should ever come is that some one wishes it to be here.

What this means is that even ontologies, of which the philosophical community has a great number, are constructed out of the "wishes" that are "fathers to the thoughts" of professional philosophers. If someone wants an ultimate principle, e.g., Jesus' *love* or Schweitzer's *life* or Marx's *dialectical materialism,* "to be here," it shall be here. So it is with values. If someone wants to introduce a value into the world, all he has to do is to live according to that value, and presto, it is "here." . . .

One may well ask at this point why we may not all be called unwitting Existentialists. If we are all subject to the "human condition" of essencelessness, what is so remarkable about Existentialism as a philosophy if its message is merely to announce this fact to us? The answer lies in a curious but exceedingly important wrinkle of semantic logic concerning the word "choice." It is this: Choosing implies awareness on the part of the chooser. One cannot, by definition, "choose unawares." Hence, by definition, it is impossible to be an "unwitting Existentialist."

Suppose an individual finds himself in a situation and pursues a course of action which we shall designate A. Then his friend comes along and inquires why he didn't choose another course of action, B. To which our man says, "Oh, I never thought of B." Now, was he choosing between A and B? Of course not. Indeed, he was unaware of choosing at all. He was even unaware of possibly doing nothing, a course we may now designate as C. In this situation, then, although various alternatives were theoretically present, they were not present in his imagination, and therefore no choosing actually took place.

It is thus with our social and moral life. We are individually confronted in every waking moment by phenomenal situations to each of which there are numberless responses we could give. But the responses must rise as possibilities in our imagination before they can play a role in genuine choosing. Moreover, no choice is possible unless the free subjectivity is aware of the act of choosing as such. This means, therefore, that the free subjectivity must be aware not only of alternatives but of the *act* of considering alternatives before one may say that choosing is actually taking place. So-called "blind choosing" is a contradiction in terms. Pinning the tail on the donkey while blindfolded is not "choosing" where to put it. Nor does sheer impulse qualify as choosing; blurting out the first thing that comes to one's mind is not choosing. Nor is any mindless stabbing in the dark really choosing. *Guessing is not choosing.* "Choice" means selecting from alternatives in a state of awareness.

The claim that awareness is a necessary condition for choosing is simple common sense. More than that, in the awareness of choosing lies the subjectivity's very freedom! Unless an individual is aware of his act of choosing, he is not a free individual. The obverse of this would be plain nonsense. How could one be free if he were not aware of alternatives—if he had, he thought, only one alternative? To have "only one alternative" is another contradiction in terms. If a putative "alternative" is the only course of action, it is not an alternative at all. And to live without alternatives is to live without freedom, which is why it is so pathetic to hear someone say, "I had to do what I did; I had no alternative." He is either telling a lie or, through an act of self-deception, forfeiting his freedom.

We may summarize, therefore, by saying that awareness, choosing, and freedom are interlocking notions. By definition, they must all be present in the same degree. And they all finally come together in *the awareness of one's own freedom* in the act of choosing.

As it turns out, it is awareness of one's own freedom which helps explain who can and who cannot claim to be an Existentialist. That is to say, what differentiates people, in an existential sense, is the degree to which they exhibit such awareness. And we may now designate this global awareness as authenticity. People differ not in their susceptibility to the "human condition"; alas, we are all equals in this susceptibility. They differ rather in the degree to which they respond to the condition authentically, i.e., are aware of their freedom, aware of their baselessness, aware of their unjustifiability, and hence aware of their personal responsibility for the way they are living their lives. Some people, obviously, are numb to this sense of freedom. They do not see themselves as free agents in the world. Instead they explain their conduct in terms of values not of their own making—their culture, their religion, the expectation of their wife's relatives. What they forget is that they *consent* to those values. And in consenting to them, they in fact adopt those values for their own lives. But they are existentially unconscious; they are not aware that they are in fact consenting to something; they are not aware that they are free not to consent.

It is imperative not to be misled into thinking that the opposite of consent is somehow more existential. This is most certainly not the case. Revolt, rebellion, apostasy are not in themselves the mark of the existential man. Even the man who consents to convention can be the existential man *if* he is *aware* of the act of consenting, and hence of the necessity that he take *personal responsibility* for living his life in a conventional way. Most of us, let us admit, are of the conventional sort. We pull our socks on every morning with the expectation of fitting into community folkways throughout the day. Now, there is nothing particularly reprehensible about this behavior.

What *is* reprehensible is our numbness to the fact that that very expectation is itself a value which we insert into our lives. So long as we do so unknowingly, unwittingly, we are nonauthentic individuals; we are not aware of making that value commitment at sock-pulling time. Multiply the foregoing by all the other moments in life when situations call for the awareness of our freedom to choose our own personal response. The point is not to find the most deviant or bizarre response and to call that the "free" response. The point is to be *aware* of all responses so that when an individual makes his own response, even if it be supremely conventional and prosaically *un-*bizarre, he will know that he has *chosen* something rather than simply fallen into it by necessity. It is the "necessity" people who will kill the human race—those people who say that this or that behavior pattern is required by God, or state, or mother-in-law. The people who say, "I couldn't help it; I had no choice," are the nonauthentics; they do not know they are human.

And who is the authentic? The individual whose example is perhaps beyond the reach of most of us: the individual who is free and who knows it, who knows that every deed and word is a choice and hence an act of value creation, and, finally and perhaps decisively, who knows that he is the author of his own life and must be held personally responsible for the values on behalf of which he has chosen to live it, and that these values can never be justified by referring to something or somebody outside himself.

It is this imperative for *answerability* which is the leitmotif of the Existential argument. But how can we understand it? To whom is the authentic man supposed to be responsible? The answer is deceptively simple, I think, for the sense in which the word "responsibility" is used by Existentialists is precisely that of common speech. When we say to someone that he will be "held responsible" for something, we mean that if anyone should ask, he must be ready to answer for what he has done. The question of who might ask is irrelevant; maybe no one will. But in case someone does, he is to be ready to speak in behalf of his own performance.

Buber has put it this way:

The idea of responsibility is to be brought back from the province of specialized ethics, of an "ought" that swings free in the air, into that of lived life. Genuine responsibility exists only where there is real responding.
    Responding to what?
    . . . We respond to the moment, but at the same time we respond on its behalf, we answer for it. A newly-created concrete reality has been laid in

our arms; we answer for it. A dog has looked at you, you answer for its glance, a child has clutched your hand, you answer for its touch, a host of men moves about you, you answer for their need.

Gabriel Marcel has developed the argument in a somewhat different way. He reminds us of the difference between making an observation and offering testimony. In making an observation, one is quite matter-of-factly speaking about events and phenomena beyond his own skin in which he has only the spectator's interest. But testimony involves observation, and more:

... my testimony bears on something independent from me and objectively real; it has therefore an essentially objective end. At the same time it commits my entire being as a person who is answerable for my assertions and for myself. ... I was present at the time and place of an accident; I can witness that the victim crossed at an island and that the car did not slow down; my testimony will throw light on the event and will help to assess the responsibility involved. I am obliged to bear witness because I hold, as it were, a particle of light, and to keep it to myself would be equivalent to extinguishing it. Can I refuse to attend the trial because of the trouble and the waste of time or because the victim was a stranger to me?—I would be guilty of betrayal, but against whom? Against society? ... against the victim? but betrayal presupposes a commitment and I have no commitment to this stranger whom I have seen by chance. ...
What concerns us is the relation in which the witness stands to the world. ...

I think the relation in which the witness stands to the world may be a clue to the manner in which the free subjectivity assumes personal responsibility for his values. The witness can refuse to testify; he can claim that he didn't see anything or that he has forgotten. The free subjectivity can refuse to feel responsibility for the way he lives his life; he can claim that he can't help it, that he has to live his life that way. In both cases there is a basic dishonesty, a lie. But it is not a lie against another, or against society. It is a lie against himself. For the witness knows that he *did* see something and that he *does* remember it; and the free self knows that he *can* help it, he *could* live his life differently. The pathos is not that the subjectivity has told a lie but that through an "intramural" lie he has wiped out his precious humanness, his freedom.

Awareness of freedom is thus the main project of every life which hopes to be existential. And it must be recognized by now that this awareness requires us to take on a burden not easily carried. It is the burden of *care*. To trade numbness for awareness is to feel the intensity of moral involvement. It is to feel *personally* about life, to feel the meaning of *personal* answerability, to *personally* care about the increase of good in the world.

American society seems to encourage just the opposite mood. Our organization complex is the victory of the *impersonal* social apparatus of the corporation over the individual self. When a colleague gets sick at Rutgers, a Committee on Social Welfare sends him a bucket of flowers and a "get well" card on behalf of the faculty. It's almost like pushing a button on a vending machine: word reaches the committee, a telephone is lifted from its cradle, an order is placed, a messenger runs it over to the hospital, an orderly delivers it to the bedside. When acknowledgment is received from the laid-up colleague and announced in faculty meeting, a soundless wave of relief surges over the group. The impersonal apparatus of the organization has taken "care" of our personal cares; and each of us, potentially capable of being made aware of that person's misadventure, is made numb again by the cold, brutal form of corporate "sympathy."

There is, I think, a developing moral numbness in American life, a growing state of unfeeling in which we lose the sense of personal responsibility for protecting the safety of fragile human values in the close-in, person-to-person human relations that make up the routine of daily life. Instead, "human relations" becomes an objective science and public relations becomes another industry.

A world governed by "human relations" in the abstract sense rather than in the I-and-Thou sense of Buber is a world in which detachment replaces attachment as the leading value. As John Ciardi explains it, the "Playboyniks" who frequent the Playboy Clubs and the "Beatniks" who linger in the coffeehouses actually share a common ideology. They scorn the world of the "square." A "square" is one "who commits affection. . . . Both Boynik and Beatnik . . . are out to play it cool, the first with elaborate accessories, the second without. For both, however, the essential religion is detachment."

In our time, it is too easy to become detached from other men. We increasingly think that Blue Cross can take care of the accident cases, CORE and the NAACP can take care of the Negro's fight for equality, and the Social Security Administration can take care of the weak and dispossessed. It's all so easy. "Care" has been incorporated; it is now a separate branch of public affairs.

Finally, to crown all, Norman Cousins of *Saturday Review,* who is otherwise a fairly sensible man, has come forward with the proposal

that there be established a Society for Individual Responsibility! The
mind boggles at such a suggestion—an organization to get
individuals to be responsible! I can think of no proposal more likely
to arouse Existential nausea, both organic and metaphysic, in the
authentic man.

Absolute Freedom   "Awareness" may be a matter of *degree.* Our lives
are so much governed by reflex and routine it is difficult to say that
anyone is wholly aware of choosing during his every conscious
moment. Moreover, in actual experience we encounter some people
who seem to have more active sensibilities toward the world than
do others; some individuals concern themselves with the world's
troubles while others are less involved. On a purely empirical basis,
then, awareness might be said to be distributed along a continuum.
But in that case freedom itself, since it rides with awareness, must
also be distributed along the same continuum. In a manner of
speaking, it is. But to grant this point may obscure another feature
of Existential freedom which we can ill afford to miss, namely, that
freedom creates its own degrees. An illustration may be helpful.
    After listening to a discussion of the Existentialist's notion of
freedom, someone is sure to ask if I am free to jump over the
Washington Monument. The ingenuousness of his question both
disarms and frustrates the argument, for it reveals an artless density
in the questioner, as if he were expecting Existentialism to announce
that the law of gravity had been repealed and thought he could
score a point by reminding everyone that it had not. Any reader
who feels that this is all Existentialism has to offer is asked to lay
this book aside; the remainder of it will mean nothing.
    I am obviously *not* free to jump over the Washington Monument.
But this limitation may be due to the fact that I am not strong
enough or to the fact that I have set out to do so. But which is
primary? Where does my lack of freedom originate? It originates and
is brought into being by my free choice to make this jump a goal of
my life.

. . . the coefficient of adversity in things can not be an argument against our
freedom, for it is by us—i.e., by the preliminary positing of an end—that
this coefficient arises. A particular crag, which manifests a profound
resistance if I wish to displace it, will be on the contrary a valuable aid if I
want to climb upon it in order to look over the countryside. . . . Without
picks and piolets, paths already worn, and a technique of climbing, the crag
would be neither easy nor difficult to climb; the question would not be
posited. . . . Thus although brute things [like the Washington Monument]
can from the start limit our freedom of action, it is our freedom itself which

must first constitute the framework, the technique, and the ends in relation to which they will manifest themselves as limits. . . . it is therefore our freedom which constitutes the limits which it will subsequently encounter.

Or consider the youngster in school who is told by his guidance counselor that his difficulties with mathematics are going to make it impossible for him to become an engineer. Just why does his lack of mathematical ability limit his freedom? The answer is foolishly simple—because he has chosen to become an engineer. It is his free choice of life goal which suddenly converts mathematical weakness into a limit. Suppose his choice had been "newspaper reporter." Would weakness in mathematics be a limit? Obviously not. It is thus the free choice of the individual which turns circumstances into either aids or limits to his freedom.

But at base, freedom is absolute because it is existential. And this freedom is the freedom to set goals. It is absolute because there are no limits to the freedom to set goals for oneself; there are no goals that one cannot choose. The setting of the goals comes first. Only later is this or that feature of the phenomenal environment recognized as a limit to accomplishing this or that aim in life.

The setting of goals may therefore be viewed as the starting point of value creation, the point at which values first peep through the soil. What then, to return to our opening question, is the practical program of living implied by the Existentialist injunction? I think it can now be stated as the project of waking up to one's freedom, of struggling up from the slumber of numbness and nonauthenticity to recognize that one is the architect of one human life and, through that life, the creator of values in the world.

It is not too early to say that an educational program built on this notion is what we shall call Existential.

*　　*　　*

Maxine Greene

Maxine Greene was born in New York City on December 23, 1917. She received the Bachelor of Arts degree from Barnard College in 1938, the Master of Arts in 1949, and the Ph.D. in 1955 from New York University. She has taught at New York University, Montclair State College, and Teachers College of Columbia University. She edited *Existential Encounters for Teachers,* from which the following selection is taken.

*　　*　　*

Questions inevitably arise. Existential writers are telling about their own personal responses to their own existence; they seem to be

---

addressing other single creatures, particularly those attuned to their own subjectivity. Their concerns seem in one sense cosmic, in another sense desperately private. What do these have to do with the humdrum, organized life of classroom and lecture hall?

"You must change your life," Rilke once wrote, referring to experience with a work of art. Perhaps this is what the existential writer demands of the one who encounters him; but, if so, it must be personal life that is to be changed, not professional attitudes or orientations. The teacher—or the teacher-to-be—who pays heed must acknowledge somehow that his effectiveness, like his authenticity, depends to some degree upon the nature of his personal commitment. He must acknowledge that he cannot live in two domains—private and professional. If he has chosen himself to teach, then teaching must become *his* "fundamental project," his means of creating himself.

There remains the question of the *use* of such an insight. What does the decision to change one's life, to recommit oneself, have to do with what is now becoming known about the teaching–learning enterprise? How is it possible for existential insights to be built into the cognitive structure that the contemporary educator needs? Is it not the case that preoccupation with one's own inwardness will distract one from theory and rational controls?

If there is an answer, it can only be found when the person engaged in teaching seeks it in the actual situations of his life. An answer can only be meaningful when an *individual* arrives at it, an individual who can maintain the vantage point of one intentionally and immediately involved.

In truth, this is the vantage point required for clarifying most educational issues; and it is one too seldom taken. Too often, those who study the subject called "education" consider the processes and phenomena to which that word refers from without. They talk and write about "education" without any feeling of responsibility for what happens in any particular school. This may be appropriate for behavioral scientists, asked to describe the institutional patterns of a society or a group. It may be appropriate, on occasion, for historians and anthropologists.

But the situation of the teacher is as different from these as is the situation of the psychotherapist from that of the statistician. No matter how deliberately, how rationally the teacher guides what happens in his classroom, he personally is involved in it; and almost everything that occurs is affected by his presence there, by his moods and gestures, his expectations and explanations, his responses to those who are trying to learn. A "true," a reliable account of a teaching situation is the one presented from that vantage point, since it is the only one which can take intention into account—the intention of the living individual who is making choices, guiding discoveries, identifying possibilities.

There is a sense, then, in which both an "inner" and an "outer" vision is required. There is a sense in which the multiple facets of the educational process can be described from both perspectives; and when one perspective is taken, the facets seen from the other need be neither eroded nor denied. This means that, if one looks existentially upon the act of teaching—taking choosing into account, and freedom, and being *there*—the strategies devised by the teacher, the tasks he identifies as learning, or the materials he uses, continue to be as consequential and "real" as the physical classroom itself.

It is important to see this after reading existential literature. It is important, too, to think about the ways in which the subjectivity of the teacher may sustain his rationality, and about the ways in which a decision to be intelligent may sustain the struggle to be.

There is no reason, therefore, to suspect dichotomy; there are no necessary either/ors where human existence is concerned. The person who is a teacher may be conscious of his own condition, his own fearful freedom, and at once behave strategically at his work. The major difference between the "inner" and the "outer" lies in the relationship between idea and action in each dimension: one can draw logical inferences from theory for teaching behavior; one can define no implications for behavior in general from encounters with existentialists.

Since this means that we can posit no existential theory or philosophy of education, given or derived, it leads us back to our earlier question: how can we put our encounters to use? We have said that they may move the one who experiences them to renewed consciousness of his life's commitment, but this gives little promise of help, if help is conceived in general, prescriptive terms. The very notion of doctrine is excluded by the existential view. Prescription is excluded by the centrality of free choice. All we can say is what we said originally: if the individual who engages with existential writers is committed to the study of teaching and learning, and to the action which is teaching, he—or she—cannot but see education with new eyes when the reading is, for the moment, done.

And he—or she—can say how it looks after such an experience. Saying, such a person will at least indicate possibilities; and these possibilities may be acted upon by others who are seeking their own vision, their own enhanced awareness of themselves. This, it is hoped, will be the response to the commentaries placed among the foregoing readings. They are personal statements; they are neither deductions nor explications. They were written by one committed to being an educator, and so they have to do with education. But there still exists a world of things to say by the others, the many others, who may also choose to see.

Education, for many people, signifies a process of unfolding. The teacher's function, according to this view, is to make it possible for a child to realize his inborn potentialities, to actualize himself. Whether this is accomplished through deliberate efforts to arouse activity in the child, through the creation of an "educative" environment, or through some non-directive, intuitive approach, the objective is to permit the child to be whatever he has it in him to be. Those who conceive education in this way are those who prize spontaneity and difference, who hope to see a society composed of autonomous individuals, each of whom is committed to his own form of "excellence," all of whom are committed to a common good.

Education, for other people, signifies a process of rearing, of deliberately cultivating certain tendencies and discouraging others, depending upon what the cultural situation demands. The end of education so conceived is productive membership. The individual, properly reared, is equipped with the beliefs, skills, and techniques of thought which are meant to enable him to function adequately in his society. Achieving identity through participation in a culture and a heritage, he is ready to take his place in history. He has been taught, and presumably he has chosen, to act upon values which are communal, to forge in the midst of the many a significant personal life.

Education, for still others, signifies a course of initiation, through which young people are enabled to form the inchoate world of experience by means of the cognitive disciplines and the arts. The primary aim of education, in this view, is to liberate and sensitize young minds for cognition, vision, innovative thought. Properly taught, they will be expected to find pleasure in the subject matters that they will discover as their store of concepts grows and as their perspectives diversify and expand. And, although there will never be an end to their learning, they will be increasingly free and competent when it comes to ordering the substance of their lives.

The emphases shift as the generations pass and the earth turns. In all the important views of education, however, there is concern for the diffuse and multiple energies of the child. There is an interest, always, in the ways in which particular children may be stimulated to learn, in the curricula conducive to the patterns of growth considered valuable, and in the human world where the child will perform his adult tasks.

Clearly there are points of contact between each of these views and the responses aroused by the readings in this book. The integrity of the individual seems central to the view of education as unfolding. Being-in-the-world seems focal to the conception of education as rearing. And those who speak in terms of initiation are concerned with the learner's own responsibility for enlarging his vision and achieving growth.

None of these views, however, seems to summon up an image of the contemporary learner under the conditions of the present age. An encounter with existentialism makes such an imaging crucial for the person choosing himself to be a teacher at this time. The import of "this time," this particular historic moment, cannot be overlooked by the one who tries to see, even for an instant, through an existential glass.

It is *now* that our teaching is to be carried on, *now,* in the second half of the twentieth century. Conscious of the now, we may consider the very process of learning to be a rebellion against the forces which abstract and depersonalize. How, having read what we have read, can we forget what these forces have done to persons? How can we overlook what it means to resign oneself to a "crowd"? We see the individual struggling against the incursions of that crowd when he is a child and when he is grown. We see ourselves as teachers goading him on to "live dangerously" for his own sake, to combat inertia, to take the risks of growth. We see a student choosing to learn only as he commits himself to achieve his own reality, only as he defines his own "fundamental project," which is to act on his own possibilities.

The principle of mere unfolding begins to seem alien, once we confront the obstacles to being: the neutrality of nature, the essential indifference of the world. But we agree that each person must act upon his own possibilities, recognizing them as such. And he must be held responsible for his choice. He must ache to learn and to grow; and we must welcome his aching and unease. We must welcome the anguish he may feel, the guilt before his own refusals. There may be no sin so great as the sin of refusing to become, to be.

Responsible as we are for indicating possibility to him, we know that all we can do is enable him to will his own freedom and make his own choices. As teachers, we can provide curricula rich enough and diverse enough to excite all sorts of youngsters to attempted mastery. We can provide a ground for the "lurch" into teachability. When the individual learner begins moving restlessly, when he shows signs of abandoning formlessness and prereflective "slime," we can acknowledge each small advance he makes, so long as it is in the direction decided on by the youngster himself with the knowledge that he is being given his single chance on earth, that he will never pass this way again.

No matter how many students we have in our classrooms, we will not (having read what we have read) treat the individual as a "specimen." We will not objectify him or make him an object of study, even when we consult the assessments made of what he can do or what he has achieved. Knowing we are "other" with respect to him, we can nonetheless work for encounters with him—for the sake of his authenticity and our own. We may succeed in entering an "I-Thou" relationship; we may dare to engage in dialogue with him and open ourselves to him as he opens himself to us. But we recognize, if we do this, that we are opening the way to tensions and anxieties, the disquietude that is so essential to growth.

We engage in relationships with young people, as with our contemporaries in an effort to release the "single one." No one of our pupils is likely to live as an isolate, not in a world where others are always present; therefore we must make it somehow possible for each to live among those others while remaining authentically himself. He will be threatened constantly by the appraising "look," the stare that demeans and objectifies. His sincerity will be put to the test by the social games he and others must continually play. But classroom situations can be made occasions for strengthening his will to be authentic and free—if, that is, we who teach are willing to open ourselves sufficiently to be *present* there. If we are, if we can stand forth as existing selves while we teach, we can transform our classrooms into exemplary places where presentness and objectivity coexist.

We can exert outselves to see through the eyes of the student "other," to take his perspective, his vantage point, even while we concern ourselves deliberately with objective things. We can, while working with the structures of subject matters, with the tasks that must be performed if our students are to learn, create an atmosphere of intersubjectivity. Tranquillity will not pervade such an atmosphere; the members of the class will not be put at ease. But neither will they be dealt with as objects, cases, specimens. Engaged as subjectivities as well as minds, they may discover the possibility of being with others and at the same time being themselves. They may learn that one is not doomed to be a thing in an objective, public domain, so long as one ventures out of coolness and separateness—so long as one rebels through questioning and forming, and insists on the right to grow.

Continuing to look through an existential glass, we find ourselves affirming the priority of consciousness at every moment of classroom life. It is, however, when we are attending to the fundamental work of teaching—arousing our students to inquiry—that we pay particular heed to that priority.

As we have seen, the child does not begin as a reflective creature. Rather, he relates to the world around him by means of his feelings and moods. He gives rudimentary meaning to things as he touches them and uses them. It is only as he learns to investigate it, to symbolize it in language, to "tell about" what he finds, that he imposes significance upon his environment. Once he begins to do this intentionally, he begins to break with the habitual and familiar; and he continues to break with the "given" as he frees himself for more diversified forming and as he learns to create the orders within which he can decently live.

As teachers, we became concerned not with *what* he knows but with *how* he comes to know, how the truths of the world and of consciousness are revealed to the "single one." We endeavor to keep ourselves and the child in touch with concrete life situations, since these represent the dimensions of the world-to-be-known. The individual comes to know as he achieves appropriate relationships with various aspects of his life situations; sometimes he relates himself as a scientist would to empirical phenomena; sometimes, as an artist would to forms which are deeply felt; sometimes, as a statesman would to the practical strategies of life.

This, too, is an area where dichotomies have no place. The object is not to choose between the intuitive and the rational-empirical, the aesthetic and the discursive, the emotive and the logical. Nor is it to establish priority for one way of knowing above all others. The teacher's concern must be for the way in which each student chooses his relationship with the various situations which arise; for if knowing is conceived as a relationship with a variety of concrete situations, the student will not be likely to take refuge in the propositions of "pure" reason and disembodied intellect. As seeker, as knower, he will be participant. He will construct orders and define meanings as he chooses to do so, as he acts upon and challenges his world.

Only as he chooses can he achieve a continuity of identity and a continuity of knowing. As a free individual, he must take his choices seriously and commit himself in the space he discovers between his limitations and his possibilities. If not, he will flounder "in the possible"; and the project which is his selfhood will become abstract and finally meaningless.

And so we who teach must give him "care" and intense concern. We must foster the freedom that he can attain as he moves dialectically between necessity and fulfillment, between the ineradicable qualities of his particular situation and the thus-far-unrealized capacities which are his. "Cast into the world" though he may have been, the individual has grown up in situations: of slum life, perhaps, of poverty, of parental dominance, of rootlessness. These need not determine him; they certainly do not define him; but they do compose the frame of reference in which his becoming must take place. He cannot make decisions in a vacuum; he cannot define his possibilities if he is unaware of limitations, of necessities.

He is caught in a dialectical movement, therefore, when he acts to learn and to create himself; and, inevitably, he will feel strain, he will suffer as he struggles to become. It is in that suffering, however, that he experiences the pain of willing and the intensity of consciousness which makes a person feel himself to be an existing creature—sharply and painfully alive. And it is in the midst of such intensity that he will be moved to shape values as he lives, to create his "ethical reality."

Values may be arbitrary at some level, but they do not appear in a vacuum. The individual must feel himself to be a distinctive person, confronting negations, caught up in the situations which give content to his life. These situations, as we teachers know, are social and political; they are economic, recreational, religious; occasionally they are situations of love, passion, friendship, faith. And they are, always, temporal situations, conditioned by history and by transiency.

The meaning and the impact of such situations are determined by the individual who encounters them; and one of our commitments as teachers is to enable him to confront them and choose appropriate action when he does. This is another reason for teaching for the widest, most varied perspectives: the young person must be equipped to perceive himself imaginatively in multiple predicaments, against diverse backgrounds. He must be, as he learns, a seeker and a wanderer. He must be adventurous enough to break repeatedly with the conventional. He must image himself in the great reaches of time and in continually expanding space. And at climactic moments of decision, he must experience the "boundary situations," where he can confront the "Encompassing," or the unanswerable, or non-being, or the absurd.

On the one hand, this implies a necessity for the most "general" curriculum, at least in the early years of his life. If he is to relate himself to novel situations as he chooses his future, he must experience himself thinking now like a scientist, now like an artist, now like a strategist. He must be given opportunities to manipulate, to experiment, to hypothesize, to test. He must be offered possibilities, as well, for knowledgeable appreciation of art forms, for vicarious identification with literary figures. He must find himself occasions for appropriating ideas, ideals, visions of possibility from a heritage made contemporary with him.

On the other hand, the prospect of confronting strange situations ought to lead the individual student to rehearse encounters with absurdity. He must not be protected, therefore, from inequity, injustice, suffering, and death—nor from the frequently unanswerable questions to which they give rise. It is only as he confronts the existence of "plague," only as he intensifies his own consciousness of "dread," that he may be moved to commitments which are ethical.

We cannot indoctrinate him with moral regulations if we intend to nurture his freedom. We cannot impose a ready-made value system upon him if we want him to choose himself. We can, however, open the way to the confrontations which will require him to make choices, choices involving conceptions of "good" and "right." In his freedom, then, he will shape a conscience for himself; he will construct a morality. And if the situations of his life (including the ones we have made) permit him to act on the possibilities he perceives, he will commit himself to the moral ideals that he has chosen. Taking responsibility, he will have achieved the hope of meaning at that point; he will have become a rebel for a cause.

This approach to the individual learner is one possible response to engagement with existential thought, as we have said. It is, significantly enough, an approach congruent with the emphasis on intellectual discovery, on autonomous learning, on "becoming" in current educational discussions. In the great centers of curriculum reform, in the offices of subject-matter specialists, in the laboratories of psychologists of learning, men are recognizing that learning is a function of teaching—and that it is an internal process conducted idiosyncratically by an individual. Even where teaching machines are being built and installed, the talk is of differential rates of speed, distinctive styles and rhythms of learning. There is anticipation of a computer center which will make "dialogue" possible for each student in the classroom, enabling him to move by means of his own questions, his own intentions, toward the kind of mastery possible for him.

The educational specialists, of course, have their eyes mainly on conceptual growth and on the subject matter appropriate to each level of development. They stress individual and developmental differences in the interests of efficiency, not because of an "I-Thou" concern. And the very nature of their investigations makes them consider the student as an abstraction, an object of study, rather than as a "fellow creature." This is wholly understandable. In situations where research takes place or experimentation, the existing human person has no place.

This does not mean that he can be obliterated. Surely it ought not to mean that his uniqueness is irrelevant in the other situations of life. As we have seen—as can be seen every day of our lives—this is precisely what young people are protesting, more vehemently than ever before.

There is a profound desire for recognition. There is a need for intense consciousness, for significant and moving experiences, and for the "courage to be" in a mute, indifferent world. Existential encounters cannot satisfy this need; but they may at least make it possible to affirm it. And they may liberate a teacher here and there for becoming and for choosing. If they do, they will serve the most important cause—the cause of life.

FURTHER READING

Greene, Maxine. *Existential Encounters for Teachers.* New York: Random House, Inc., 1967.

Grene, Marjorie. *Introduction to Existentialism.* Chicago: University of Chicago Press, 1959.

Kneller, George F. *Existentialism and Education.* New York: John Wiley & Sons, Inc., 1964.

Morris, Van Cleve. *Existentialism in Education; What It Means.* New York: Harper & Row, Publishers, 1966.

Soderquist, Harold O. *The Person and Education.* Columbus, Ohio: Charles E. Merrill Publishing Company, 1964.

Vandenberg, Donald. *Being and Education: An Essay in Existential Phenomenology.* Englewood Cliffs, N.J.: Prentice-Hall, Inc., 1971.

eleven

PHILOSOPHICAL ANALYSIS

Philosophical analysis, a contemporary movement in educational philosophy, is the examination and classification of the language of both common discourse and scientific expression. Philosophic analysts who are concerned with educational philosophy seek to examine critically the language associated with teaching and learning and with the formulation of educational goals and policies.

This movement differs in its intent and method from the older Idealist, Realist, and Thomist systems which are grounded on metaphysical conceptions of an antecedent reality. The more traditional speculative philosophers attempted to construct world views that systematized all human experience and knowledge into a unitary and systematic philosophy. They sought to discover an ultimate principle or first cause that was the source of all existence. The analysts reject the system building of the speculative philosophers, which they claim has produced only philosophical chaos and confusion. They contend that the so-called systematic philosophies, which were supposed to unify, merely succeeded in dividing the intellectual world into a bewildering variety of conflicting "isms."

As they work to examine, classify, and verify ordinary and scientific language, the Analytical philosophers seek to establish meaning rather than to create new systems. As a means of resolving controversy, the analyst seeks to point out and to clarify the fundamental assumptions of contending points of view. He does this by asking for operational definitions of the terms used. Unlike the speculative philosophers, the analytical philosopher is exclusively concerned with the problem of meaning. He does not consider it to be his function to advise people on life's prescriptive or normative issues. The function of Analytical Philosophy may be examined more clearly by turning to the origins, development, and educational implications of this method of inquiry.

ORIGINS OF ANALYTICAL PHILOSOPHY

G. E. Moore and Bertrand Russell are frequently cited as the founders of the analytical movement in philosophy. Although both Russell and Moore were interested in analyzing the language of common discourse, Russell sought to discover the logical structure that he believed is present within any given language. For Russell, the task of philosophy is to find and formulate the logical rules underlying language usage. In seeking to develop an analytical system of symbolic, or mathematical, logic, Russell sought to understand the nature and meaning of discourse. Russell, in effect, proposed a set of mathematical symbols that represent words, concepts, and propositions which, when processed mathematically, would render solutions that are unaffected by the subjectivism of personal preferences and emotions.

Language analysis was also pursued by a group of Viennese philosophers, the Vienna Circle. Foremost among these philosophers was Ludwig Wittgenstein, who had been a student of Russell. Wittgenstein developed a system of analysis that seeks to establish the meaning of propositions.[1] By constructing a language based on irreducible facts, discourse could be so constructed that it yields true, or verifiable, propositions about reality. The logical positivists, as the members of the Vienna Circle are called, devised a method whereby language can be analyzed according to a criterion of verifiability. They hold that sentences are either analytically true or synthetically true.

Analytical statements are true by virtue of the terms that they contain. An example of such a statement is "$1 + 1 = 2$"; the terms in this statement can be reversed: $2 = 1 + 1$. It is tautological in that it tells nothing beyond that which is already implicit in the meaning of the terms.

Synthetic statements are either true or false because they can be verified empirically. The truth of such statements is not *a priori* (implicit), but is *a posteriori* (discovered afterwards). An example of a synthetic statement is "John weighs 170 pounds." John can be placed on a scale and the assertion that he weighs a given number of pounds can be tested. Or, "The population of the Soviet Union in 1962 was 218,-000,000 persons." This statement can be verified by examining Soviet census figures and can be judged as either true or false. A synthetic

---

1. For a description of the function of analytical philosophy, see Ludwig Wittgenstein, *Tractatus Logico-Philosophicus.* New York: Humanities Press, 1955.

statement is meaningful only when it can be tested empirically through the means of some empirical data or by observation.

The language analyst's assertion that meaningful statements are either analytic or synthetic eliminates a number of statements that do not fulfill the requirements of either category. Such statements as "The world is mind," or "God is love," are not analytical tautologies but bear a superficial grammatical resemblance to synthetic statements. The difficulty with these statements is that there is no evidence that could possibly be gathered to determine their truth or falsity. They are not true by definition. Such statements are neither true nor false; they are literally senseless or nonsense since no empirical data can be found to determine their validity. The meaning of a statement is found in its method of verification. If there is no method of verification, it has no meaning.

If the analyst's principle of verification is adopted, then most traditional philosophy is nonsense. Idealism, Realism, Thomism, and Existentialism all rest upon what the analyst would call pseudo-propositions. When an Idealist states that "Reality is Mind," or when a Realist asserts that "Nature contains a moral law," or when an Existentialist claims that "Existence precedes Essence," they are all talking nonsense. They are making claims that cannot be verified by sense or empirical tests. For the analysts, the metaphysical disputes that comprise so much of the history of philosophy are without meaning. Philosophy should not spin castles in the air, nor build world views, nor construct metaphysical grand designs. It should deal with the consequences of man's language.

The statements that are found in much of metaphysics, theology, and even the social sciences merely express opinions or personal preferences. When one says that "Democracy is the best political system," or that "There are three persons in God," or that "Man is Rational," he is merely voicing his preference that this is the way things should be. Of course, individuals have the freedom to make such statements about politics, religion, and philosophy if they wish to do so. But such statements are not genuinely meaningful for anyone else because they will not have the same meaning for another person. They are emotive statements, personal preferences, or poetical statements rather than factual statements. Although teachers are certainly free to use such language, they should make certain that they do not confuse poetry, preference, or prejudice with fact.

The relevance of Philosophical Analysis as a method of working with language can best be found by an examination of the conditions of modern life and education that make such an approach a useful one. It should be remembered that the Analysts do not wish to create a new philosophical system. They are concerned with eliciting the meaning of our language.

SEARCH FOR ORDER AND CLARITY

Modern man, living in a highly specialized technological society, finds himself beset by problems of understanding and communication. Specialization has resulted in the rise of specialized occupational and professional groups, each of which has developed its own language. While they are able to communicate with each other in the languages of their specialities, specialists are often unable to communicate with those who are outside of their areas of specialization. The analytical philosopher sees his role as aiding in the communication of people across their specialties.

Modern man also lives in an era in which the channels of communication have been multiplied through the development and sophistication of such various media as the newspaper, journal, radio, and television. Indeed, modern man is bombarded by a steady flow of information and just plain noise. Although the explosion in communication systems has quickened the pace of national and international communication, one may raise the serious question of whether men are any better related to each through meaningful communication than they were in the past.

The problems of understanding and communication are not only those of sorting out messages received by the various media. They are also problems of deciphering and of separating image from reality. Modern man's political, social, and economic life, in a mass society, is largely determined by those who seek to shape his opinions and influence his decisions. In the United States, candidates for public office have frequently had their images made so they have an appeal on the television screen. The modern television commercial that appeals to emotions rather than to critical intelligence conveys its message through the form of slogans. Political and consumer campaigns become a matter of selling a product rather than conveying the information that would appeal to sensible people. When it is broadly conceived rather than pedantically structured, the task of the analytical philosopher can be one of helping to defuse the propaganda and to examine the substance of the many slogans that beset modern man.

Professional education is a discipline which has borrowed much from the various social sciences of anthropology, economics, psychology, sociology, and political science. Like these social sciences, the language used in educational writing is frequently an uncritical blending of the descriptive or factual elements and prescriptive ones. The analytical philosopher can perform a service by clarifying the language used in teaching and learning situations. He can examine the formulation of educational policy statements and make their meaning clear to educators. He can do this if he dispels the jargon that frequently besets writing in education and in the other social sciences.

Education is related to broad personal, social, national, and international purposes. In the United States, education has always been in the public domain and has always been subject to public scrutiny. The school is a major cultural agency which has social and political consequences. In twentieth century America, educators and educational institutions—from the elementary school to the university—are subjected to social, economic, and political pressures. School administrators and teachers find themselves in situations that are no longer solely pedagogical but that have social, political, and economic implications. Contemporary educators have not only to deal with questions of curriculum and methodology—with alternative approaches to the teaching of reading, mathematics, social science; they also must be concerned with issues of community control of schools, racial integration, foreign policy, and other crucial sociopolitical issues. Educational issues frequently become framed in slogans that lend themselves to propagandizing rather than to learning. Among the terms that the popular media have used to portray educational controversies are "quality education," "meaningful education," "relevant and irrelevant education," "generation gap," "confrontation," and "new left." Analytical philosophers can do much to examine such terminologies so that they can become useful to understanding educational controversy rather than confusing it.

Professional educators, too, need to clarify their language so that their own terminology becomes meaningful rather than a pedantic jargon. If one surveys educational literature for the past decade, the following terms can be found in hundreds of articles—"learning by doing," "creative expression," "culturally disadvantaged," "culturally different," "urban child," "meaningful life experience," "life adjustment," "equality of educational opportunity," "quality education," "education for international understanding," "education for freedom," and countless other catchy phrases. Again, the analytical philosopher can perform a service by reducing such phrases either to sense or nonsense.

Further, much lecturing and writing about education has been homiletic and has taken the form of preaching in which the speaker or writer seeks to inspire younger teachers. Such discourse, which is often merely the statement of a person's educational preferences, is often presented as a descriptive and factual account of the actual conditions of schooling. Examples of such preaching often take quite different forms. For example, lectures by superintendents and principals on such subjects as the "Duty of the Teacher," "Professionalism and Teachers," and

"Educators and Change" are often notorious examples of prescription in the guise of description. Perhaps a more serious source of uncritical language and ideas is the deluge of anecdotal paperback books which consist of a narrative about the success of a beleagured teacher who succeeds in winning the hearts and then the minds of students in a difficult teaching situation, usually an inner-city school attended by disadvantaged youth. The key to success is usually found in the narrator's concern for his students and in his use of creative methods. The villains of such pieces are usually members of a pedantic and unsympathetic faculty and a bureaucratic school administration. While such anecdotal accounts may make interesting reading, they, too, need cool and critical examination.

Simply stated, then, the Analytical philosopher can serve education by encouraging the critical examination of its language and terminology. He can aid by exploring the verbal interactions that go on in teaching–learning situations. He can help to clarify the goals and policies that direct the course of education.

CONCLUSION

Philosophical Analysis is a new method of working with language and of trying to clarify and establish its meaning. It does not attempt to create new philosophical systems or world views that embrace all of man's experiences. Through the methodology of empirical verification, the Analytical philosopher seeks to classify our language statements. He dispassionately seeks to disentangle description from prescription. His service to education has been that of examining the concepts, language, and strategies that deal with the formulation of policies and the elaboration of teaching–learning strategies.

SELECTIONS

Jonas F. Soltis

Dr. Jonas F. Soltis was born in Norwalk, Connecticut on June 11, 1931. He received his Bachelor of Arts degree from the University of Connecticut in 1956, his Master of Arts in teaching from Wesleyan University in 1958, and his doctorate in education from Harvard University in 1964. He teaches philosophy and education at Teachers College, Columbia University. His books include *Seeing, Knowing, and Believing* (1966), and *The Language of Visual Perception: Psychological Concepts in Education* (1967). In the following selection, Professor Soltis uses language analysis to examine the concept of education, values in education, and educational aims.

*   *   *

In a way, I suppose, students and teachers may feel that to ask such ridiculous questions as: "What is meant by 'education'?, 'subject matter'?, or 'learning'?," is like asking a housewife to reflect on the meaning of "cooking," "cleaning," or "washing dishes." After all, the ordinary terms which refer broadly to what students and teachers actually do each day of their lives hardly seem to call for an unnecessary strain of brain power, especially when there are unsettled and perplexing problems which place more immediate demands on their time.

Nevertheless, I would argue that many of us who at least have been students, if not yet teachers, would be hard pressed if asked to spell out in simple words the ideas which are contained in such ordinary concepts of education as teaching, learning, or subject matter. Yet these very concepts are basic to any thought or discussion about education. Furthermore, I believe that such an attempt to explicate these ideas would invariably result in the unveiling of nuances of meaning which we unconsciously assume in our discourse and in our actions as students or teachers. As a result, we would not only become more sophisticated and careful in their use, but would also gain a deeper insight into education as a human endeavor in which all men take some part sometime in their lives.

Definitions of Education   I do not mean to give the impression, however, that few if any ever try to *define* education. From A to Z, from Admirals to Zealots, we find almost everyone, in or outside the field of education, not only ready to talk about education, but also most willing to offer *his* definition of education. In fact, it is not *a* definition of education which is lacking. Part of the problem involved in talking and thinking about education is the variety of definitions and views of education which is offered to us on all sides. We are, in fact, literally bombarded with a multitude of competing definitions which tempt us to choose among them, to mix an eclectic set of fragments from them, or even, rejecting them all, to find *the* "real" definition of education for ourselves.

Under this barrage of definitions, however, a very crucial assumption is frequently hidden. That is, we assume that there is *a* definition of education or *the* definition of education. We act as if we were searching for that definition much as a big game hunter

Jonas F. Soltis, AN INTRODUCTION TO THE ANALYSIS OF EDUCATIONAL CON-CEPTS, 1968, Addison-Wesley, Reading, Mass. pp 1–7.

searches for an elephant, confident that he will recognize one when he sees it and net himself a most valuable trophy. But what if we are really more like a sincere but misguided centaur hunter who, even with his fully provisioned safari and his gun kept always at the ready, nonetheless will never require the services of a taxidermist? Could it be that *the* definition of education is more centaurlike than elephantlike? Is there such a thing as *the* definition of education?

Instead of directly attacking this last question, let us turn to an examination of the idea of definition itself in an attempt to throw a bit more light on this problem of defining education. In his book, *The Language of Education,* Israel Scheffler discusses three types of definition, the stipulative, the descriptive, and the programmatic. Although in practice these may not always be found in their pure forms, Scheffler ascribes certain distinguishing features to each.

A stipulative definition is one which is *invented,* or better perhaps, one which is given by its author who asks that the defined term be consistently taken to carry this stipulated meaning throughout his discussion. One might, for instance, say, "Look, I know that there are various definitions and views of education currently in vogue, but in order to keep things straight, I shall use the word 'education' throughout my discussion (speech, article, book, etc.) to refer only to that social institution created and maintained by a society in order to perpetuate certain aspects of its culture through purposeful teaching and learning." This is a stipulation. It is saying, "This is precisely what I will mean by the word 'education' regardless of what others may mean."

The essence of a descriptive definition, however, is not a stipulative assertion that such and such will be *my* use of the term, but rather, such a definition purports to adequately *describe* what is being defined or the way in which the term is used. In effect, a dictionary attempts to provide descriptive definitions, and thus, not infrequently, we find several definitions given for a word because many words have multiple descriptive meanings. However, the dictionary does not offer us several to choose from in any arbitrary way; it provides us with the different ways in which a word *is* used in differing contexts. Consider the word "run," for instance. It has many definitions, each of which is appropriate only to some specific context. If John *runs* a footrace, we expect him to physically propel himself as fast as he can, whereas if he *runs* for president such a description of his activities seems quite inappropriate. Moreover, if Susan's stocking *runs* or if the colors in her dress *run,* we have two more different and noncompeting descriptive definitions of the word "run" exemplified by application to different contexts. In the first, "run" means an unsightly separation of woven strands, whereas in the second, we use "run" to mean a spreading and mixing of dyed colors. Thus, there is not *a* descriptive definition of the word "run," but many definitions describing the appropriate uses of that word in differing contexts.

We should now notice that the stipulative definition of education offered above was also a descriptive definition in that it referred to our use of the word "education" to describe that special institution created and maintained by a society in order to transmit aspects of its culture by means of purposeful teaching and learning. There can be no doubt that this definition describes *a* very broad use of the term "education," which ranges in proper application from the formal schooling which takes place in a complex society such as ours to the informal setting of an aborigine village where a father teaches his son to make weapons or to hunt game. But this is only *one* of the descriptive definitions of education. There are also contexts in which the term is used quite appropriately even though purposeful teaching and learning are not integral characteristics of such situations.

One example of such a context would be the autobiographical account of one man's "education" to be found in *The Education of Henry Adams* or, more generally, the kind of thing referred to by the phrase "being educated in the school of hard knocks" (education by means of experiences had and suffered through and not by some function of purposeful teaching and learning). It would seem foolish to argue that the first definition referring to purposeful teaching and learning is the true definition since both usages are proper descriptions of what we mean by education in differing contexts. To stipulate that the first definition will be used throughout a discussion is not to legislate out of existence the second nor any other proper descriptive definition. Stipulation of this sort is merely a device or convention for keeping things straight. Moreover, it seems that we should have little room for real disagreement over definitions which are descriptive, and, if we did, it should not be too difficult a matter to resolve them in some objective way. After all, the objective description of anything is but an attempt to be true to what is in the public domain.

Why, then, we might wonder, do we have such varying and competing definitions of education which lead to, or form the basis for, vehement disagreements over educational aims? Could it be that they are but competing stipulations? It hardly seems possible that we should have such quarrels over stipulations about how a term is to be used temporarily, but should it not be equally true that it would be foolish to argue over the correctness or "truth" of descriptions of how a term is *in fact* used in different contexts? An answer, I think, can be found in Scheffler's notion of the *programmatic definition,* a definition which tells us overtly or implicity that this is the way things *should* be. To say what something *should* be is quite different from trying to say what it actually is *or* merely saying, "I'll use *this* to mean *it* for now." But more than this, definitions of education which are programmatic are frequently mixtures of the *is* and the *ought,* of the descriptive and the prescriptive. Consider, for example, a definition of education which might be offered as "the means by which a society attempts to develop in its young the capacity to recognize the good and worthwhile in life."

Here we not only have the descriptive element of education as an instrument or institution of society, but we also have a program suggested. Implicit in this definition is the prescription or normative statement: "Education *ought* to develop in people the capacity to recognize the good and worthwhile in life." Notice also that there appears to be another auxiliary prescription embedded in the above definition which is: "Once the educated person is able to recognize the good and the worthwhile, he ought to pursue it in life."

Now, on a moment's reflection, it should not be surprising to anyone that definitions of education frequently contain, either explicit or implicity, certain programs or norms or prescriptions or values. After all, education is a human enterprise in which people attempt to do something in a purposeful, thoughtful, and careful way. Acting purposefully with some end or procedure in mind is, in one sense at least, holding that end or procedure as valuable, good, desirable, etc. Just as the doctor tries to cure his patient because he values health over disease, so the educator tries to produce open-mindedness in his students because he values that quality over the closed mind. We could enumerate many other instances of the way in which certain values enter into purposeful human activities, but at this point that hardly seems necessary. Instead, let us turn back for a moment to the questions which we left earlier regarding *the* definition of education.

With these ideas about types of definition squarely before us, it seems that, at the very least, our definitional question is ambiguous. In asking if there is such an animal as *the* definition of education, we might mean: Is there any such thing as *the* stipulative definition of education, or *the* descriptive definition, or *the* programmatic definition? Seen in this light, our question now really constitutes three questions. To recognize this seems to be a step in the right direction, for if someone were to answer "Yes" to the original question, we wouldn't know which question was being answered affirmatively.

We might do well therefore to examine just what an affirmative answer might mean in each case. In terms of a stipulative definition, an unqualified "yes" answer would seem foolish, for the very essence of stipulation is the freedom of pronouncement. Logically any definition could serve as the stipulated definition of education, and so here, obviously, a request for *the* stipulative definition of education either is out of place or deserves a negative response. (Unless, of course, a stipulative definition had already been given, and one was merely asking to refresh his memory or check his notes.)

But if the question is asked with the intent of seeking *the* descriptive definition of education, an affirmative response implying that there is one and only one true descriptive definition would be puzzling at this stage of the game, for we have already seen the possibility of multiple descriptive meanings of "education" for varying contexts and purposes. But let's say that we could produce a definition (such as "education is learning," perhaps) which would fit all appropriate contexts; such a definition might possibly please all, but by the same token it would say very little to anyone. (One can learn to be a burglar as well as to be a lawyer, or learn from experience as well as from a teacher.) In essence, then, we might be able to produce a single, all-purpose descriptive definition of education. It may very well leave us cold, though, for when we ask for *the* definition of education it hardly seems that what we have in mind is such a broad, indiscriminate, and nonevaluative use of the term.

Rather, and this is the intended upshot of this discussion, a search for *the* definition of education is most probably a quest for a statement of the *right* or the *best* program for education, and as such is a prescription for certain valued means or ends to be sought in educating. In my view, asking for *the* true programmatic definition of education is very much like asking "Which is *the* true religion of man?" or "Which is *the* true flavor of ice cream, chocolate or vanilla?" I juxtapose ice cream and religion not to be irreverent, but merely to indicate the range and complexity of value questions in education. Some, like ice cream flavors, are pure and simple preferences of taste, while others, like religion, are firm beliefs around which some grounds and rational superstructures have been developed. To argue that the school should teach good manners is closer to the "ice cream" end of the continuum, but to advocate the school as the prime teacher of democratic values is closer to the "religion" end. Whether students should be taught to rise whenever the principal enters the room is a less crucial value decision to make than to decide whether or not they should be taught to be responsible and loyal democratic citizens. While there can be no doubt that decisions of value must be made in education, and that some will be most crucial decisions, to make them *by definition* seems hardly to be the most rational approach. Important questions of value require critical and careful judgment, not merely solution by definitional fiat.

*   *   *

Israel Scheffler

Dr. Israel Scheffler, who was born in Brooklyn, New York, in 1923, received his Bachelor of Arts degree in 1945 and his Master of Arts degree in 1948 from Brooklyn College. He was awarded a Ph.D. in 1952 from the University of Pennsylvania. He is a member of the school of education of Harvard University. His publications include *The Language of Education* (1960) and *Philosophy and Education* (1966). In the selection which follows, Professor Scheffler analyzes the cognitive terms knowing and believing in relation to the educational terms learning and teaching.

*   *   *

How are the cognitive terms *knowing* and *believing* related to the educational terms *learning* and *teaching?* The question is not as simple as it may seem, and our consideration of it in this section will introduce several points of relevance throughout our discussions.

We might, as a result of attending to certain simple cases, suppose *learning that* to imply *knowing that.* If a student, for example, has *learned that* Boston is the capital of Massachusetts, we should normally say he has come to *know that* Boston is the capital of Massachusetts. Yet we cannot generalize from such cases that whenever a person X has learned that Q, he has come to know that Q.

Consider a student in some distant age or culture in which disease has been attributed to the action of evil spirits. Such a student may well have learned from his tutors that disease is caused by evil spirits, but we should not be willing to describe him as having come to know that disease is caused by evil spirits. *He* may, to be sure, have been perfectly willing to say "I *know* that evil spirits cause disease," but nonetheless *we* will not wish to describe him as having come to know that evil spirits cause disease, for we should then ourselves be admitting that evil spirits *do* cause disease. For us to say that some person knows that such and such is the case is, in general, for us to commit ourselves to the embedded substantive assertion that such and such *is* the case. Where such a commitment is repugnant to us, we will accordingly avoid attributing knowledge, though we may still attribute belief. In the present case, we will deny that the student in question has come to know that evil spirits cause disease, but we may safely describe him as having come to believe that evil spirits cause disease, for our belief attribution does *not* commit us to the substantive assertion in question. In our earlier example, by contrast, since we were perfectly willing to agree that Boston is the capital of Massachusetts, the stronger attribution of knowledge to the student did not commit us to an embedded substantive claim we found repugnant.

We are thus led to contrast *learning that* and *knowing that* in the following way: To say that someone has come to know that Q, commits us generally to the substantive assertion represented by *"Q."* For example, if we say of a pupil that he has come to know that Cornwallis surrendered at Yorktown, we are ourselves committed to the substantive assertion, "Cornwallis surrendered at Yorktown." To say that someone has learned that Q, does not so commit us; we are, in general, limited only to the claim that he has come to believe that Q.

There are, to be sure, certain uses of *learning that* which do, in fact, commit us substantively in the manner we have been discussing. Consider the following statement, for example: "Reporters, after extensive investigation, learned that secret negotiations had been in progress for three weeks before the agreement was announced publicly." The force of "learned that" in this statement approximates that of "found out that" or "discovered that," which do commit us substantively. We may label such a use of "learn that," a *discovery use,* and contrast it with the *tutorial use,* in which the expression refers (without committing us substantively) to what people come to believe in consequence of schooling. The existence of the tutorial use suffices to show that a *learn that* attribution does not, in general, commit us to the embedded substantive assertion. And as we saw earlier, this is sufficient to *block* the generalization that what *X* has learned he has come to know, permitting only the weaker generalization that what *X* has learned he has come to believe.

The weaker generalization, in other words, unlike the stronger one, frees us from commitment to repugnant substantive claims in all those cases where we attribute *learning that* tutorially but reject the content learned. The student mentioned earlier may well be admitted to have learned, and to have believed, that evil spirits cause disease, but he cannot well be admitted to have come to know this. Suppose, now, that we consider all and only those cases where (i) X has learned that Q, and where (ii) we concur with the substantive assertion represented by "Q." Should we be willing in all these cases, at least, to say that X has indeed come to know (and not merely to believe) that Q?

This question raises a point of general importance regarding the attribution of knowledge: Some writers on the subject have recognized a weak and a strong sense of *know that*. The answer to our question will depend on which sense we have in mind. In the weak sense, *knowing that* depends solely on having true belief; in the strong sense, it requires something further—for example, the ability to back up the belief in a relevant manner, to bring evidence in its support, or to show that one is in a position to know what it affirms. If we take the weak sense of *know that*, we shall then answer our question in the affirmative. If X has learned that Q and has therefore come to believe that Q, and if, further, we are willing to concur with the claim made by "Q" (i.e., to affirm it as true), we must acknowledge that X has come to believe truly, hence to know (in the weak sense) that Q.

If we take the strong sense of *know that*, however, we must answer our question in the negative. For a person may believe correctly or truly that Q, and yet lack the ability to provide adequate backing for his belief or to show that he is in a position to know that Q. Though he has learned that Q and has come to believe truly that Q, he will then not *really* know, or know in the strong sense, that Q. He has, for example, learned in school that $E = mc^2$ but cannot, unless he can supply suitable supporting reasons, be said to know (in the strong sense) that $E = mc^2$.

We may summarize our discussion to this point as follows: If X has learned that Q, he has come to believe that Q. If we deny "Q," we will directly rule out that X has also come to know that Q, no matter how well X is able to support "Q." On the other hand, if we grant that "Q" is true, it is not directly ruled out that we shall say X has come to know that Q. We shall, indeed, say this immediately if we employ the weak sense of *know*, but only upon the satisfaction of further conditions if we employ the strong sense of *know*.

Often, perhaps typically, however, we do not make a direct test to determine whether these further conditions have indeed been satisfied; we operate rather on general presumptions that seem to us plausible. The presumption that the relevant conditions have been satisfied varies, for example, with the difficulty, technicality, or complexity of the subject. Thus, it seemed quite natural to us earlier to say that a student who has learned that Boston is the capital of Massachusetts has indeed come to know this. Nor does this seem to be simply a result of using the weak sense of *know*. The question "He has learned it, but does he really know it?" springs less easily to our lips in this case than in the case of "$E = mc^2$." For what sort of complex technical backing could possibly be needed here? Granted that the strong sense of *know* is operative, we are more likely to presume, on general grounds, that a student who has learned a "simple" fact can support it appropriately than we are likely to make the same presumption for a relatively "complex" or technical affirmation.

Another source of variation seems to be the method by which the belief has been acquired. To have merely been made aware or informed by somebody that Q leaves open the practical possibility that one does not really know (in the strong sense) that Q, even where "Q" is true. To have found out for oneself that Q, lends greater credence to the presumption that one really has come to know that Q, for it suggests, though it does not strictly imply, that one has been in a good position to realize that Q, either relatively directly or on the basis of clues or reasons pointing to "Q."

This suggests why the discovery use of *learning that* seems to imply *knowing that* in the strong sense. Consider again our reporters, who learned (found out) after extensive investigation that the negotiations had been in progress for three weeks before the publicly announced agreement. The question "Granted they found out, but did they really know?" does not strike us as immediately relevant or natural. Those educators who stress so-called discovery and problem-solving methods in schooling may, in fact, be operating upon the general presumption that such methods lead to strong knowing as an outcome. And emphasis on *teaching*, with its distinctive connotations of rational explanation and critical dialogue, may have the same point: to develop a sort of learning in which the student will be capable of backing his beliefs by appropriate and sufficient means. To have learned that Q as a consequence of genuine teaching, given that "Q" is true, does seem to lend some weight to the presumption that one has come to know.

The notion of "teaching," unlike "learning," has, typically, *intentional* as well as *success* uses. That is to say, teaching normally involves trying, whereas learning does not. To say of a child that he is learning to walk, that he is learning several new words every day, that he is learning how to conduct himself socially, that he is learning to express himself well in speech, does not in itself normally convey that he is *trying* to accomplish these things. It does not even convey that he is engaged or occupied in them, in the sense of thinking of what is going on, focusing his attention, and acting with care. Learning, it might thus be said, is not an *activity* but rather more nearly a *process.* We may surely distinguish the different stages of a process, and we may separate those situations in which the process has run its course to completion from those in which it has not. But such analyses do not presuppose either deliberateness or intention, although the latter *may,* in particular circumstances, be involved. We *can* try to learn this or that, but we often learn without trying at all; there is, moreover, no general presumption that any given case of learning is intentional.

Teaching appears quite different, by comparison. To say of someone that he is teaching conveys normally that he is engaged in an activity, rather than caught up in a process. It is to imply contextually that what he is doing is directed toward a goal and involves intention and care. He is, in short, trying, and what he is trying to bring about represents *success* in the activity, rather than simply the end-state of a process. We can, to be sure, speak of so-called "unintentional teaching," in which a person actually brings about a certain sort of learning, although without trying or even awareness on his part. But such reference will require that the word *teaching* be suitably qualified (e.g., by the word *unintentional*), or that supplementary explanation of the case be offered. Without such further information, a bare ascription of *teaching* contextually implies intention, whereas a success use of the verb (e.g., "Jones has taught his son how to swim") signifies intention brought to successful fruition.

What does teaching have as its goal? What does a person engaged in teaching intend or try to bring about? Obviously, an appropriate bit of learning. In the particular case of *teaching that* with which we have so far been concerned, a person X teaching Y that Q, is trying to bring about Y's learning that Q. As we have seen, this involves Y's coming to accept "Q" or to believe that Q. If X has been successful in teaching Y that Q, Y has indeed learned that Q, has come to believe that Q.

The converse, of course, does not hold: One may learn that Q without having been taught it by anyone. Furthermore, we must not suppose that teaching can be *reduced to* trying to achieve someone's coming to believe something. One may try to propagate a belief in numerous ways other than teaching—for example, through deception, insinuation, advertising, hypnosis, propaganda, indoctrination, threats, bribery, and force. Nor must we be quick to identify teaching with schooling generally, for formal agencies of schooling have employed and often do employ methods other than teaching—for example, indoctrination, suggestion, threats, and force. Thus, if we think of *learning that* as referring to the acquisition of belief just in the context of schooling, we still cannot take teaching as simply directed toward learning as its goal, although teaching does have learning as its goal.

What distinguishes teaching, as we remarked earlier, is its special connection with rational explanation and critical dialogue: with the enterprise of giving honest reasons and welcoming radical questions. The person engaged in teaching does not merely want to bring about belief, but to bring it about through the exercise of free rational judgment by the student. This is what distinguishes teaching from propaganda or debating, for example. In teaching, the teacher is revealing his reasons for the beliefs he wants to transmit and is thus, in effect, submitting his own judgment to the critical scrutiny and evaluation of the student; he is fully engaged in the dialogue by which he hopes to teach, and is thus risking his own beliefs, in lesser or greater degree, as he teaches.

Teaching, it might be said, involves trying to bring about learning under severe restrictions of *manner*—that is to say, within the limitations imposed by the framework of rational discussion. Since teaching that Q presupposes that the teacher takes "Q" to be true (or at least within the legitimate range of truth approximation allowable for purposes of pedagogical simplification and facilitation) and since the activity of teaching appeals to the free rational judgment of the student, we might say that the teacher is trying to bring about knowledge, in the strong sense earlier discussed. For the presumption is that a person who is encouraged to form his beliefs through free rational methods is likely to be in a position to provide proper backing for them. The teacher does not strive merely to get the student to learn that Q, but also to get him to learn it in such a way as to know it—i.e., to be able to support it properly.

We must, however, admit that there will generally be differences of opinion as to the success or failure of the whole teaching operation. Cross-cultural cases provide the clearest illustrations. Consider the teacher of a distant age who strove to teach that evil spirits cause disease. He was (we have said) *trying* to get his students really to know this. Now we may admit that he was successful in getting them to believe that evil spirits cause disease and even in supporting this belief in a way that may have been reasonable in their cultural environment. We cannot, however, admit his *success* in getting his students to *know* that evil spirits cause disease, for *we* hold this doctrine to be false.

Is there not a difficulty here from the point of view of appraisal of teaching? We want to distinguish successful from unsuccessful teaching in this ancient era, but our present analysis forces us to judge all of it (at least with respect to such false doctrines as we have been considering) to have been uniformly unsuccessful. To meet this problem, we may propose a secondary or "subjective" notion of success to supplement the primary or "objective" notion we have been using. According to this secondary or subjective notion of success, we assume that the truth of the doctrine taught is to be judged from the teacher's point of view; we also judge the question of proper backing in a way that makes allowances for the prevalent standards and available data in the culture in question. Then we judge success in the normal manner. We can now make the wanted cross-cultural distinctions between successful and unsuccessful teaching even where, from an objective point of view and judged from our standpoint, it has been unsuccessful.

Any teaching is geared to what the teacher takes to be true, and his aim is not merely that his student learn what he takes to be true but that he be able to support it by criteria of proper backing taken to be authoritative. Insofar as the teacher is *teaching,* he is, in any event, risking his own particular truth judgments, for he is exposing them to the general critique of these criteria and to the free critical judgment of the student's mind.

One point of general importance should be especially noted. *Knowing that* attributions reflect the truth judgments and critical standards of the speaker; they commit him substantively to the beliefs he is assigning to others, and they hinge on the particular criteria of backing for beliefs, which he adopts. Thus, unlike attributions of *belief, learning that,* and *teaching that,* they reveal his own epistemological orientation to the items of belief in question; in this sense, they do more than merely describe the person to whom knowledge is being attributed.

We have, in sum, connected the educational ideas of learning and teaching with the cognitive ideas of knowledge and belief, as follows: Learning that Q involves coming to believe that Q. Under certain further conditions (truth of "Q" and, for the strong sense of *knowing*, proper backing of "Q"), it also involves coming to know that Q. Teaching that Q involves trying to bring about learning that (and belief that) Q, under characteristic restrictions of manner, and, furthermore, knowing that Q, as judged by the teacher from his own standpoint.

Now, there are certain classes of counterexamples that might be offered in opposition to these generalizations. A student might say, in reporting what he had learned on a certain day, "I learned that the gods dwelt on Olympus," or, if a student of philosophy, "I learned that the world of sense is an illusion." These reports might indeed be true, without the student's actually coming to *believe* that the gods dwelt on Olympus or that the world of sense is an illusion. Such reports are, however, plausibly interpreted as elliptical. What is really intended is, "I learned that it was believed (by the Greeks) that the gods dwelt on Olympus," or, "I learned that it was said (by such and such a philosopher) that the world of sense is an illusion."

Another sort of counterexample is provided by the case of X, who is teaching Y that metals expand when heated but who does not really care whether Y believes this or not. He is not trying to get Y to believe or to qualify (from his point of view) as knowing that metals expand when heated. He is only preparing Y to do what is necessary to pass the end-term examination. He may not even care about that; he may only be trying to get through the day. First, as to the latter case, it is quite possible for a *teacher* not to be engaged in *teaching* at a given time. To be called a teacher is, typically, to be described as having a certain institutional role in the process of schooling, rather than as engaging in teaching activity; we must avoid the assumption that whatever a teacher does on the job is properly describable as teaching. Secondly (as to the former case), we might well differentiate teaching Y that metals expand when heated from teaching Y how to handle examination questions relating to this subject in order to facilitate passing. It is, in fact, possible to do one of these without doing the other; from the time of the Sophists (at least), it has been recognized that teaching might be geared not toward knowledge of propositions taken as true but rather toward the acquisition of skills in handling the outward manifestations of such knowledge. There are analogous cases, moreover, where the latter aim is quite respectable—for example, where teaching is geared toward the development of skills in handling and applying theories rather than toward acceptance of these theories as true.

FURTHER READING

Ayer, Alfred. *Language, Truth and Logic.* New York: Dover Publications, Inc., 1946.

Broudy, Harry S. "The Role of Analysis in Educational Philosophy," *Educational Theory.* *14*:4 (October, 1964), pp. 261–70.

Feigl, Herbert. "Aims of Education for Our Age of Science: Reflections of a Logical Empiricist," in Nelson B. Henry (ed.), *Modern Philosophies and Education.* 54th Yearbook, Part I, National Society for the Study of Education. Chicago: University of Chicago Press, 1955.

Feigl, Herbert and Sellars, Wilfrid (eds.). *Readings in Philosophical Analysis.* New York: Prentice-Hall, Inc., 1953.

Kneller, George F. *Logic and Language of Education.* New York: John Wiley & Sons, Inc., 1966.

O'Connor, D. J. *An Introduction to the Philosophy of Education.* London: Routledge and Kegan Paul, 1957.

Scheffler, Israel. *Conditions of Knowledge.* Chicago: Scott, Foresman and Company, 1965.

Soltis, Jonas F. *An Introduction to the Analysis of Educational Concepts.* Reading, Mass.: Addison-Wesley Publishing Co., Inc., 1968.

Smith, B. Othanel and Ennis, Robert H. *Language and Concepts in Education.* Chicago: Rand McNally & Co., 1961.

White, Morton. *The Age of Analysis.* New York: Mentor Books, 1955.

twelve

OPEN EDUCATION AND
DESCHOOLING SOCIETY

This chapter examines the educational theories of those who have advocated the radical transformation of educational structures. While such educational philosophies as Idealism, Realism, Thomism, and Experimentalism conceive of education in the broad sense as the total formative experience of a human being, they emphasize particular approaches to formal education in the school. The educational theories of Essentialism, Perennialism, and Progressivism concentrate almost exclusively on particular approaches, contents, and methodologies for use within the school context. In contrast, educational theorists such as John Holt and Ivan Illich have proposed a learning revolution designed to bring about radical change in educational structures and processes. This chapter analyzes the educational theories of Holt and Illich in order to discern certain of the new directions in philosophy of education.

John Holt's educational theories grew out of his experience as a classroom teacher in elementary schools in the United States. Dissatisfied with the constraints imposed by traditional school structures and bureaucracies, he criticizes the educational establishment and suggests reformation in such books as *How Children Learn, How Children Fail, The Underachieving School,* and *What Do I Do Monday?* His informal and engaging speaking style has made him a popular lecturer on behalf of educational reform and change.

Holt's *Freedom and Beyond* (1972) presents a theoretical and practical examination of his concept of educational reform by means of open learning. While Holt has recommended the reformation of the school by creating opportunities for open learning, he has also come to support Illich's plan for "deschooling" society.

HOLT AND THE SCHOOL'S FUNCTION

Holt's theory of open learning can best be approached by first consider-ing his conception of the nature of the child. By their nature, he says, children are "smart, energetic, curious, eager to learn, and good at learn-ing."[1] They do not have to be tricked, enticed, or coerced into learning, as frequently happens in conventional schools where there are far too many restrictions and prescriptions. Continual and unnecessary inter-ventions in the child's affairs restrict the opportunities for and freedom of choice that he needs to grow as an intelligent and humane person. Like the child-centered Progressive educators, Holt insists that children learn best when they are happily involved and interested in what they are doing.

In Holt's educational theory, the school's function is determined by the nature and needs of the child who it is intended to serve. The school has the primary and legitimate mission of promoting the growth of the children who attend it. Holt urges teachers to be true to the educative mission of helping every child to grow to the "fullest extent of his capacity" in "awareness, responsiveness, curiosity, courage, confidence, imagination, resourcefulness, patience, generosity, sympathy, skill, competence, and understanding." It is such qualities that will enable people to frame and to choose intelligently from a wide range of choices. Such qualities will bring "freedom, dignity, and worth" to those who possess them.[2]

In holding that schools ought to be concerned exclusively with the growth of the child, Holt's view is similar to that of John Dewey, who saw the purpose of education as that of growth. For both Dewey and Holt, education's sole end is to extend the learner's capacities in all directions so that a fuller range of choices becomes available to him. Holt also resembles the Existentialist educators who see the task of education as that of bringing the learner to an intensity of awareness and responsibility regarding the choices that are available to him. The environment that Holt suggests in the open classroom is one that creates and has present in it wide possibilities of choice so that the child may learn by pursuing his interests, uncoerced either by the classroom situa-tion or the teacher.

Unfortunately, the school's primary task of promoting the learner's growth has been obscured by other functions that have been imposed upon or accepted by professional educators. Instead of promoting child growth and development, schools act as custodians of children. They sort, indoctrinate, and assign social roles to their students instead of

---

1. John Holt. *Freedom and Beyond.* New York: E. P. Dutton & Co., Inc., 1972. p. 2.
2. *Ibid.*, pp. 242–43.

liberating them. In its custodial role, the school removes children and adolescents from the larger society and keeps them from interfering with adults. Diametrically opposed to the humane function of growth, the custodial function inhumanely expresses the "adult's general dislike and distrust of the young."[3] In Holt's opinion, compulsory school attendance laws make schools an alternative to jail. Schools must spend large amounts of money and expend a great energy in dealing with masses of students who would prefer to be elsewhere.

Schools also exercise a selective function as they sort out individuals according to levels of academic ability and grade and label them. School people frame the definitions of academic competence and incompetence which are used to label people. As a selection agency, the school determines the occupational and social roles that children will have upon reaching maturity. Schooling becomes impersonal and degenerates into an inhumane assembly line that reduces people to products. Academic transcripts and school records are then used to determine the occupation and frequently social status that one will have as an adult. An even more pernicious consequence of the school's selective function is that education degenerates into a competitive race which has only a few victors but many losers.

Holt also charges that schools deny their humane function by serving as agencies of indoctrination which enculcate the moral, economic, political, and sexual values which have been approved by the dominant groups in society. As agents of indoctrination, professional educators either censor or approve of ideas and books.

More subtly, schools condition students to accept certain economic attitudes. Students are conditioned to believe that they want and need certain products. The consumer and marketing attitudes which are cultivated lead to a sense of alienation which artificially separates the worlds of play and work. Before schooling has had its effect, the child's life is of one piece and not separated into work and play. In school, however, work, play, and learning are considered to be separate and independent of each other. As commodities, they are exchanged for praise and approval and are measured and evaluated by grades. Children are indoctrinated into rejecting their play culture in favor of the adult work culture. When separated from play, work is seen as the necessary but onerous pain of performing tasks at the command of others, under their supervision, for payment or other extrinsic rewards.[4] If schools are to be places of open learning, they must throw off the custodial, selective, and indoctrinating functions that dehumanize learning. If they are

---

3. *Ibid.*, pp. 244–45.
4. *Ibid.*, pp. 251–56.

to be places of open learning, they must again become humane institutions which seek only to encourage and promote the growth of children.

FREEDOM AND THE OPEN CLASSROOM

Essentially, the open classroom is a learning situation which encourages and enhances the widest possible range of alternatives so that the child can choose what and how he will learn. In *Freedom and Beyond,* Holt argues for self-directed learning which is initiated and carried on by the students themselves. An open classroom has an environment and a teacher that create and encourage the possibility and opportunity for such learning to occur. Although free from authoritarianism and coercion, the open classroom has structure. Indeed, Holt asserts, all human situations have a structure which is simply those elements or aspects that give order to experience. In the broad sense, the classroom structure consists of the climate of the school, the human interactions between peers and between students and teacher, and the requirements imposed by the task, issue, or involvement that the student wishes to pursue. Disagreeing with those who see open education as completely unstructured, Holt contends that every human situation has its own structure and is simultaneously a part of a larger structure.

Holt's concept of structure can be illuminated by examining it in relationship to both the traditional and open classroom. It is important to note that: (1) while both the traditional and open classrooms have structures, they have different ones; (2) the open classroom is not a structureless learning situation as some of its advocates contend.

Holt finds that the structure of the traditional classroom has only two elements: the teacher and the students. Since the structural elements are limited, the possibilities of choice are also limited. The conventional classroom is "inflexible, rigid, and static," in that students, despite their individual differences, are expected to perform the same tasks and do the same things. The structure in the traditional classroom is extrinsic to the interests and needs of both students and teacher since it has been imposed by school or community authorities, frequently operating from a distance and through a bureaucratic chain of command. In the traditional classroom, the teacher, who has his orders, is supposed to follow the curriculum guide, giving commands and transmitting information, which the children can either passively receive, accept, or reject. Of course, acceptance is rewarded and rejection is punished. Rewards become grades, grades become the academic record, and the academic record becomes the occupational and social determinant which often follows the child throughout his life as an adult.

In contrast to the two basic elements of the traditional classroom, the open classroom is complicated and richly varied in its structure. It has as many elements as there are teachers and students within it. Since the differences of students are genuinely recognized and their individual choices are encouraged and respected, none of the elements can be identical. If it is genuinely open in practice and not just in name, the open classroom must be flexible and dynamic. Growing out of the interests, needs, and problems of the individuals who comprise it, the structure of the open classroom is evolutionary, organic, and internal. The relationships between the children change daily as do those of the teacher and the students.[5]

Since all life has structures, it must also have constraints. Each man is limited by his nature, conception of reality, way of relating to others, and by his hopes and fears. The real question, says Holt, is one of choice within limits. A person's choice may be limited further by either the prescriptions or proscriptions of others. Prescriptions indicate what one must do; proscriptions indicate what he must not do. The tyrannical situation, whether political or educational, has many vague prescriptions. When limits are ill-defined, despots enter into as many areas of life as possible. A free society, whether it is in or out of school, has clearly and specifically defined limits. In a free society and in the open classroom which is its educational correlative, the rules are kept to a necessary minimum and are mostly proscriptive injunctions framed to safeguard an individual's freedom from arbitrary infringement by others. Since they are clearly and specifically stated, the rules of the open society and classroom need little or no interpretation. Citizens and students do not have to guess about the limits of power and the degree of authority which will be exercised over them.

Holt also asks how, when classrooms are closed to individual choice and when schools are coercive of personal liberty, they can be opened to give greater freedom to people? Although it is impossible for one to give freedom to another, it is possible to create opportunities for choice by removing the coercions and restraints which impede it. What an individual does with his opportunities is his own affair. The crucial issue for the open society and classroom is to guarantee that the opportunity is present. Like the Existentialists, Holt argues that choosing involves tension and risk. When a person is free to choose, only he is responsible for the choice and its consequences.

DISCIPLINE AND FREEDOM

In *Freedom and Beyond,* Holt answers those critics who fear that open education will lead to an undisciplined people living in an undisciplined society. Examining the concept of discipline which is common to west-

---

5. *Ibid.,* p. 11.

ern societies, he finds that human experience has been divided into work or play, into the easy or the difficult, and into the agreeable or the disagreeable. The Puritan ethic, ingrained in the American historical experience, holds that work is better than play. Furthermore, valuable work is to be unpleasant and to require difficult effort. In contrast, Holt argues against dividing learning or any other human activity into parts. All activity should be regarded as an unbroken flow of human experience. In many respects, Holt's attack on separating work and play resembles Dewey's attack on the dualisms that have divided theory from practice, fine art from popular art, and liberal from useful education. For both Holt and Dewey, man's interest in his freely chosen projects will lead to the efforts needed to complete them. Only when another's project is imposed coercively is extrinsic motivation necessary to arouse the needed effort. Holt's view of interest and effort, like that of the Progressive educators, opposes the methods of the Perennialists and Essentialists who argue that in many instances effort must be expended before interest arises.

The problem of interest and effort leads to the matter of discipline. Holt condemns the conventional conception of discipline, which asserts that it is proper to give unquestioning obedience to an authority. This concept of discipline is based on the assumptions that: (1) obedience is necessarily good for one's character; (2) it is desirable to follow orders regardless of one's own interests; (3) one's role in life should be accepted without complaint; (4) punishment is necessary and should be applied to disobedient individuals.[6] Although long associated with traditional schooling, it is obvious that such a concept of discipline is alien to a democratic and free society. Indeed, it is more appropriate to despotism.

While rejecting the dogmatic discipline often associated with traditional schooling, Holt recognizes that properly constituted, legitimate discipline is a necessary part of living and learning. He identifies three kinds of legitimate discipline: (1) of nature or reality; (2) of culture or society; (3) of superior force.

The most important kind of discipline, that of nature or reality, is imposed on what we do by the real world and by our necessity of conforming to it. For example, if children have a terrarium with growing plants in it and then neglect to provide sufficient water to sustain the plants, the plants will die. The consequences of such negligence will be clear and apparent and indicate the needed correction to the learners. If a girl who wants to sew a dress fails to follow the pattern or to measure her material correctly, then the dress will not fit. The results of careless measuring will be apparent in the feel and appearance of the garment.

---

6. *Ibid.,* pp. 100–101.

The results will be plainly visible to the learner. The needed corrections are impersonal and can be applied without guilt. Whenever a learner tries to do or make something—be it the simple planting of a flower or the execution of a complicated chemical experiment—nature's discipline is present. While much of Holt's educational theory resembles Progressivism and Existentialism, his conception of the Discipline of Nature is similar to that of Realist philosophy, which asserts that man's common sense leads him to know and to conform to the patterns and laws of an antecedent and independent reality.

Holt identifies culture or society as exerting a disciplining force upon children. Sensing the intricate network of social relations, customs, and manners which is around them, children want to understand, be involved in, and participate in their culture. Wanting to do that which is socially approved, they observe and try to emulate the social amenities of their culture. In so doing, they acquire a cultural heritage.

The Discipline of Superior Force comes into play when a superior commands a subordinate. Although adults frequently exercise this kind of discipline over children, Holt contends that it is used legitimately only to protect the child's well being. Its exercise should be restricted to those occasions when it is necessary to protect a child from a danger that he does not fully comprehend. Adults legitimately administer this discipline to children because by nature they have greater experience and understanding and not merely because they are older and bigger. Holt warns that the Discipline of Superior Force should be used cautiously and reluctantly. By inhibiting the child, the constant fear of punishment locks him into the immaturity of babyhood. Only by learning "to take responsibility for his life and acts" can a person grow up. Rather than being good for the child's character, Holt asserts that the threat of superior force "is never good for anyone's character."[7]

John Holt recommends the open classroom, where learners are free to initiate and complete the projects that interest them. Open learning takes place only when people are free of coercion and authoritarianism. Educators who would follow Holt's advice will seek to open the closed learning situations so that the learner has the greatest possibilities for exercising the widest range of choices.

Although he once believed that reform would be wrought within the structure of formal education, Holt has grown wary of attempts to reform schools. He has come to see Ivan Illich's proposals for deschooling society as offering the best hope for achieving genuine educational freedom. The remainder of this chapter examines Illich's arguments for the deinstitutionalization of education and the deschooling of society.

---

7. *Ibid.*, p. 104.

ILLICH AND THE DESCHOOLING OF SOCIETY

Among contemporary educational theorists, Ivan Illich, co-founder of the Center for Intercultural Documentation, has offered a radical approach to social and educational change. Unlike those who recommend educational innovation and reform within the school context, Illich calls for the abolition of the school and the deschooling of society. While his larger social theory aims to deinstitutionalize society, Illich sees deschooling as the initial thrust in creating a new social order. His basic thesis is that the values of contemporary society have become encased in institutionalized structures. Institutionalized values are measured as the outputs or products of particular institutions such as factories, hospitals, or schools. Losing his identity as a value creator, man's own value is reduced to consuming and demanding products and services. Illich states, "When values have been institutionalized in planned and engineered processes, members of modern society believe that the good life consists in having institutions which define the values that both they and their society believe they need."[8] In the process of institutionalizing values, Illich finds the school to be particularly pernicious, because it contributes to personal alienation and to psychological impotence.

Illich's attack is directed against the concept that all important learning is conducted in institutions of formal education. In pointing out that primitive man was governed by the facts of the environment and the necessity of survival, Illich seeks to restore the tone of primitive education, when learning was informal and direct rather than formal and indirect. Rather than certified teachers, the best educators are the objects of the environment, members of the peer group, and experienced adults who possess special skills and knowledge.

Illich's plea for a return to the spirit of primitive education rests on his rejection of modern man's attempt to construct a totally manmade environment. He is repelled by the contemporary ideal of a totally planned world in which all human interactions are the result of the social engineer's calculation and manipulation. In a technological society, trained specialists perform specific functions. Around these specialists have grown specialized institutions which produce the goods and services specified by the planners and social engineers. These institutions and the specialists within them are maintained by what Illich calls the myth of "unending consumption," which holds that valuable products have been produced and should be consumed. The myth promises that greater human progress will result if more products and services are produced and consumed. The school exercises a key role in perpetuating

8. Ivan Illich. *Deschooling Society*. New York: Harper & Row, Publishers, 1971. pp. 113–14.

the myth by indoctrinating people to accept the theory of unending consumption, preparing and certifying specialists, and training people to accept their institutionally defined roles. If society is to be deinstitutionalized, it must first be deschooled by an educational revolution.

ILLICH'S CRITIQUE OF SCHOOLING

Illich, an unyielding critic of schooling, defines the school directly and simply as an "age-specific, teacher-related process requiring full-time attendance at an obligatory curriculum."[9] Although education has been frequently confused with schooling, he contends that the school's antieducational effects have caused a variety of personal and societal ills. The blurring of the distinctions between schooling and education has led to the naive but popular belief that education must be expensive, complicated, and entrusted only to pedagogical specialists. By monopolizing the financial and human resources which society has available for education, the school has discouraged other institutions from participating in the educational process.

The school's educational monopoly rests on three unchallenged tenets that Illich seeks to explode: (1) behavior acquired in the presence of a teacher is of special value to the pupil and society; (2) man is properly socialized as an adolescent in the school; (3) young people have the special responsibility for bringing about social change, but only after their completion of school.[10] These three assumptions make it possible for educators to restrict the freedom and creativity of learners by setting, specifying, and evaluating their personal goals.

Agreeing with Illich's attack on schooling, Holt also contends that children are educated much more by the whole society and the general quality of life than they are by the school. In a schooled society, he argues, most of the learning tools and resources are locked up in schools. A schooled society creates obstacles for individuals who have learned outside of the walls of the school. In a society which is deschooled, learning will be restored to the general fabric of life.

Illich continues his attack on schooling by asserting that the school's usurping of education is founded on the false syllogisms that: (1) everything in life is secret; (2) life's quality depends on knowing the secret; (3) these secrets can be revealed only by teachers in an orderly and sequential fashion. Disputing the school's instructional monopoly, Illich counters that most people acquire most of their knowledge outside of the school in a casual rather than in a structured and programmed manner.

9. *Ibid.,* pp. 25–26.
10. *Ibid.,* pp. 67–68.

Schooling, the initial exposure to institutions, causes people to rely on institutionalized life. Once the dependency is formed, it is transferred to other institutions, with the result that the person and society are institutionalized. Through its ritual game of graded promotions, the school helps to sustain the social status quo and structure. By merging instruction with certification, schools have confused learning with the assignment of social roles. In an institutionalized society, promotion within institutions and society depends upon holding a certificate. Unfortunately, certificates are based on others' opinions.

The school's educational monopoly is the same throughout the world. Whether in an emergent or modernized nation, the school system has the same structure, hidden curriculum, and consequences. It has the effect of shaping a consumer's mentality and attitude in its students by encouraging them to value institutional commodities over the friendly assistance of concerned but uncertified neighbors. The school convinces its clients that the administrative bureaucracies of coercive institutions are really scientific, objective, efficient, and benevolent. The habits acquired in school lead to a dependence on institutions and an acceptance of institutional rankings.

Condemnation of Compulsory Schooling   In urging the deschooling of society, Illich attacks compulsory education as a "dull, protracted, destructive, and expensive" initiation rite supported by a system of regressive taxation in which the elite is supported by the mass. The advocates of compulsory education have insisted that children belong in, learn in, and can be taught only in school.[11] Rather than learning from the programming of schools and teachers, Illich claims that students actually do most of their learning without and often in spite of teachers.

When he attacks compulsory education, Illich also condemns middle-class conceptions of childhood and the authoritative and frequently authoritarian teacher. In the past, children learned directly by being involved in the work of their parents. The middle classes, arising out of the industrial revolution, invented the concept of childhood to take their children out of the work situations which they themselves had created. Other social classes, imitating the middle classes, have either voluntarily or through coercion removed their children from contact with the daily experience of work. Parents have surrendered their children to the school, an age-specific and obligatory institution. When society has been deschooled, Illich believes, childhood, too, will disappear and the arbitrary segregation of children will cease.

In Illich's opinion, the contemporary teacher–student relationship has exaggerated the teacher's authority by removing the safeguards of indi-

11. *Ibid.,* p. 26.

vidual liberty. The teacher's presence in the school has led to a blurring of the distinctions between moral, legal, and personal values. In the school setting, the teacher is a powerful figure who enters into the student's personal and private life. As a social custodian, the teacher is a master of ceremonies who guides the students through the drawn-out ritual which is supposed to be an initiation to life. Acting *in loco parentis,* the teacher becomes a guardian who substitutes for the parents and state. Most dangerously, the teacher can exercise the role of therapist. Sure of his therapeutic powers, the teacher convinces his students that he can help them by delving into the inner-most aspects of their lives, persuading them to submit to his conception of truth and right.[12]

Critique of the Curriculum   Illich's rejection of schooling also involves a critique of the school's curriculum. In a consumer's world, educators have constructed a curriculum in which subject matters, purporting to be knowledge, are planned and packaged like other products. The contemporary school's curriculum, consisting of a "bundle of planned meanings" and "a package of values," is so designed as to have a "balanced appeal" which makes it marketable to enough consumers to justify its production costs. Each curricular subject is so packaged and programmed that the learner must continue to consume additional courses each year. Thus, the modern school curriculum is a series of prefabricated, measurable blocks transmitted by a teacher to students who have no choice but to submit to the programming of the educational establishment.

In trying to imitate the scientific method, schools attempt to initiate students into a world where everything is quantifiable, impersonal, and measurable. In a situation where knowledge and values are held to be measurable, then people, too, are quantified. With quantification, all sorts of gradations and rankings emerge as people are conditioned to assume assigned roles and also expect others to assume and play their assigned roles. Rejecting the notion that people, knowledge, and values can be quantified, Illich denies the worth of a curriculum of packaged, prefabricated meanings and values. In contrast, he insists that personal growth and creativity are not measurable and that learning's true prize is "immeasurable re-creation."[13]

EDUCATIONAL REVOLUTION

Illich's proposal for the deschooling of society is really a call for an educational revolution to deinstitutionalize learning and instruction. He

---

12. *Ibid.,* pp. 30–32.
13. *Ibid.,* pp. 40–43.

expects that such a revolution will serve as a catalyst bringing about sweeping social transformation. Compulsory schooling and a packaged curriculum will be replaced by relational structures, enabling "each man to define himself by learning and by contributing to the learning of others."[14] Illich proposes that the coming educational revolution be guided by (1) abolishing the control which people and institutions have over the access to objects and their educational values; (2) liberating the sharing of skills by guaranteeing freedom to teach or exercise them on request; (3) liberating critical and creative resources of people by returning to them the ability to call and to hold meetings; (4) liberating the individual from the obligation of shaping his goals according to the specifications required by any established profession and thus giving him the opportunity to draw on the experience of the peers, teacher, guide, or adviser of his choice.[15]

Illich's new relational structures are to be those of the emergent counter-culture, which values the unpredictable outcome of the self-chosen encounter above the certified quality of professional instruction. A good educational system, in his opinion, will require constitutional guarantees that free learners from submission to an obligatory curriculum, eliminate discrimination based on possession of a certificate or a diploma, and free the public from supporting a huge professional apparatus of educators and equipment through a system of regressive taxation.[16]

ILLICH ON LEARNING

Illich's educational revolution and its emergent relational structures will replace the school. The distinction between formal education as represented by the school and informal education will be eliminated as all learning becomes informal and as the learners interact with their environment, peers, and elders. The elimination of the distinction between formal and informal education will mark a return to the spirit of the primitive education of the pre-institutionalized society.

Illich sees the learning process as a two-faced one which can be differentiated into either drill training or "liberal education." Drill training is designed to facilitate the acquiring of particular skills such as reading, swimming, or computer programming. Illich defines liberal education as the "open-ended, exploratory use of acquired skills."

14. *Ibid.*, pp. 40–71.
15. *Ibid.*, p. 104.
16. *Ibid.*, pp. 75–76.

Drill Teaching In advocating drill teaching for the learning of specific skills, Illich claims that the strongly motivated students who want to learn a complex skill will benefit from the discipline necessary to the learning task. He urges the creating of the circumstances where people can choose from hundreds of definable skills at public expense. Progress in acquiring a skill can be easily verified and measured by one's ability to perform that particular skill.

Certification of teachers would be removed as an unnecessary impediment in skill learning. A plentiful supply of teachers for drill training in specific skills would be recruited from those who competently demonstrate the skill. Illich recommends that skill centers be established in work places, factories, and industries where the employer and the work force can supply the instruction. Illich seems to be recommending the kind of on-the-job training that has been practiced by the armed services and private industry. In such situations, the individual learns particular skills by performing them under the tutelege of a competent practitioner.

As they argue for what is really a return to primitive education, in which no distinction existed between formal and informal learning, Illich and Holt seem to be suggesting a return to the system of apprenticeship. Holt, for example, claims that schools are expensive and wasteful in that they do not really produce anything. Apprentices, such as in drill training or learning, would be making a product as well as learning a skill.

Although Illich insists that his plan for deschooling society applies to both advanced and emerging nations, his stress on skill teaching seems more suited to the developing nation in the initial stages of modernization than to the industrially and technologically advanced nation. Developing nations, embarking on industrialization, usually have an elite which has been educated in conventional ways along the lines of European literary education and an uneducated, often illiterate mass. Such nations lack the semi-skilled workers and technicians needed to maintain the machines of industry. Illich's skill learning is an approach to training those who are needed as craftsmen and technicians. As technology becomes more complex, it is questionable if an immediate set of basic operational skills will be adequate, however.

Illich's drill training bears some superficial resemblances to the "learning by doing" approach which has been associated with John Dewey and progressive education. Like the Progressives, Illich apparently wants to integrate learning with the consequences that come from action. The results of an action can be verified directly by the learner's performance of the skill. In contrast with Illich, Dewey is more concerned with the learner's acquiring of the problem-solving attitude. For

Dewey, the method of intelligence or problem solving is a generalized method of inquiry that involves the transference and application of the method to various problem-centered tasks. When dealing with drill training, Illich apparently is concerned with training an individual to competently perform a specific task rather than with the generalized method.

Educational Webs or Exchanges   Although Illich stresses skill training as one type of needed learning, "liberal education" requires still other kinds of instructional arrangements. In place of the school, he would create "opportunity webs, or networks" which would provide learners with access to educational objects, models, peers, and elders. These webs, available to all, are intended to equalize the opportunity for learning and teaching. According to Illich, the four channels of things, models, peers, and elders would contain all the educational resources needed for genuine learning. The child grows up in an environment of objects and is surrounded by persons who can serve as models for skills and values. His peer group, a potent educational agency, challenges him to argue, compete, cooperate, and understand. Experienced elders can provide the needed corrective criticism.[17]

Illich's learning networks are buttressed by four types of educational resources. In addition to skill teachers and centers, there will be reference services to educational objects, peer matching, and reference services to educators-at-large.

In his examination of formal education, Illich asserts that schools remove the objects of the immediate environment from the learner's inspection and use. The objects of the environment which might be expected to be used in everyday life are either absent or remote from the conventional classroom. With deschooling, the objects of the general physical environment must again be made available to learners. In the kind of self-directed learning advocated by Illich, the objects of the environment become basic learning resources. Both the quality of the environment and the relationship of the person to that environment determine how much a person can learn incidentally. To facilitate the learner's access to a variety of learning objects or educational artifacts, Illich would create a reference service to them. His broadened definition of learning objects would include tool shops, libraries, laboratories, photo labs, office equipment, films, art exhibits, and factories.

To create peer groups and to locate concerned adult critics, Illich has formulated a plan for a communications network to bring people together to discuss, investigate, and work out their own unresolved prob-

---

17. *Ibid.,* p. 76.

lems and interests. When using the proposed peer matching network, a person would identify himself and describe the learning activity in which he wishes to engage; then the network custodians would assist in locating partners for the inquiry. A computer would send the names and addresses of individuals who had indicated the same interest, concern, or involvement. The peer groups which form would cluster around specific interests or problems. Their duration and intensity of involvement would depend upon the participant's degree of interest in the issue or the time needed to solve a problem. Illich believes that such groups would be free of the coercion or compulsion associated with schools, since they would be entirely voluntary. Based upon the mutuality of the learners' interests, education would become a dialogue which occurs when people meet to discuss and to share a commonly felt emotional, social, political, or intellectual issue.

Illich's attack on the school also involves a condemnation of the authoritarian teacher who holds power over his students, because of compulsory attendance laws which compel them to attend his classes and because of certification requirements which protect his status and role. In place of the certified teacher associated with the school, Illich forsees the rise of the independent educator who can serve as a designer, facilitator, and administrator of learning situations and circumstances. Those aspiring to build educational networks would have to assess the special genius of non-interference with other people's plans and learning. Their task would be to facilitate encounters between learners and other students, skill models, peers, elders, and educational objects and leaders.

Listed by their names, addresses, and self-descriptions in an educational directory, the educators-at-large would include professionals, paraprofessionals, and free-lancers. They would provide learners with three basic kinds of services: (1) administrators would create and maintain the educational exchanges and networks; (2) pedagogical counselors would guide students and parents in using learning networks by judging learning proficiency, aiding in textbook selection, and suggesting appropriate study methods; (3) educational initiators would provide special leadership for undertaking difficult intellectual undertakings.

The educational initiator or leader would exercise a key role in the deschooled society. In fact, the initiators would become the leadership elite in such a deinstitutionalized social order. Described by Illich as a master or true leader, the initiator would be first among his peers. Having the capacity to exercise a prophetic vision based on entirely new standards, the leadership of the educational initiator would depend on "superior intellectual discipline and imagination and the willingness to associate with others in their exercise."[18] The initiator and his followers would be related in a master–disciple relationship. Characterized by its "priceless character," the master–disciple relationship is a form of meaningful activity devoid of ulterior motivation or extrinsic compensation. The disciple is willing to follow the master's initiative and to become an advocate of his progressive discoveries.

EPIMETHEAN MAN

As indicated earlier, Illich's plan for deschooling society is not solely a pedagogical matter but involves the creating of a deinstitutionalized social order. This new society will be led by an emergent and growing minority, an elite of Epimethean persons.[19] Living a life of "postindustrial conviviality," the new men will demonstrate an intensity of action rather than fall victim to the contemporary routine of production, consumption, and role playing. Rejecting a life of planned consumption, the Epimethean man will have a life which is simultaneously spontaneous and independent but also related to others. In rejecting the bankruptcy of contemporary life, the Epimethean man will abandon false hopes promised by scientific utopians, ideologists, and the institutionalized distributors of prepackaged goods and services.

CONCLUSION

Advocates of radical educational reform such as Holt and Illich contend that the school is not a viable agency for bringing about a learning revolution. They urge that a process of deschooling society be inaugurated to free learning from the restraints that have been imposed by schooling. Society's learning resources would be made available to more people by creating educational exchanges and networks to replace the school. If this is done, they argue, education will be opened and made more responsive to the desires, interests, and needs of individuals. The demise of the school will equalize the educational opportunities of all people, particularly the poor, who are the most frequent victims of schooling.

---

18. *Ibid.,* p. 100.
19. For Illich's description of Epimethean man, see *Deschooling Society,* pp. 105–16. Epimethean man is derived from Epimetheus, who in Greek mythology married Pandora. While Promethean man seeks to construct social institutions designed to solve each of the problems or ills released from Pandora's box, Epimethean man is a spontaneous person who has a trusting faith in the goodness of nature.

SELECTIONS

Ivan Illich

Ivan Illich, proponent of the deschooling of society, was born in Vienna, Austria, in 1926. He studied theology and philosophy at the Gregorian University in Rome and received his Ph.D. in history from the University of Salzburg. A Roman Catholic priest, he served as an assistant pastor in New York City. From 1956 to 1960, he was vice-rector of the Catholic University of Puerto Rico. Illich is a cofounder of the Center for Intercultural Documentation in Cuernavaca, Mexico. Since 1964, he has devoted himself to the search for institutional alternatives in a technological society. In addition to articles on education and development, his books include: *Celebration of Awareness: A Call for Institutional Revolution* (1970) and *Deschooling Society* (1970). In the following selection, Illich argues for the disestablishment of the school.

*   *   *

The escalation of the schools is as destructive as the escalation of weapons but less visibly so. Everywhere in the world school costs have risen faster than enrollments and faster than the GNP; everywhere expenditures on school fall even further behind the expectations of parents, teachers, and pupils. Everywhere this situation discourages both the motivation and the financing for large-scale planning for nonschooled learning. The United States is proving to the world that no country can be rich enough to afford a school system that meets the demands this same system creates simply by existing, because a successful school system schools parents and pupils to the supreme value of a larger school system, the cost of which increases disproportionately as higher grades are in demand and become scarce.

Rather than calling equal schooling temporarily unfeasible, we must recognize that it is, in principle, economically absurd, and that to attempt it is intellectually emasculating, socially polarizing, and destructive of the credibility of the political system which promotes it. The ideology of obligatory schooling admits of no logical limits. The White House recently provided a good example. Dr. Hutschnecker, the "psychiatrist" who treated Mr. Nixon before he was qualified as a candidate, recommended to the President that all children between six and eight be professionally examined to ferret out those who have destructive tendencies, and that obligatory treatment be provided for them. If necessary, their re-education in special institutions should be required. This memorandum from his doctor the President sent for evaluation to HEW. Indeed, preventive concentration camps for predelinquents would be a logical improvement over the school system.

Equal educational opportunity is, indeed, both a desirable and a feasible goal, but to equate this with obligatory schooling is to confuse salvation with the Church. School has become the world religion of a modernized proletariat, and makes futile promises of salvation to the poor of the technological age. The nation-state has adopted it, drafting all citizens into a graded curriculum leading to sequential diplomas not unlike the initiation rituals and hieratic promotions of former times. The modern state has assumed the duty of enforcing the judgment of its educators through well-meant truant officers and job requirements, much as did the Spanish kings who enforced the judgments of their theologians through the conquistadors and the Inquisition.

Two centuries ago the United States led the world in a movement to disestablish the monopoly of a single church. Now we need the constitutional disestablishment of the monopoly of the school, and thereby of a system which legally combines prejudice with discrimination. The first article of a bill of rights for a modern, humanist society would correspond to the First Amendment to the U.S. Constitution: "The State shall make no law with respect to the establishment of education." There shall be no ritual obligatory for all.

To make this disestablishment effective, we need a law forbidding discrimination in hiring, voting, or admission to centers of learning based on previous attendance at some curriculum. This guarantee would not exclude performance tests of competence for a function or role, but would remove the present absurd discrimination in favor of the person who learns a given skill with the largest expenditure of public funds or—what is equally likely—has been able to obtain a diploma which has no relation to any useful skill or job. Only by protecting the citizen from being disqualified by anything in his career in school can a constitutional disestablishment of school become psychologically effective.

Neither learning nor justice is promoted by schooling because educators insist on packaging instruction with certification. Learning and the assignment of social roles are melted into schooling. Yet to learn means to acquire a new skill or insight, while promotion depends on an opinion which others have formed. Learning frequently is the result of instruction, but selection for a role or category in the job market increasingly depends on mere length of attendance.

Instruction is the choice of circumstances which facilitate learning. Roles are assigned by setting a curriculum of conditions which the candidate must meet if he is to make the grade. School links instruction—but not learning—to these roles. This is neither reasonable nor liberating. It is not reasonable because it does not link relevant qualities or competences to roles, but rather the process by which such qualities are supposed to be acquired. It is not liberating or educational because school reserves instruction to those whose every step in learning fits previously approved measures of social control.

Curriculum has always been used to assign social rank. At times it could be prenatal: karma ascribes you to a caste and lineage to the aristocracy. Curriculum could take the form of a ritual, of sequential sacred ordinations, or it could consist of a succession of feats in war or hunting, or further advancement could be made to depend on a series of previous princely favors. Universal schooling was meant to detach role assignment from personal life history: it was meant to give everybody an equal chance to any office. Even now many people wrongly believe that school ensures the dependence of public trust on relevant learning achievements. However, instead of equalizing chances, the school system has monopolized their distribution.

To detach competence from curriculum, inquiries into a man's learning history must be made taboo, like inquiries into his political affiliation, church attendance, lineage, sex habits, or racial background. Laws forbidding discrimination on the basis of prior schooling must be enacted. Laws, of course, cannot stop prejudice against the unschooled—nor are they meant to force anyone to intermarry with an autodidact—but they can discourage unjustified discrimination.

A second major illusion on which the school system rests is that most learning is the result of teaching. Teaching, it is true, may contribute to certain kinds of learning under certain circumstances. But most people acquire most of their knowledge outside school, and in school only insofar as school, in a few rich countries, has become their place of confinement during an increasing part of their lives.

FURTHER READING

Dennison, George. *The Lives of Children*. New York: Random House, Inc., 1969.

Featherstone, Joseph. *Schools Where Children Learn*. New York: Liveright, 1971.

Freire, Paulo. *Pedagogy of the Oppressed.* New York: Herder and Herder, Inc. 1971.

Holt, John. *Freedom and Beyond.* New York: E. P. Dutton & Co., Inc., 1972.

_____. *How Children Learn.* New York: Pitman Publishing Corp., 1964.

_____. *The Underachieving School.* New York: Pitman Publishing Corp., 1967.

_____. *What Do I Do Monday?* New York: E. P. Dutton & Co., Inc., 1970.

Illich, Ivan. *Celebration of Awareness: A Call for Institutional Revolution.* Garden City, N. Y.: Doubleday & Company, Inc., 1970.

_____. *Deschooling Society.* New York: Harper & Row, Publishers, 1971.

Kohl, Herbert R. *The Open Classroom.* New York: A New York Review Book, 1969.

_____. *36 Children.* New York: The New American Library, Inc., 1967.

Kozol, Jonathan. *Death at an Early Age.* Boston: Houghton Mifflin Company, 1967.

Epilogue

In the preceding chapters, the major schools of philosophy of education are examined and analyzed. Selections from the writings of philosophers and theorists identified with particular philosophies are presented so that you can analyze the sources from which I drew my conclusions. Such schools of educational philosophy as Idealism, Realism, Perennialism, Essentialism, Experimentalism, Progressivism, Reconstructionism, Existentialism, and Philosophical Analysis are treated as are the theories of "open learning" and "deschooling." While such an array of philosophical and educational "isms" may seem unnecessarily confusing to you, these philosophical alternatives are presented to lead to the examination of educational theory and practice.

In their most obvious form, the various educational philosophies constitute alternatives in education. Providing a common heritage of philosophical and educational wisdom, these theoretical positions are the foundations from which new alternatives in education are likely to emerge.

Although some of the readers of this book may decide to give their allegiance to one of the philosophies of education presented, my major intention was not that of persuading anyone to believe in or to give their personal and professional allegiance to any one of them. It is quite possible that you may become interested enough in a particular philosophy of education to do further reading, to examine, and perhaps even embrace it. If commitment results from deliberate reflection and examination, there can be no objection to it. Rather than encouraging discipleship, the various philosophical alternatives in education are presented to encourage examination and speculation as to their meaning for man's personal and social growth.

As alternatives to educational theory and practice, the various philosophies illustrate that different solutions may be formulated honestly, seriously, and intelligently in response to the same problem or issue. These alternatives are valuable in that they illuminate the variety of views that have been expressed on such basic issues as man's place in the universe, the nature of the learner, the meaning of education, the role of the school, the validity of knowledge and values, and the place of discipline and authority. It should be remembered that these are only a few of the questions that concern the educational theorist.

While they may appear bewildering in their number and complexity, I hope that the students of these educational philosophies will note the ebb and flow that has occurred in educational theory as these philosophies gained and then lost momentum. Such, for example, is the case of Idealism. Once a commanding philosophy of education, its residues can be detected only tangentially in certain school practices. One can discern the flavor of the progressive educators of an earlier time in the arguments presented by proponents of the open classroom. The rise and decline of educational theories in influence and popularity may cause students to pause and to reflect before giving their loyalty to particular educational positions and movements.

Although the words *liberal education* are often loosely used and have been defined differently by the various philosophers treated in this book, it is possible to suggest that the study of educational philosophy may have a liberating influence on those who are involved in it. If a liberal education is that which makes one free, the liberal study of educational philosophies may serve to make one free in regard to education. To be free means that one can shape and choose from alternatives. If an intelligent life is an examined rather than an unexamined one, an intelligent education will be an examined one in which the individual is free to reflect on educational alternatives and choices. By examining the philosophical alternatives in education of both past and present, students of education can be stimulated to examine their own beliefs and values. As they reflect on their own educational condition, they can use the wisdom of the various educational philosophies to create, to illuminate, and to extend their own alternatives in education. If it does no more than to stimulate reflection about the possibilities and alternatives available in education, educational philosophy will have fulfilled its promise.

Concerned as it is with the broadest and most general educational issues and problems, philosophy of education is a valuable instrument in examining the internal and external conflicts that effect educational practice. By removing them from the urgency of immediate pressures, issues and conflicts in education can be examined against the framework provided by systematic inquiry. By asking the most general kinds of questions, the study of educational philosophy may stimulate the teacher to examine the activities occurring in his own classroom. It may cause him to speculate on the broad consequences that these practices may have for the individual child and for the society.

I have suggested earlier that the life of the liberally educated person is an examined one. I have further suggested that the liberally educated teacher examines education by creating and choosing between educational alternatives. While recommending adherence to no one particular philosophy of education, I would like to raise some questions that can be asked by the teacher in order to speculate on the most general consequences that educational practice will have on the personal and social life of students and teachers.

(1) What is the rationale for a particular educational practice, attitude, or commitment? In other words, why is something being done? What is the basis for this particular rationale? Does it rest on a particular conception of reality? Does it rest on a particular social, political, or economic philosophy? What will be the immediate effects of the implementation of the rationale? What can be anticipated as the long range and most general consequences?

(2) What curriculum has been designed to fulfill the requirements of the rationale? Does the curriculum reflect a particular conception of reality and man's place in it? Does it purport to convey that conception of reality to students? Is there a hierarchy in the structure of the curriculum or are all subjects and experiences considered to be equally valuable? Is the curriculum effective in providing the means to achieve the educational purposes, aims, and goals that emerge in the rationale? In the most general sense, what kind of man or woman is likely to be the product of such a curriculum? Does this person conform to or diverge from the model that I have of the ideally educated person? What are the personal and social consequences of the curriculum?

(3) What is the method of instruction being used in a particular educational situation? Does the method rest on a particular conception of knowledge and of knowing? What method of instruction is likely to achieve the ends specified in the rationale? Is the method genuinely appropriate to the rationale and the curriculum? Does the method effectively unite teaching and learning? Does the method of instruction enhance or diminish the possibilities for personal and social growth of the individual?

(4) Is the means of evaluation used a genuine test of the effectiveness of instruction? Does it relate to the rationale used to guide educational

practice? Does the means of evaluation select students? What is the basis for such selection? What are the personal, social, political, and economic consequences of such selection?

(5) What kind of teacher am I? Is my self-concept as a teacher an examined one? Have I searched for, framed, and evaluated my teaching in terms of the general consequences that it has for children and others who encounter me?

(6) What is my conception of the child, the learner, the adolescent, and the person? Is this conception consistent with my view of man and the universe? Am I able to see the student against the matrix of the ideally educated person and still see him as a unique individual?

These questions are designed to suggest the initial means of creating a philosophy of education. When posed against the framework of the wisdom and alternatives of the various philosophies, they may lead teachers and other students of education to examine what they believe, value, and do and to create and extend alternatives in education.

Index

Charles E. Merrill Publishing Company
A Bell & Howell Company
Columbus, Ohio